Spirituality and Corporate Social Responsibility

Corporate Social Responsibility Series

Series Editors:
Professor Güler Aras, Yildiz Technical University, Istanbul, Turkey
Professor David Crowther, DeMontfort University, Leicester, UK

Presenting applied research from an academic perspective on all aspects of corporate social responsibility, this global interdisciplinary series includes books for all those with an interest in ethics and governance, corporate behaviour and citizenship, regulation, protest, globalization, responsible marketing, social reporting and sustainability.

Forthcoming titles in this series

Creating Food Futures
Trade, Ethics and the Environment
Cathy Rozel Farnworth, Janice Jiggins and Emyr Vaughan Thomas
ISBN: 978-0-7546-4907-6

Spirituality and Corporate Social Responsibility
Interpenetrating Worlds
David Bubna-Litic
ISBN: 978-0-7546-4763-8

Global Perspectives on Corporate Governance and CSR
Güler Aras and David Crowther
ISBN: 978-0-566-08830-8

The Gower Handbook of Corporate Governance and Social Responsibility
Güler Aras and David Crowther
ISBN: 978-0-566-08817-9

Corruption in International Business
Sharon Eicher
ISBN: 978-0-7546-7137-4

Wealth, Welfare and the Global Free Market
I. Ozer Ertuna
ISBN: 978-0-566-08905-3

Spirituality and Corporate Social Responsibility

Interpenetrating Worlds

Edited by

DAVID BUBNA-LITIC
University of Technology Sydney, Australia

GOWER

Gower Applied Business Research
Our programme provides leaders, practitioners, scholars and researchers with thought provoking, cutting edge books that combine conceptual insights, interdisciplinary rigour and practical relevance in key areas of business and management.

Published by
Gower Publishing Limited
Wey Court East
Union Road
Farnham
Surrey, GU9 7PT
England

Ashgate Publishing Company
Suite 420
101 Cherry Street
Burlington,
VT 05401-4405
USA

www.gowerpublishing.com

British Library Cataloguing in Publication Data
Spirituality and corporate social responsibility :
  interpenetrating worlds. – (Corporate social responsibility
  series)
  1. Social responsibility of business 2. Work environment
  3. Spirituality 4. Management - Religious aspects
  I. Bubna-Litic, David
  658.4'08

  ISBN: 978-0-7546-4763-8

Library of Congress Cataloging-in-Publication Data
Spirituality and corporate social responsibility : interpenetrating worlds / [edited] by David Bubna-Litic.
     p. cm.
 Includes bibliographical references and index.
 ISBN 978-0-7546-4763-8
 1. Spirituality. 2. Social responsibility of business. I. Bubna-Litic, David.
 BL624.S6867 2009
 201'.73--dc22
                                                                    2008049213

Mixed Sources
Product group from well-managed
forests and other controlled sources
www.fsc.org Cert no. SA-COC-1565
© 1996 Forest Stewardship Council

Printed and bound in Great Britain by
MPG Books Ltd, Bodmin, Cornwall.

Contents

List of Tables

List of Contributors

C. Murat Alpaslan is an Assistant Professor teaching strategic management at the College of Business Administration and Economics, California State University at Northridge. His research focuses on corporate governance, stakeholder theory, business ethics, crisis management, rhetorical theory and the philosophy of organizational science.

Charles Birch has been an Emeritus Professor at University of Sydney, Australia since 1983. In 1961 he was honoured as a Fellow of the Australian Academy of Science and in 1980 as a Fellow of the American Association for the Advancement of Science. He became a member of the Club of Rome in 1980 and is an Honorary Life Fellow of the British Ecological Society. He is also an Honorary Life Member of the Ecological Society of America. He was awarded the Eminent Ecologist Award in 1988 and the Templeton Prize in 1990. Professor Birch is a member of the Center for Process Studies, the American Center for a Post Modern World and the World Council of Churches and has written nine books, and 60 publications on science, religion and human existence.

David Bubna-Litic is a renaissance thinker with degrees in Psychology and Commerce and Social Ecology. A Senior Lecturer in Strategic Management at the University of Technology, Sydney, he teaches in the area of sustainable management, organization theory and strategy. David embodies the transdisciplinary nature of the emerging new economics paradigm. An innovative educator, he was the original designer of the award-winning Australian Business Week programme. His doctoral dissertation reformulates Buddhist economics, drawing on postmodern thinking to develop a theory of 'appreciative economics'. He is author of many book chapters and journal articles that explore new ways of thinking about Buddhism, management and strategy and has presented numerous conference papers in North America, Europe and the Pacific Rim. David's research interests are transdisciplinary, incorporating East Asian thinking to form new understandings relevant to strategy, organization theory, economics and sustainability.

Nicholas Capaldi, the Legendre-Soule Chair in Business Ethics has written six books and more than 50 articles, and has edited six collections. His principal research and teaching interest is in public policy and its intersection with political science, philosophy, law, religion and economics. He is a recent recipient of the Templeton Foundation Freedom Project Award. In addition, he is an internationally recognized Hume scholar and a domestic public policy specialist on such issues as higher education, bioethics, business ethics, affirmative action and immigration.

David Crowther BA, MBA, PhD, FCMA, CPFA has worked in industry and commerce for over 20 years, first as an accountant and subsequently as a systems and business consultant and general manager, before becoming an academic. His doctoral thesis on the corporate reporting of social and environmental performance was completed while working as a lecturer in accounting at Aston University. He is now Professor of Corporate Responsibility at London Metropolitan University, and has acted as an adviser or consultant to a wide range of organizations. His research interests cover a wide area but are primarily concerned with issues surrounding the accountability of organizations to their wider stakeholder community such as: the effect of environmental influences on corporate reporting; the measurement and evaluation of corporate performance and the implications of specific measurement systems for corporate behaviour; the regulation of privatized industries; and accounting for the wider environment and stakeholder influences upon corporate reporting systems.

Dexter Dunphy has been a Distinguished Professor, University of Technology, Sydney. Professor Dunphy's main research and consulting interests are in corporate sustainability, the management of organizational change and human resource management. His research is published in over 70 articles and 18 books, including the Australian bestsellers: *The Sustainable Corporation: Organisational Renewal in Australia* (co-authored with Andrew Griffiths), Allen and Unwin, 1998; *Sustainability: The Corporate Challenge of the 21st Century* (co-edited with others), Allen and Unwin, Sydney, 2000; and *Organisational Change for Corporate Sustainability*, (with A. Griffiths and S. Benn), Routledge, London, 2003. Professor Dunphy has acted as consultant to over 150 private and public-sector organizations in Australia and elsewhere in the world. He has been a recipient of a Fulbright Senior Scholar Award, the University of New South Wales' Vice-Chancellor's Award for Teaching Excellence and, on leaving the University of New South Wales in 2000, was appointed Professor Emeritus. In 1998 he was awarded the Australian Human Resources Institute's Mike Pontifex Award for Outstanding Contribution to the Human Resources Profession and the Australian and New Zealand Academy of Management's Distinguished Member Award for contributions to management research, scholarship, education and leadership. In 2001 he was elected a Fellow of the Academy of Social Sciences in Australia and in 2007 was made a member (AM) of the Order of Australia for his service to education in the fields of organizational change, corporate sustainability and business management.

Terri D. Egan, Associate Professor of Applied Behavioral Science, Pepperdine University, teaches courses on the topics of leadership, team effectiveness, managerial decision-making, critical thinking, business ethics, appreciative inquiry and organizational change and development. Her award-winning research has been published in a number of academic journals including *Administrative Science Quarterly*, *Organization Science*, *Journal of Public Administration*, *The Information Society Human Relations* and *The Appreciative Inquiry Practitioner*. In 2000 Dr Egan combined her love of horses with her expertise and experience in management and leadership development to co-found Saddle Sojourns, (www.saddlesojourns.com) a full-service organizational development and change management consultancy.

Dr Egan's current work focuses on an expanded model of leadership and organizational development that supports the evolution of individual and organizational consciousness as a means for increasing creativity and capacity.

Ana-Maria Davila-Gomez is a Professor in the Department of Administrative Sciences at the Université du Québec en Outaouais (UQO), Canada, where she teaches management and organizational change and conducts research on the managerial challenges facing more social responsible organizations. She holds a Ph.D from the École des Hautes Etudes Commerciales de Montréal and an MBA and a degree in Industrial Engineering from the Universidad del Valle, Colombia. For seven years she worked for various private and public organizations in Latin America (in governmental service as well in telecommunications and manufacturing industries), supporting and implementing information technology (IT) and business process re-engineering projects. She has recently completed doctoral research on the human implications of IT in management education.

Sandy E. Green is Assistant Professor in the Management and Organization Department, Marshall School of Business, at the University of Southern California. He has a Ph.D in management from the Harvard Graduate School of Business. His research interests include rhetoric, neo-institutional theory and corporate governance.

Winton Higgins is a graduate of the Universities of Sydney, Stockholm and London. Following an early career as a lawyer, he joined the Politics Department at Macquarie University where he became an Associate Professor specializing in political economy, political theory and comparative genocide studies. He is the author of many articles and several books, both academic and creative non-fiction. He is now a Visiting Research Fellow at the Institute for International Studies, University of Technology, Sydney.

David Loy is Besl Family Chair of Religion and Ethics, Xavier University, Cincinnati, USA. He has studied Zen for over 25 years and is a qualified Zen teacher. He is the author of *Lack and Transcendence: The Problem of Death and Life in Psychotherapy, Existentialism, and Buddhism* (1996) and *Nonduality: A Study in Comparative Philosophy* (1988). His most recent publications include *A Buddhist History of the West: Studies in Lack* (2002); *The Great Awakening: A Buddhist Social Theory* (2003); and *The Dharma of Dragons and Daemons: Buddhist Themes in Modern Fantasy* (2004). Dr Loy also sits on the editorial boards of *Cultural Dynamics, Worldviews, Contemporary Buddhism*, and the *Journal of Transpersonal Psychology*. Dr Loy's research has uniquely combined the study of Buddhist philosophy with Western existentialism and psychotherapy. His comparative study, *Nonduality*, has become a standard work in Buddhist philosophy, and his book, *Lack and Transcendence*, complemented this with existential phenomenology to produce a powerful diagnostic tool which lays bare the value orientations operating in postmodern societies.

Pankaj Mishra completed his MA in English Literature at the Jawaharlal Nehru University in New Delhi and is a Visiting Fellow at the Department of English, University College, London. In 2004–2005 he received a fellowship at the Cullmen Center for Writers and Scholars, New York Public Library. He is author of *An End to Suffering: The Buddha in the World* (2004), *Temptations of the West: How to be Modern in India, Pakistan and Beyond* (2006) and *India in Mind* (2005). Mishra writes literary and political essays for the *New York Times*, the *New York Review of Books*, the *Guardian* and the *New Statesman*, among other American, British and Indian publications. His work has also appeared in the *London Review of Books, Times Literary Supplement, Financial Times, Washington Post, Boston Globe, Time*, the *Independent, Granta, The Nation, N+1, Poetry, Common Knowledge, Outlook, Travel & Leisure, The New Yorker*, and *Harper's*. He divides his time between London and India, and is presently working on a novel.

Ian I. Mitroff, Harold Quinton Distinguished Professor of Business Policy and Director of the USC Center for Crisis Management, earned his Ph.D in

Engineering Science and the Philosophy of Science from the University of California at Berkeley. He has published over 200 articles and 11 books. He contributes regularly to the *Los Angeles Times* and other major newspapers and is a frequent guest on national radio and TV programmes. His research interests involve the study and prevention of large-scale, human-induced crises; managing and bringing about creative large-scale change; and the design of moral/ethical work environments, and organizations.

Julie A. Nelson is author of *Economics for Humans* (2007) which dismisses the view that markets are inexorable 'machines' and discusses how a better understanding of the relation of economics and values could improve both business and care work. She is also author of *Feminism, Objectivity, and Economics* (1996) and co-editor of *Beyond Economic Man: Feminist Theory and Economics* (1993). Formerly a government researcher, an Associate Professor of Economics at the University of California-Davis and at Brandeis University, she is currently a Senior Research Associate with the Global Development and Environment Institute at Tufts University. Julie is interested in the economics of care and the application of relational ontologies to the economic and physical worlds.

David Paul is Consultant and previously a Senior Lecturer at the Australian Centre for Educational Studies at Macquarie University. He is co-author, with Charles Birch, of *Life and Work: Challenging Economic Man* (2003). David's research interests include: complex organizational change management; deep cultural transformation; organizational communication and relational networks; organizational psychological frameworks; Eupsychian leadership; work–fife balance and quality of life.

Acknowledgements

I would like to thank Winton Higgins, in particular, for his enormous help with the editorial work. I would also like to thank Cleo Lester, Stewart Clegg and Siggi Gudergan of the Centre for Management and Organisation Studies, University of Technology, Sydney for their support of the project. Thanks are also due to David Paul, who prompted me to discuss the possibility of the book with other colleagues, and to John Cameron, Stewart Clegg, Dexter Dunphy, Samiul Hassan, Stewart Hill, and Tyrone Pitsis for their advice and encouragement.

I would also like to thank the series editors Güler Aras and David Crowther, in particular David Crowther, who was instrumental in helping identifying some important contributors and eventually agreed to submit a paper of his own. In addition, I wish to thank Peter Lang AG, International Academic Publishers for permission to use Julie Nelson's chapter 'The Relational Firm: A Buddhist and Feminist Analysis' in Zsolnai, Laszlo and Knut Johannessen Ims (eds), *Business within Limits*, Bern: Peter Lang, 2006: 195–217.

Finally, I would like to thank my sons Matthew, Anton and Akira, who have endured my preoccupation with this book and for the never-ending source of support and love, my wife and 'soul-mate', Subhana Barzaghi.

Preface

It is hard to pinpoint the origins of this book, as it has had a momentum of its own, seemingly always one step ahead of me, and never entirely in my control. Thus, the chapters have co-arisen with a harmony that could not have been planned, but still met with my intentions, which were twofold. First, I wished to stimulate a re-engagement with the driving questions of the great spiritual movements founded on a mature knowledge of modernity. This new mature sensibility recognizes the limitations of a singular cultural view of modernity and brings a fresh openness to readdressing questions that remain unsatisfactorily answered. This approach echoes the rekindled attention that is being paid to consciousness, where Douglas Hofstadter and others are breaking new ground in thinking about what it is to be human. In a similar vein, the chapters of this book represent a re-engagement with 'hard problems' of the secular divide in creative ways. The contributors have been chosen because they are not afraid to think differently. This is may be unsettling, as with John Shelby Spong's promotion of a historically informed understanding of the Gospels, or Brian Victoria's exposé of the complicity of the Zen establishment in the Japanese War effort, and it takes a certain maturity to recognize that such explorations may be farsighted attempts to encounter new understandings by those who recognize that historically legitimated beliefs do not always bear up against critical scrutiny. Yet to concede, for example, that Darwin's careful investigations of the origin of species is a far more convincing explanation than the Abrahamic construction of the world does *not* mean that Christianity, Islam or Judaism have nothing valuable to contribute. On the contrary, it might prompt us to explore how their fundamental concerns might be answered in light of this new knowledge.

My second intention was to re-examine our assumptions about the nature of corporate life from this new perspective. Modernity has shown us how institutions in general, including religious institutions, create narratives of power and control to maintain their legitimacy. The new spiritual inquiry must also take stock of these historical and organizational narrative legacies, as they structure how we collectively think about the non-human world and ourselves. This opens the path for new options in corporate life, which may enable us to meet our deepest spiritual aspirations. These aspirations go beyond the personal to include the possibility of corporate action for a better world. In this regard, I have attempted to bring together contributions from a range of leading thinkers, and it is my hope that this book will stimulate the reader to join in what has already begun to be a very interesting and necessary conversation.

David Bubna-Litic

Introduction

David Bubna-Litic

Why Spirituality and Corporate Social Responsibility?

Following decades in which spirituality in the workplace has been a taboo subject, a new interest in it has arisen in both academic and business circles (see Bolman and Deal, 2001; Conger, 1997; Defoore and Renesch, 1995; Fox, 1994; Giacalone and Jurkiewicz, 2003; and Mitroff and Denton, 1999a, 1999b). In these writings spirituality is about something new; these authors use it in a markedly contemporary sense. Today's spirituality, Biberman and Whitty (1997) argue, brings a postmodern perspective on working life. This perspective is postmodern in that it goes beyond the modern suspicion of religion, but it also encompasses something broader than religion, even if it returns us to some familiar religious questions. The new spirituality raises questions informed by scholarship and by the desire to develop an understanding which can be integrated into other contemporary thinking.

Mainstream management discourse still dismisses the new interest in spirituality as swimming against the tide of the typically modern concerns of today's organizations, which, for the most part, not only remain disinterested in spirituality, but are also resistant to its inclusion in corporate life (Grant, O'Neil and Stephens, 2004; Gull and Doh, 2004; Jurkiewicz and Giacalone 2004). This book challenges that exclusion.

The Religious Foundation of Secularism

The exclusion of spirituality and moral sentiments from organizational life has a long history. Since the Industrial Revolution, numerous writers have raised questions about the impact of corporations on the quality of life and their tendency to create 'dark satanic mills', as opposed to what Schumacher (1973), for instance, would see as an economic system geared to real human needs. The exclusion of the spiritual dimension from modern secular organizations goes to the heart of today's debate about the ultimate direction of capitalism. It may well be that present-day critics, in breaking the taboo against raising spiritual issues, constitute just one more protest against that direction. On the other hand, they may be something more significant – the first step towards a transformation. Either way, the writings in question raise central issues about the nature of the economic system.

The contemporary aversion towards things spiritual in corporate life can be traced back to early-modern religious ructions in European history, which appear to have motivated the rise of rationalistic secular society. Undoubtedly the present orthodoxy, which regards the separation of religion from public institutions as a prerequisite for both rational management and individual freedom, insists that religion now remain in the confines of the individual's private world and not invade the public realm of work and economy. The secular assumptions about religion implicit in neo-classical economics sprang from early liberal thinking about choice and freedom. The primary concern of liberal philosophers, according to Eisenach (1981), was not to insulate civil government from religious convictions; rather, it arose out of the Protestant impulse to banish religious hierarchies from public life and to limit their influence to guiding individual believers' private relationship with God. This cultural shift paved the way for religious tolerance through an expansion of private freedoms incorporating not only religion, but also freedom of speech, property and association.

The proponents of these private freedoms did not intend to exclude religion from cultural and institutional organizations, but to free privatized religious observance from institutional control. The later banishing of religious concerns from organizational life expresses the subsequent influence of the 'disenchanted' scientific world-view of the nineteenth and early twentieth centuries. Social scientists also eschewed paradigms that invited spiritual questions as they struggled to gain legitimacy in an intellectual milieu dominated by the natural sciences. This disenchanted view moulded conceptions of 'rational' management. First, the former was seen as a prerequisite for dispensing with the bias and superstitions of religion; second, it accommodated rational legal structures which rewarded merit, not religious persuasion.

This shift coincided with the rise of Western European power, which diffused it well beyond that continent. Secularism is now an established part of the culture of global capitalism and, as such, it surfaces in a variety of cultural contexts. Secularism manifests globally in shopping malls, workplaces, business and government organizations, and in many homes. In these milieux there is very little to suggest that there is more to life than a hedonic journey.

Together with religion's symptomatic absence from these key domains, we see how the modern period has maintained a parallel stream of thinkers who have pathologized religion and spirituality, notably Freud (religious belief as neurotic symptom), Marx (as a form of mass stupefaction) and, more recently, Richard Dawkins (2006) who has polemicized against theistic belief as 'the god delusion'. These critiques have presented formidable challenges, particularly to mainstream religions. Despite this, the resilience of religious adherence points to the limits of rationalism's power; the transformation of any major institution rarely results from outsiders attacking its core positions, particularly positions which its adherents feel obliged to defend. Change is certainly occurring in some contemporary religious institutions, but through far less adversarial means, while religiosity, as such, persists. As Berger (1998: 782) notes, '[m]ost of the world today is as religious as it ever was and, in a good many locales, more religious than ever'.

A simple explanation for why such attacks fail might be that they do not address the core questions and needs that draw people to religions in the first place. These core questions evoke the enduring conundrums of the human condition – ubiquitous ones that are collectively experienced and of public significance. People directly encounter recurring dilemmas in identifying and pursuing the good life; these dilemmas go to the heart of the new thinking about spirituality and have important implications for how we perceive the current direction of global capitalism. Alvesson and Wilmott (1996) explore the possibility of emancipation from instrumental rationality, the dominant ethos of corporate life that isolates individuals, creating tensions between how we live our lives in the private sphere, on the one hand, and in the organizational sphere on the other. They argue that these spheres *interpenetrate* and that we need to work towards a coherent relationship between the instrumental–technical and moral–practical dimensions of social life. This interpenetration also occurs, as David Whyte (2000: 15) suggests, because '[w]ork … is not something we do, but a great pilgrimage of identity by which we discover larger and larger perspectives on our self and the world we inhabit'. Issues of work and identity attract the most fundamental and timeless questions, such as 'Who are we?' and 'Why are we all here?'.

The new openness to spiritual questions in management and organizational thinking, which announced itself in the late 1980s, follows changes in the way other disciplines began to think about these questions. Whilst some management authors attribute the shift to factors such as the changing age composition of the workforce, the loss of community, changes in religious institutions and the growth of interest in non-European religious ideas, these elements seem to divert attention from a deeper change, one that has been emerging for over a century and encompasses far more than the sphere of religious thinking. It reflects a shift in how we think about all human endeavours in the context of growing scepticism towards the assumptions of modernity.

The contemporary interest in spirituality is just one of the fruits of this new sensibility, which many writers flag – *faute de mieux* – with the prefix 'post' attached to the name of an intellectual framework now under critical review. Terms such as 'postmodernity' and 'post-structuralism' signal a deepening suspicion that modernity can never deliver on its promise of liberation from suffering. Science and technology have already provided significant material benefits, and yet we remain far from fulfilled. Thus, despite many nations' attaining relative affluence, as Hamilton (2003, 2005) points out, we find that this success has failed to deliver its promised emancipation; despite our apparent progress, we may be no happier than our ancestors.

The prospect at the beginning of the twenty-first century, although still full of possibilities, does not evoke the same optimism that earlier generations espoused. The present century contrasts with the last in that we now temper our commitment to technical progress with insights into its limits. It often only brings us fleeting satisfactions at the cost of terrifying risks (Beck, 1992). Contemporary science has not dispelled our ignorance, although it has revealed an even stranger universe – one in which old assumptions unravel and even greater mysteries replace them. This vastly enhanced knowledge *about* the world and the power that it bestows has left us far from secure; in fact, it has brought 'an age of anxiety' and 'the risk society' in its wake. 'Modernity has developed alongside an extensive desacralisation of social life,' Mellor and Schilling (1993: 411) point out, 'yet has failed to replace religious certainties with scientific certainties.' In recognizing increased risks associated with modernity, we no longer feel comforted by its assurances, particularly as security is one of its key emancipatory promises. In late modernity, life is increasingly fragmented and accelerating with consequent effects on our sense of self. According to Anthony Giddens (1990: 98):

> *Ontological security and routine are intimately connected, via the*
> *pervasive influence of habit ... The predictability of the (apparently)*

minor routines of day-to-day life is deeply involved with a sense of psychological security. When such routines are shattered – for whatever reason – anxieties come flooding in, and even very firmly founded aspects of the personality of the individual may become stripped away and altered.

Thus, despite the benefits of a century of modernization, our hearts are not at rest, and collectively there remains a familiar spiritual longing, one expressed by the question: 'Is there not more to life than this?'

At the heart of this question lies a re-evaluation of the quest of modernity. Willmott (2000) suggests that the modern 'purchasing' of relief from existential anxiety through the practices and institutions of modernity has, to some extent, entailed a 'sequestration of experience'. This transaction, according to Giddens (1991: 156), enables modernity to be complicit in 'an exclusion of social life from fundamental existential issues which raise central moral dilemmas for human beings'. The desire to transcend these existential concerns is not new: the legend of the Buddha's life reflects the very same themes of transcending the human condition. After hearing a prophecy that his then infant son would either be a king or a saint, the Buddha's father expressed a very modern anxiety in his attempts to prevent his child taking an interest in spiritual things by shielding him from experiences of sickness, old age and death (Bubna-Litic, 2000). Despite his wealth and power, the Buddha's father failed to keep him from confronting these core existential questions, which visit every human life.

As Bauman (1998) points out, the modern pretence that life is amenable to sharp distinctions and definitional precision cannot be sustained, and so any attempt to sequester aspects of the human condition inevitably fails. It seems that new technology creates new problems (such as isolation, lack of exercise and obesity); we cannot escape the pain of inhabiting bodies. To take another example: as Palmer (2006) suggests in *Toxic Childhood*, modern life is having a negative influence on children's development. Once again, we must face dilemmas around rapid technological development and social adaptation to it.

In short, the renewed interest in spiritual questions is a response to these failures of modernity to transcend the human condition. Yet we need to be cautious about trading one promise for another. As Zizek (2001) reminds us, we need to be suspicious of all promises of transcendence. The spirituality of transcendence may not differ in kind from today's antidepressant drugs which cultivate 'an inner distance and indifference towards the mad dance of this accelerated progress [of late capitalism]' (Zizek, 2001: 13).

The various re-evaluations of modernity do not speak with one voice, and, according to Charlene Spretnak (1999), their antecedents lie in a number of social movements that date back to the eighteenth century. In the 1960s, however, many of these ideas resurfaced in a conglomeration of anti-modern sub-cultural movements which Theodore Roszak (1969) dubbed 'the counter culture'. This composite social movement comprised a variety of social experiments which sought radical alternatives to modern life. A significant theme was renewal of religious sentiment which, as Roszak (1972: xx) suggests, was:

> ... not that of the churches; not the religion of Belief and Doctrine, which is, I think the last fitful flicker of the divine fire before it sinks into darkness. Rather, I mean religion in its perennial sense. The Old Gnosis. Vision born of transcendent knowledge. Mysticism, if you will – though this has become too flabby and unrefined a word to help us discriminate among those rhapsodic powers of the mind from which so many traditions of worship and philosophical reflection flow. My purpose is to discover how this, the essential religious impulse, was exiled from our culture, what effect this has had on the quality of our life and course of our politics and what part other energies of transcendence must now play in saving urban-industrial society from self-annihilation.

Despite the obvious naivety of many of these efforts, valuable experience was gained which, according to Lattin (2003), has since continued to diffuse into mainstream society. These themes have now clearly surfaced in recent management literature on spirituality.

Despite Roof's (1999: 74) suggestion that '[w]e stand much too close in time to grasp fully this transition,' the general thrust of the change can be understood as one of perspective. Almost half a century after the 1960s we can see the change more clearly; and we have lived with modernity long enough to be more than suspicious of its pretensions. We know its game and are no longer seduced. The new sensibility carries a number of consequences, the first of which is precisely our distrust of modernity's promises, and now we hear growing demands for ameliorative action, not only from those it has marginalized, but also, by those much closer to its centre. The second consequence of the new sensibility is a renewed openness to critically re-examining premodern and even romantic solutions.

'Romanticism' denotes a broad, long-lived strand of opposition to disembodied scientific knowledge. It embraces a distinctive revision of the central human project in which typically modern knowing – predictive and thus controlling – is seen as incomplete. The romantic sensibility proposes that there are other ways of knowing, particularly knowing as a way of being in the world and embracing the mysterious nature of life. Recent romantic approaches emphasize that the experience of our embodiment brings with it a presence that is a 'given' in our sense of being, which David Abram (1997: 65) suggests is no isolated being, but 'inter-being' with nature:

> [W]e gradually discover our sensory perceptions to be simply our part of a vast, interpenetrating web-work of perceptions and sensations borne by countless other bodies – supported, that is, not just by ourselves, but by icy streams tumbling down granitic slopes, by owl wings and lichens, and by the unseen, imperturbable wind.

This way of flesh and shell is linked to the romantic contention that the modalities of understanding the world offered by modernity fail to *touch* us, and they are unlikely ever to do so. The late Douglas Adams (1995) cleverly dramatizes this limitation in his science fiction fantasy *Hitchhiker's Guide to the Galaxy*, in which he imagines that a race of highly intelligent beings in another world have built a super-computer of unparalleled power in the history of the galaxy. The computer, called 'deep thought', can be seen as a teleological end or ultimate artefact of scientific achievement. One day its owners ask it to answer a human question, *the* big question 'about life, the universe, and everything'. After several thousand years of processing, the intelligent inhabitants of the galaxy eagerly assemble to hear the computer reluctantly pronounce that the answer is … 42. The assembly is hugely disappointed with this answer, and whilst we can laugh at the absurdity of such a meaningless answer there is a powerful allegorical dimension regarding the impotence of *any* scientific answer to satisfy the embodied human desire for meaning. For the very objective nature of scientific explanations is fundamentally separate from the experiential and embodied reality of being human.

Philosophers have not overlooked this limitation, as a similar problem arises with art. As Gadamer (2000: xxii–xxiii) explains,

> … *scholarly research pursued by the 'science of art' is aware from the start that it can neither replace nor surpass the experience of art. The*

fact [is] that through a work of art a truth is experienced that we cannot attain in any other way.

This critical reexamination of romanticism, however, is very different from the old adversarial and rejecting stance of modernity. Critics doubt the overenthusiastic promises of romanticism, just as they voice similar concerns about the emancipatory promises of modernity. This does not necessarily entail cynicism, but rather, as Charlene Spretnak (1999: 1) suggests, 'fresh perceptions and creative alternatives … where previously deadlock and despair held sway'. My own research on Buddhist insight suggests that spiritual experiences are rarely complete in themselves, but require a significant amount of reflection and a foundation in everyday practice. Through constant revisitation, a growing confidence arises, and from this confidence comes the wisdom we associate with mature spirituality.

Modernity's sequestration of human experience forecloses alternative ways of knowing – ways that offer new sources of wisdom. In this context, a new perspective on spirituality offers a fresh approach to central existential questions, and, for this reason, there is a philosophical parallel in the status of personal and private knowledge as contrasted with the public, objective kind. Michael Polyani (1962) recognized the importance of personal participation in objective knowledge, but for spirituality this distinction is something of a misnomer; as David Chalmers (1996) points out, fundamental questions about the nature of our personal private experience – the phenomenon of consciousness – and its relationship to the physical brain remain unanswered.

What we understand to be 'spiritual' arises from the ordinary experiences of our lives. It could be in the form of nagging doubts, which might wake us at night and perplex us with the seeming meaninglessness of life. Spiritual questions might arise from an unbidden event, one which changes our lives in ways outside our control. This may happen without warning, perhaps with a screech of brakes or with an unexpected phone call that disturbs the stillness of the night. Such events remind us of the possibility that at any time, no matter who we are, our lives are subject to an existential uncertainty, which we can neither conceive of in advance nor plan against. Whether it be an accidental death, a cancer diagnosis or a masked assailant, suddenly everything that was once taken for granted is no longer possible.

Catalysing events are not the only source of such questions; some people find spiritual questions arise unexpectedly, apparently for no reason, leaving them touched by life in a way they are at a loss to explain. Overcome with tears of joy, a completely new vista opens before them, for which they find poetry more useful than philosophy. Such experiences are mysterious; for instance, the poet Elisabeth Bishop, then aged seven, was reading a magazine in a dentist's waiting room when she suddenly experienced a profound intimacy with life which set her life on an entirely new course. As she puts it in her poem, 'The Waiting Room', for her 'nothing stranger had ever happened … nothing stranger could ever happen' (Bishop, 1979).

Whatever brings these questions to the surface, they are alien to modern conceptions of corporate life in which questions of life and death and the sacred are banished. Following his heart attack, Burkard Sievers (1990) describes how he was personally confronted by how his experience was 'diabolized' – in the original Graeco-Roman sense of being split off or dissociated – from his work life. Mellor and Shilling (1993: 419) suggest that a consequence of modernity is 'a general privatisation of meaning and experience, leaving individuals alone to construct and maintain values to guide them through life and death, a situation prone to reality-threatening ontological and existential anxieties'.

For people faced with this isolation and collective division, spiritual questions hold great potential for nourishing and rewarding relationships. It is through spiritual encounters that some people learn there are solutions. The term 'self-actualization', coined by Abraham Maslow (1971), arose out of his interview material and implied 'seeing sacredness in all things'. For him, this process amounted to the actualization of the highest human potential. In the form of peak experiences available through cultivation, however, self-actualization did not necessarily create people who were well suited to modern institutional life.

The sudden surge of writers interested in revisiting spirituality in corporate life does not always reflect an understanding of a broader historical context, such as the one I have been attempting here. Similarly, critical reviewers of the literature, according to Biberman and Coetzer (2005), point to a number of ways in which spirituality can be misused. These critiques pick up on some old themes. The first is that spirituality is a form of delusion and functions in a psychological sense to avoid or deny reality. As Marx observed, 'Religion is the sigh of the oppressed creature, the heart of a heartless world, just as it is the spirit of a spiritless situation. It is the opium of the people' (Marx and Engels, 1982: 42).

The second criticism of spirituality in work life is that organizations may use their power to impose spiritual or religious beliefs on employees. The third concern is that spirituality could be used as another form of control by which management might manipulate employees. In this context the latter are understood as exemplifying Foucault's (1994) formally sovereign and normatively self-disciplining subjects who, on the basis of internalized 'truths', become motivated and compliant self-managing employees.

There is no doubt that spirituality is susceptible to such abuses, but that does not refute the key message of the new literature, that we might find new ways of working with our vital existential questions in the context of our working lives. As much as we need to be aware of the pitfalls, workplace spirituality can prove emancipatory and enable individuals to explore a new relationship with work.

The literature also attracts the criticism that it lacks clarity around the meaning of spirituality, which can seem so broad as to be almost useless (Brown, 2003). This criticism fails to recognize that the term is not being used to denote some*thing*, but rather *to name a dialogic space* (see Hattam, 2004). A dialogic space is not simply a dyadic encounter, but rather a space inhabited by different voices and different languages (Bakhtin, 1981). In this sense, the dialogic space of spirituality sets its disparate concepts in a conversation with modernity to form something new, which is informed by a dialogic interaction between the corresponding disciplines. It is through this process that spirituality is undergoing a metamorphosis to something which will unfold in time. Yet we can already discern that it is no longer synonymous with religion, or some perennial truth, but rather invokes a new openness to our interiority. This openness invites in religion too, in that it reframes it as just one contribution to how we think about fundamental issues that confront human existence in general. It allows us to meld modern critical analysis with personal experience to produce, for example, a 'critical subjectivity' (Reason and Rowan, 1981). This perspective honours our capacity to reflect critically on our experiences and engages with the hermeneutics of how we interpret our experiences. Hermeneutics has long problematized the interpretation and meaning of texts and arguably can be applied to narrative accounts of experience as well.

The 'spiritual' dimension, understood as a new openness, is a novel artefact of contemporary challenges to modernity. But it is also born out of modernity's relationship with religion, as modernity has been defined *inter alia* as *other* to the premodern world of religion – particularly Christianity. The openness of present-day spirituality rejects this old family feud and proposes forms of reconciliation. For example, Biberman and Coetzer (2005) suggest the appreciative-inquiry approach for it. However, reconciliation will not occur unless both sides are prepared to give up some ground. As Foucault (1970, 1972) pointed out, different bodies of knowledge do not simply posit the real existence of the objects they purport to describe and theorize, but also prescribe the system of rules and practices which circumscribe what is studied and how it is studied. The suspicion that Foucault and others express is that all discourse thereby intrinsically sets up relations of power. Yet power relations not only inhere in practices of normalization; they also manifest in the practices of *liberation* (Foucault, 1988).

In this sense we can acknowledge that the worlds of work and of the spirit interpenetrate and that the future of the most powerful is bound up with the future of the weak. The groundswell for change comes from the increasing recognition of interpenetration – inter-being – which leads both sides to pose the central ethical question, 'What is it good to be?'. The new ethos thus has deep implications for how we live, work and organize; it implies a new order of things in ways that few have imagined.

Corporate Social Responsibility

'The movement of the [sacred][1] is full of power,' declares the Chinese classic, the *I Ching* (the *Book of Changes*) (Wilhelm and Baynes, 1951: 6). This power arises from 'the primal depths of the universe' and reaches its potential only when it accords with 'what is right'. These observations about the nature of human affairs, written millennia ago, refer to the creative energy that can arise when people touch on the sacred or spiritual. Some corporate managers have not overlooked this potential, according to Mitroff and Denton (1999b: 83) who 'believed strongly that organizations must harness the immense spiritual energy within each person in order to produce world-class products and services'. History is full of examples of changes wrought because a sense of what was right moved people to action. Yet there is no definition of the sacred or specification of what is right in the *I Ching*, which leaves its readers to discover what spirituality means through dialogic reflection on their own lives in the light of the text. What is right for any reader depends on the context of his or her own life. The longevity of this Chinese classic may rest on its avoidance of

---

1   Wilhelm Baynes's translation uses the word 'heaven' here, but 'sacred' better captures the intention of the work.

rigid principles – its acknowledgement that individuals' lives are complex and that their actions mesh with collective processes in subtle ways. Harmony is a key trope in the *I Ching*; it recommends that we realize it in all the complexities of our lives.

Corporate social responsibility – now the subject of a burgeoning literature – also rests on a sense of doing what is right, which no set of rules can express. As Zeller (2006) reminds us, for instance, carefully crafted ethical principles in force at Enron amounted to very little in practice. Many people seek their understanding of what is right through deep inquiry into questions concerning the sacred or spirituality. Spiritual inquiry, at its best, goes beyond the creation of a set of rules for living by and challenges us to meet the open-ended question 'What is it good to be?'. This meeting occurs at the most fundamental level, the level of being. As Charles Taylor (1989) has argued, selfhood and moral action are 'inextricably intertwined themes'.

This relationship informs the pursuit of corporate social responsibility, which contradicts the neo-classical economic claim, exemplified by Milton Friedman's work, that the sole purpose of a corporation is to serve the financial interests of its owners. In pointing to the lack of rigour in discussions about the 'social responsibilities of business', Friedman criticizes the tendency to reify the corporation as something separate from its constituent parts. For most legal purposes a corporation is an artificial person, but it differs from a human person in every other way; it cannot be said to have responsibilities, even in this vague sense, he argues. Yet Friedman assumes that corporate success arises from idealized arms-length transactions – the stuff of neo-classical economics – between these various parts. This way of looking at the social world also sees a corporation as created through a nexus of contracts (Williamson, 1990), one negotiated around established property rights – a central plank of liberal philosophy since John Locke that neo-classical economics relies on. An economy and society based on contract are in themselves democratic, neo-classicals argue, since they support the sovereignty of the individual consumer. However, the doctrine (to say nothing of policy based on it) reinforces the distance between individuals and obscures the degree to which individual consciousness is part of social consciousness. As Naomi Klein suggests in her recent book, *The Shock Doctrine: The Rise of Disaster Capitalism* (2007), any social system fails when human relations break down, and a successful economic system depends on the integrity of its actors. A successful market system requires the ethical and responsible operation of markets, and that this ethos informs corporate organization.

Nowadays managers are coming to see the unrealism inherent in the neo-classical view of the firm. Corporations operate in an economic environment characterized by complex, multiple linkages which affect value creation and thus profit. Very little commerce is based on the simple market transactions that informed early economic thinking, before mass advertising and the consumer society. These days consumer choices are known to involve far more complex interactions, including participation in marketer-created symbolic fantasies, rather than rational evaluation of a product's worth.

The close link between products and identity is not new; back in the 1950s, Levy (1959) recognized the symbolic importance of consumption. Recent research (Capra, 2002) shows how complex the vital linkages between elemental activities in the economy are, which is hardly surprising given the dynamic, interactive and multifaceted nature of social life today. Recognition of this complexity reveals a dimension which extends Porter's (1980, 1985) notion of strategy based on an isolated value-chain. Porter (1980, 1985), in focusing on competitive advantage, narrowed the complexity of the strategy process, overlooking the potential for a multidimensional *matrix* view of value-adding activities. Linkages may not only occur vertically, but also horizontally and diagonally across a multiplicity of value-chains. In this new conception, string-like linkages can create value for a corporation in unpredictable ways. This cooperative perspective suggests that the locus of control does not lie entirely with management, but in networks of relationships. These networks explain the impact of relatively small non-government organizations such as Greenpeace on large multinational corporations and how its strategic and symbolic actions can have an immense impact on public perceptions.

This complex systems-view of the firm does not fit easily with neo-classical assumptions about rational decision-making, in which individual agents manifest as independent entities guided by an economic calculus in turn designed to maximize their wealth in a conceptually simple context. Rather, we now see organizational outcomes emerging out of a dynamic interplay in a complex and interdependent system. From the social responsibility perspective, the interests of shareholders cannot be neatly divided off from those of other stakeholders; all these interests co-arise in a complex, dynamic process. This process-based paradigm refutes the essentialization of the individual by highlighting interdependence in a network of hidden connections, which Capra (2002) suggests link even the most primitive cells to the global economy. The spiritual thus interpenetrates the consciousness of corporations, whose survival depends on a vast web of circumstances and whose existence arises not only from financial capital, but also natural, social and symbolic 'capital'. These new categories of capital in today's managerial thought represent attempts to grapple with the several aspects of the multilayered context which now confronts corporate management.

At its heart, a multidimensional perspective challenges proponents of corporate social responsibility to develop new ways of thinking about what is right, by moving from what it is good to do, to what it is good to be. Corporate social responsibility thus demands an open inquiry into spiritual questions. Clearly, such an inquiry problematizes the secular divide as it uncovers the shared underlying assumptions of the traditionally secular and religious realms respectively – assumptions on which the authority of traditional religious institutions once rested, but which have also legitimated a secular and impersonal society that encourages the pursuit of material wealth at the expense of human well-being and nature.

The new wave of questioning suggests that many of the old conceptual divisions are false, that human consciousness does not transcend the body, but is shaped critically by our physical nature and our bodily experience (Lakoff and Johnson, 1999). The new spiritual questioning reopens the possibility of transcendence by questioning the assumed limits on what it means to be human. We are now free to draw on the wisdom that runs through almost all religions – a wisdom that counsels humility in the face of the mystery of life and an acknowledgement of our deep interconnection with the universe.

Technology has merely extended the shoreline of knowledge. For many astronauts, the direct seeing into the immensity of the universe at first hand obliged them to speak about the spiritual. Ultimately, the recognition of how deeply we are immersed in this mystery prepares us for far less pretentious projects than those spawned by the European Enlightenment – ones that embrace a more practical, 'make-do' approach, are more humble in their aims and are more communitarian. The new approach recognizes that our individual or group worlds are not independent, but interpenetrating. In this interpenetrating world, the old divide between self and other no longer convinces.

The essays collected here set out to renegotiate the political divide that secularization sets up in the culture of global capitalism. They do not call for a return to premodern political structures, but seek to examine spirituality and corporate social responsibility through the metaphor of interpenetration.

The various chapters seek to explore the interrelationship and interplay of what have previously been treated as isolated spheres. Today's exploration of spirituality is not ready for sharp definitions, and so, like the *I Ching*, I choose to leave spirituality itself underspecified, allowing its content to unfold in what follows. This decision emanates from my own long experience of spiritual practice and reflection, and an understanding that modernity's pretensions to precision, while appropriate in some contexts, do not always apply in the social sciences.

We are still engaged in a multidiscursive struggle that is beginning to recognize that corporate social responsibility interconnects with our spirituality and vice versa. The essays in this book draw upon important contemporary insights with roots in a variety of traditions.

About This Book

Much academic work goes beyond the call of duty, and the contributions to this volume in particular bear a gift. Almost every contributor to it has followed 'the road less travelled', giving something more of themselves than academic life usually requires. The essays collected here offer more than intellectual reflections; they have come about through each contributor's personal inquiry and practice. Inspired by contrasting traditions including Buddhism, Christianity and Hinduism as well as non-religious ones such as humanism, each essay grapples with truth which, Alain Badiou (2003) suggests, is where something happens which does not fit with our knowledge. For many of the contributors to this book, their understanding comes from such an encounter – an encounter that precipitated a foundational shift in themselves; the authors represent a growing international fellowship which has found that the human experience of inter-being, interiority and sacredness does not fit within modern science. Each contribution reflects a positive scepticism about the shibboleths of modern academic thinking.

ISSUES

Part I of this book consists of chapters which explore the broader issues of spirituality, organizational life and corporate social responsibility.

In Chapter 1 Pankaj Mishra contrasts the modern ideals and training of secular intellectuals with the spectacular mishaps their elite has wrought in

American foreign policy. Mishra wonders if there is not something awry in the logocentric preoccupations of Western intellectuals who, despite their erudition and professional dedication, signally lack wisdom. Their unwisdom points to the distortions of the culture of modernity, with all its rationalistic pretensions, and leads to an instrumental view of humanity. This culture fosters arrogance towards history and other cultural points of view; it assumes that the rational human will can and should shape the lives of others. Mishra reminds us how alien this attitude has been to the great spiritual intellectuals who have changed the course of history. These intellectuals have wrought positive social changes though their courage, sacrifice and adherence to what they believed was right. Their political modus operandi, Mishra argues, has respected human interdependence, to which their own spirituality has borne witness. The greatness of leaders like Mandela and Gandhi arose from how they themselves manifested in the world. Their presence, awareness and humility won the day, not political calculations and smart strategies.

Charles Birch's and David Paul's essay (Chapter 2) builds on the work of Alfred North Whitehead, Paul Tillich, Reinhold Niebuhr and Charles Hartshorne, who have explored different perspectives on Christianity. Birch and Paul question the mechanistic conception of reality at the heart of modern science. Drawing on Whitehead's realization that in order to understand any specific phenomenon we need to understand the whole context, they propose an alternative view of science which seeks understanding in relationship to the whole. If we want to understand lips, we need to widen our research to the physiological structure of the face. If we were to stop at the face, however, our understanding would be incomplete, as a more complete understanding would need to continue on to higher levels of the system, including the nature of gender relations, as lips are not only used for eating, but also for expressing emotion verbally and non-verbally through facial expressions, and, of course, for kissing, all of which might explain aspects of their physiology. We might then ask how these various uses developed over human evolutionary history. As we extend an inquiry in this way, we see into the interconnection that links all parts of the system. Birch and Paul explain this interconnection as dynamic: humans are constantly in a process of becoming. To be human is to be forever in a process of becoming something different, just as lips change with how they are used, how they are decorated and how we, as their owners and witnesses, feel. Ultimately, we humans can never fully understand ourselves in isolation from our myriad interconnections with the universe we inhabit. This has consequences for management, which Birch and Paul explore, including the need to create meaningful work, to work towards ecological sustainability and to welcome creative adventures.

Birch's and Paul's essay contributes to our understanding of how spirituality can enrich our understanding of corporate social responsibility. By linking our subjective experience to the great web of interconnection, our perspective on corporate affairs shifts from a mechanistic view to an organic one. From a theistic standpoint, they argue, this interconnection connects us to the universal (God) – a view which resonates with many other spiritual traditions.

Winton Higgins has contributed two valuable chapters to this book. In the first of them (Chapter 3), he takes up the relationship between business and society, which has presently become a pressing issue following the large scale government economic interventions across the world. What social conditions make private enterprise possible? The theory of civil society sets forth these preconditions, which are often assumed as the normal context of capitalism. But this relationship must not be left on automatic pilot, and certainly not to the mercies of 'business fundamentalists' who cannot see it and do not respect it. For Higgins, Western society rests on moral values embodied in the institutions of civil society and democracy. If corporations evade their social responsibilities, they threaten the social conditions of their own existence. In this way, the agenda of corporate social responsibility sensitizes us to a vital form of social embeddedness that must now move to centre-stage in managerial thinking. Civil society requires engagement with organized action, and the quality of this engagement has more to do with how we manage negative behaviours, which create misery in others. In this regard, Higgins sees dangers in economics' dismal view of social relations as founded upon an acceptance of such behaviours as natural. For most spiritual traditions, these behaviours are the least highly regarded, and, in contrast, spiritual development occurs through the cultivation of other more positive natural tendencies, such as love, generosity and compassion.

Nicholas Capaldi opens his essay (Chapter 4) with an historical discussion of 'the technological project' – how civilization seeks to control nature through technology. René Descartes, in particular, significantly shaped this project; he pointed to a 'hidden structure' that undergirds the physical world. Descartes assumed that the human mind (or more importantly, the soul) is outside the physical structures of the world. This framework sets up a foundational problem, which is that the quest for control assumes that we, as humans, are outside nature's domain and therefore a special case. Transposed to human affairs, 'the technological project' sought to create an optimal society based on rational management. The project rode on the assumptions of the Enlightenment with its disregard for religion. Capaldi explores how the collapse of Enlightenment thinking opens up new doors for the sacred and reveals a new place for Christian revelation. Revelation permeates the experience of human beings who open themselves to its possibility by learning to listen deeply. This listening is something that need not be confined to Abrahamic religious traditions; many other traditions encourage the requisite openness as well. Capaldi explores its implications for organizational life in the conviction that the technological project still beckons and that its current reconceptualization offers a new direction for management.

In Chapter 5 Buddhist philosopher and academic David Loy confronts us with certain contemporary social trends, including what he calls the 'religion of the market', which pervades the global economy promising 'salvation through consumerism'. He demonstrates the way in which the pervasive causes of human suffering that Buddhism identifies have become institutionalized in late modernity. Much of our conduct in the world springs from a deep sense of incompleteness – a pervasive experience of not being quite 'OK'. This sense of not being fulfilled drives people to actions which go far beyond their basic needs, since we create an identity out of the things we consume and display.

Loy extends his argument to collective selves, which are manifest in the form of institutions, and even nation-states, suggesting that these are also established to ameliorate the experience of lack. Just as we identify with our own stories, we also identify with collective stories about gender, race, ethnicity, nation and so on. Loy demonstrates how the nature of these collective institutions arises out of the same dysfunctional motives that infect us at the individual level: greed, ill-will and delusion. Yet he takes a new slant in which individual remedial actions are not enough; rather, we need to work towards a society which encourages generosity and compassion, virtues grounded in a wisdom that recognizes our interconnectedness.

In Chapter 6, Julie Nelson continues the theme of interconnectedness, drawing on Buddhist and feminist thinking to challenge the conventional view of the firm as an independent entity. Traditional rationalistic modes of thinking about the firm assume that its characteristics derive from what is 'inside' it – its assets, human resources and managerial skills. By contrast, the alternative way of seeing the firm highlights its relational existence, presenting it not so much as a separate entity but as a process that cannot be separated from its environment. Critics of capitalism also fall into the trap of understanding firms as non-relational and fixed in their nature. A relational view of the firm sees the potential for firms to reflect different relations both inside *and* outside the firm. The burgeoning area of stakeholder thinking illustrates how relationships and mutuality can moderate firm behaviour.

PATHWAYS FOR CHANGE

Part II of this collection explores ways in which openness to the interpenetrating nature of self and nature, self and the world can find expression in action in the workplace.

In Chapter 7 Ian Mitroff, Terri Egan, Murat Alpaslan and Sandy Green suggest that managers and management academics can glean much from the discipline of animal 'whispering' as they pursue their goal of producing healthy people and integrated organizations. Human interiority, while distinct from that of animals, nonetheless contains remnants from our evolutionary development, which today allows us to sustain a high level of communication ('whispering') with domesticated animals. We can learn a lot about our own social interactions from learning how to interact with horses and dogs in particular. If we enter into the discipline of animal whispering, we discover that animals also thrive when all their emotional and social needs are appropriately met. Whispering sets up a two-way relationship and requires close human attention to all aspects of the animal in training.

Like animals, people in organizations can lose touch with their own instinctual compass and emotional needs. When organizing people we need to recognize how to work with both sides of the relationship. Managers intent on building effective organizations need to be able to understand and respect their own interiority before they can deal with relationships at work, and this process calls on them to go beyond 'the games people play' and enter into genuine two-way communication. Ian Mitroff and his colleagues unfurl the various dimensions of organizational relationships, including the spiritual dimension – an experiential contact which reveals a deep interconnection between animal and human.

Dexter Dunphy's essay (Chapter 8) relates his own attempts to engage with the spiritual questions of his life in the context of his work as a tertiary educator and management consultant. This wonderful essay reveals an engaged spiritual practice. It shows how our spirituality comes to us, bit by bit, like the strange things we find on the beach as we walk beside the great mysterious ocean. A close friend of mine creates marvellous works of art out of things she picks up from the beach, and then she gives them to her friends. In like manner, Dunphy passes on what he finds 'on the beach', now worked into highly evocative poetry. It expresses an interiority all the more impressive for its authenticity. We are entering a period in which a new world-view is needed, he suggests – one that precisely acknowledges our deep interconnections. Competition cannot be the dominant aspect of work life, because life, as such, expresses itself through love, caring and compassion. These emotions invoke our subjective experience as a whole and demand our embodied engagement with others, including the others with whom we enter into relationship in our work. Dunphy calls on us to experience how disengagement – typically in the form of fear and greed – fails us. Hence his deeply personal poetry has important ramifications for organizational life.

In Chapter 9 Ana Maria Davila Gomez and David Crowther bring an important practical dimension to the discussion by tackling the transformative potential of management education. The latter needs to develop the whole person in a way that raises the spiritual issues which an authentic engagement with life poses – something that makes some practices central to a number of religions relevant to management education. My own research into the experience of senior Buddhist meditation teachers revealed that spiritual insights arise not just in formal meditation practices, but also from using their benefits to more fully engage with other aspects of life (Bubna-Litic, 2007). Drawing on the long tradition of humanistic education, Gomez and Crowther criticize the current narrow thrust of management development, which closes minds rather than opening them up to the human potential.

In Chapter 10 Winton Higgins discusses the ongoing project to standardize corporate social responsibility currently being undertaken by the world's premier standards body, the International Organization of Standardization (ISO). Modern standardization, a form of rule-making, evolved in the context of physical production and construction, but from the late 1980s it has broadened out to address more and more aspects of organizational life. ISO's interventions into organizational life began when it published its quality management standards (ISO 9000) in 1987, but its development of a standard for social responsibility (ISO 26000, due for publication in 2009) marks a qualitatively higher level of ambition, one with an obvious relevance to the focus of this book. Can social responsibility be reduced to a single written standard? And, if so, can it contribute to a global economic culture with real leverage into boardrooms,and thus make sustainable development more feasible? Higgins's chapter poses the fundamental question about whether corporations are capable of generating a moral view and course of action internally, as a number of the contributors to this volume suggest, or whether social responsibility must depend on external institutional and cultural constraints powerful enough to mould corporate management's forms of calculation. In short, is social responsibility something that needs to be imposed? Standards development itself depends on a dialogic process, and the large international meetings involved in the drawn-out process of crystallizing the future standard for corporate social responsibility illustrates just how much dialogue must take place to produce a workable and authoritative standard in this new area.

Interpenetrating Worlds

Collectively, these contributions reflect the growing perception that a new sensibility around spiritual questions is emerging. Some observers, such as Gordon Lynch (2007: 1) see this as being 'one of the most significant religious transitions for centuries'; however, as he expands, how we view this change depends on our perspective. Although the contributors to this book represent a variety of different spiritual perspectives there are some recurring ideas and general themes. The growing perspective on the ideas and assumptions of modernity which have had time to unfold over the past two centuries has allowed the contributors to question the value of modernity's vision in relation to spirituality from the vantage-point of hindsight. Mostly, they have engaged in the debate by questioning the governing assumptions that both explicitly and implicitly drive our modern system, which is a refreshing shift from debates on postmodernity that remain within modernity's governing assumptions – a common source of misunderstanding.

In the context of spirituality, several distinctive themes can be identified. Most prominent is the theme of interconnectedness. In the spiritual context, I prefer the term 'interpenetration' because it speaks to the experiential dimension – as a felt sense of oneness. Varela, Thompson and Rosch (1993) have argued that contemporary consciousness studies need to enlarge their horizon to encompass lived human experience, which is an idea that has since gained considerable momentum. Similarly, spirituality ultimately rests in the experienced world. Poets and mystics often describe their view of the world as oneness, something the Buddhist teacher Thích Nhất Hạnh calls inter-being, from the perspective of lived experience.

The experiential sense of interpenetration puts us in touch with the world in a profound way – a way that is more easily conveyed by poetry, than logic. Blake

(1977: 128), for example, expresses this sense of how our lives interpenetrate with the world:

> I wander through each chartered street,
> Near where the chartered Thames does flow,
> And mark in every face I meet
> Marks of weakness, marks of woe.
> In every cry of every man,
> In every infant's cry of fear,
> In every voice, in every ban,
> The mind-forged manacles I hear.
> How the chimney-sweeper's cry
> Every blackening church appals;
> And the hapless soldier's sigh
> Runs in blood down palace walls.
> But most through midnight streets I hear
> How the youthful harlot's curse
> Blasts the new-born infant's tear,
> And blights with plagues the marriage hearse.

Blake's passionate sense of social responsibility has two levels: the first speaks to an objective point of view and how our concepts and rationalities blind us to our interconnectedness, and how the plight of others inevitably has an effect on ourselves. This could not be more poignantly exemplified than by the Australian prime minister's recent apology for laws and policies which had 'inflicted profound grief, suffering and loss on these our fellow [indigenous] Australians'. In acknowledging the pain and suffering, Mr Rudd also declared that the apology was being made to 'remove a great stain on the soul of the nation'. Although this statement provokes some very interesting questions about what he meant by the 'soul' of the nation, the speech made it clear that Australians, despite their efforts to bury the past, have come to recognize that their future well-being is interdependent with that of the indigenous people. Rudd's use of the word 'soul' points to a more subtle level of this interconnection, one that reflects the experience of an inside–outside view, where one's sense of self is diffused into the world. This view sees human beings not as disconnected individuals, but as deeply interpenetrated by all things, including trees and stones. The fourteenth-century Islamic poet Mahmud Shabestari expresses such a perspective:

> Every particle of the world is a mirror,
> In each atom lies the blazing light
> of a thousand suns.

Cleave the heart of a rain-drop,
a hundred pure oceans will flow forth …
Though the inner chamber of the heart is small,
the Lord of both worlds
gladly makes [a] home there.

(*Trans. Harvey, 1997*)

Both aspects of interpenetration suggest a different perspective from that which has predominated in modernity since Descartes. If the modern approach to understanding the sovereign individual is suspect, this implies a shift at the very centre of our thinking. The scientific study of consciousness has yet to solve the hard problems of consciousness; however, there is growing sense that the mind can no longer be conceived independently, but rather must be viewed as a biological system rooted in bodily experience and interconnected with bodily action and interaction with other individuals (Garbarini and Adenzato, 2004). Thomas Metzinger (2003) goes further to suggest that what we understand as the self is simply a cognitive construction and is not a thing, but an ongoing process. If the notion of sovereign individual is under review, then so is modernity's promise of increasing control over life through scientific knowledge and rational management.

Mishra regards this presumption of control as a form of hubris in Western secular thinking and contrasts the sense of control of Western secular intellectuals to the humble stance of spiritual leaders, who, despite their modesty, elicit enormous popular enthusiasm for change. Mishra argues that the belief that personal attributes, such as humility and wisdom of the heart, have no distinctive advantages over expertise is one that pervades Western thinking. This assumption belies the power that elemental human drives, such as greed and hatred, have on reason. These inclinations too easily delude people into a sense of self-righteousness and control, which are ways of responding that inevitably lead to destructive consequences. We find this theme arising again with Loy's concern that avarice and antipathy have become inculcated over time into the culture of modern institutions. Underlying this challenge is the second aspect of interpenetration, and Loy suggests that the focus on the individual in modernity carries through to personal spiritual practices. Buddhist liberation is a challenge to the notion of the individual self and is based on awakening to one's sense of being a self that is *not* separate from others and the world. The cognitive default of an 'I' is a mental contrivance that, once recognized as such, no longer has the same hold over us. Loy suggests that full liberation brings forth a deep compassion that goes beyond an individual sense of self. From this viewpoint, the theme of interpenetration and interconnection expands to include collectively created institutions which create unnecessary suffering. A further implication of Loy's writing is a challenge to modern assumptions about a private relationship with the sacred. For Loy, spiritual development is not simply a private affair, because our own well-being is integrally connected to society's institutions, and thus we must work together to free ourselves. This relational nature between the organized corporate world and the selfless love and compassion that can be experienced through most spiritual practices highlights the interpenetration of spirituality and corporate life.

Nelson takes up a different aspect of the interpenetration theme, examining the business firm from this perspective and finding links to feminist discourse. Contemporary discussions on gender recognize that, to make progress in gender relations, a truly relational understanding between men and women needs to be achieved. A key obstacle to this understanding is that the neat distinctions between men and women – like 'us and them' – are unstable narrative categories. In recognizing interpenetration and interconnection, feminist discourse has begun to open up deep ontological questions. Nelson draws on the Buddhist concept of co-dependent origination to re-examine the notion of the individual. From this viewpoint, an individual is neither a unique, robust and separate self nor a socially constituted one. The implications challenge views of corporate social responsibility based on deliberative rationality as found in economic thinking about organizations, and reorientates us to a mutual view of the business firm as an entity interpenetrated by its social milieu and vice versa. Thus, social responsibility is an appreciation that our personal well-being and that of our business institutions are fundamentally interconnected to society. This interconnected view is also present in Birch's and Paul's Christian discussion of process thinking and its implications for management.

Higgins similarly asks whether the locus of corporate social responsibility lies outside the political culture of the society, challenging modernity's tendency to individualize corporate decision-makers. The theme of interpenetration and interdependence runs through his chapters at the level of the corporation, and he argues that corporate social responsibility depends on a proactive interrelationship with society. As modern technology advances, as it magnifies the impacts of the global economy and exposes humanity to ever-greater risks of destruction, it becomes increasingly obvious that environmental destruction does not respect human borders. Each actor in the economy must recognize his or her power and responsibility to work towards a sustainable future. Spiritual maturity calls upon us to recognize that our responsibility to protect the world interpenetrates with our being, that who we are is a reflection of this world, and that how we maintain the world is deeply interconnected with our own consciousness. In the practice of everyday life we can engage in spiritual practices to expand our horizons and develop our awareness.

The contributions in Part II, 'Pathways for Change', provide some specific maps in which spirituality and corporate social responsibility can be brought together. One theme that arises, as Davila Gomez and Crowther suggest, is the need to take action in light of a sense of our interconnection. They argue that contemporary management education fails us in the sense that it orients students to think instrumentally rather than reflect on the relationship of their actions to society and on their whole person. This applies not only to the content but also to the very process of educating, since how an individual is treated throughout their education is crucial to their development as a person. This sub-theme recognizes that the modern preoccupation with rational instrumental action is a limited view that ignores other important aspects of life, including our spiritual development.

The long evolutionary interconnection between humans and animals may provide important clues as to how people can draw on more abilities than just their reason to lead and manage organizations. Mitroff et al. have found that animals have an uncanny ability to attune to our interiority, and skilled trainers use this shared understanding to work with their animals. This 'felt sense' also forms the basis of many somatic therapy techniques which rely on the therapist using awareness of their own interiority to mirror that of their clients. In their exploration of horse-whispering, Mitroff et al. found that the skills people use in this highly effective training of animals can also be applied to human relationships. These findings highlight the psychological interpenetration of humans and animals and implicitly question the modern distrust of human interiority. This is not a rejection of reason, however; as Mitroff et al. demonstrate, the careful observation of working with animals can provide many valuable insights into human organization and leadership. At a deeper level, our interiority speaks of an interpenetrating sense of being one with the mystery of all creation. Dunphy's poetic reflections bring us back to this important theme and its many dimensions, with which the contributors to this book have fruitfully engaged. Dunphy celebrates his sense of this shifting awareness and suggests that a shift towards an appreciation of interpenetration may be necessary for a sustainable future.

References

Abram, D. (1997), *The Spell of the Sensuous: Perception and Language in a More-Than-Human World* (New York: Vintage Books).

Adams, D. (1995), *Hitchhiker's Guide to the Galaxy* (New York: Bantam Books).

Alvesson, M. and Wilmott, H. (1996), *Making Sense of Management: A Critical Introduction* (London: Sage).

Badiou, A. (2003), *Infinite Thought: Truth and the Return of Philosophy*, trans. J. Clemens and O. Feltham (New York: Continuum).

Bakhtin, M.M. (1990), *The Dialogic Imagination: Four Essays*, trans. C. Emerson and M. Holmquist (Austin: University of Texas Press).

Bauman, Z. (1998), 'Postmodern Religion?' in P. Heelas (ed.) with D. Martin and R. Morris, *Religion, Modernity, and Postmodernity* (Oxford: Blackwell).

Beck, U. (1992), *Risk Society: Towards a New Modernity*, trans. M. Ritter (London: Sage).

Berger, P.L. (1998), 'Protestantism and the Quest for Certainty', *The Christian Century*, 115:23, 782–85.

Biberman, J. and Coetzer, G. (2005), 'Can Critical People also be Spiritual? Reconciling Critical and Spiritual Approaches', *Tamara: Journal of Critical Postmodern Organization Science*, 3:5, 70–75.

Biberman, J. and Whitty, M. (1997), 'A Postmodern Spiritual Future for Work', *Journal of Organizational Change Management*, 10:2, 130–38.

Bishop, E. (1979), 'In the Waiting Room', *The Complete Poems 1927–1979* (New York: Farrar, Straus and Giroux, Inc).

Blake, William (1977), 'London' in William Blake, *The Complete Poems*, ed. Alicia Ostriker (Harmondsworth: Penguin).

Bolman, L. and Deal, T.E. (1995), *Leading with Soul: An Uncommon Journey of Spirit* (San Francisco: Jossey-Bass).

Brown, R.B. (2003), 'Organizational Spirituality: The Sceptic's Version', *Organization*, 10:2, 393–400.

Bubna-Litic, D. (2000), 'Buddhism Returns to the Market-place' in D. Keown and C.S. Prebish (eds), *Contemporary Buddhist Ethics* (Honolulu: University of Hawaii Press).

Bubna-Litic, D. (2007), 'Opening a Dialogic Space between Buddhism and Economics: An Empirical-experiential Exploration of the Relationship between Insight and Action' Ph.D. thesis (Department of Social Ecology, University of Western Sydney).

Capra, F. (2002), *The Hidden Connections: A Science for Sustainable Living* (New York: Random House).

Chalmers, D. (1996), *The Conscious Mind: In Search of a Fundamental Theory* (Oxford: Oxford University Press).

Conger, J.A. (1997), *Spirit at Work* (San Francisco: Jossey-Bass Publishers).

Dawkins, R. (2006), *The God Delusion* (Sydney: Bantam).

Defoore, B. and Renesch, J. (eds) (1995), *Rediscovering the Soul of a Business: A Renaissance of Values* (San Francisco: New Leaders Press).

Eisenach, E.J. (1981), *Two Worlds of Liberalism: Religion and Politics in Hobbes, Locke and Mill* (Chicago: University of Chicago Press).

Foucault, M. (1970), *The Order of Things: An Archaeology of the Human Sciences*, trans. A. Sheridan (New York: Random House).

Foucault, M. (1972), *The Archaeology of Knowledge*, trans. A. Sheridan (London and New York: Routledge).

Foucault, M. (1988), 'An Aesthetics of Existence', in L. D. Kritzman (ed.), *Foucault: Politics, Philosophy, Culture: Interviews and other Writings 1977–1984* (New York: Routledge, Chapman & Hall).

Foucault, M. (1994), *Power: Essential Works of Foucault, 1954–1984*, Vol. III, ed. J.D. Faubion, trans. P. Rabinow and R. Hurley (London: Allen Lane: The Penguin Press).

Fox, M. (1994), *The Reinvention of Work: A New Vision of Livelihood for our Time* (San Francisco: Harper).

Frohlich, M. (2007), 'Critical Interiority', *Spiritus*, 7, 77–81.

Garbarini, F., and Adenzato, M. (2004). 'At the Root of Embodied Cognition: Cognitive Science Meets Neurophysiology', *Brain and Cognition*, 56, 100–106.

Gadamer, H.G. (2000), *Truth and Method* (2nd edn), trans. J. Weinsheimer. and D.G. Marshall (New York: Continuing Publishing Corporation).

Giacalone R.A. and Jurkiewicz, C.L. (eds) (2003), *Handbook of Workplace Spirituality and Organizational Performance* (Armonk, NY: M.E. Sharpe).

Giddens, A. (1990), *The Consequences of Modernity* (Stanford, CA: Stanford University Press).

Giddens, A. (1991), *Modernity and Self-Identity: Self and Society in the Late Modern Age* (Stanford, CA: Stanford University Press).

Grant, D., O'Neil, K. and Stephens, L. (2004), 'Spirituality in the Workplace: New Empirical Directions in the Study of the Sacred', *Sociology of Religion*, 65:3, 265–83.

Gull, G.A. and Doh, J. (2004), 'The "Transmutation" of the Organization: Toward a More Spiritual Workplace', *Journal of Management Inquiry*, 13:2, 128–39.

Hamilton, C. (2003), Growth Fetish (Sydney: Allen and Unwin).

Hamilton, C. and Denniss, R. (2005), *Affluenza: When Too Much is Never Enough* (Sydney: Allen and Unwin).

Harvey, A. (ed.) (1997), *The Essential Mystics: Selections from the World's Great Wisdom Traditions* (San Francisco: HarperSanFrancisco).

Hattam, R. (2004), *Awakening-Struggle: Towards a Buddhist Critical Social Theory* (Flaxton: Post Pressed).

Jurkiewicz, C.L. and Giacalone, R.A. (2004) 'A Values Framework for Measuring the Impact of Workplace Spirituality on Organizational Performance, *Journal of Business Ethics*, 49, 129–42.

Klein, N. (2007), *The Shock Doctrine: The Rise of Disaster Capitalism* (London: Allen Lane/The Penguin Press).

Lakoff, G. and Johnson, M. (1999), *Philosophy in the Flesh: The Embodied Mind and its Challenge to Western Thought* (New York: Basic Books).

Lattin, D. (2003), *Following our Bliss: How the Spiritual Ideals of the Sixties Shape our Lives Today* (New York: Harper).

Levy, S.J. (1959), 'Symbols for Sale', *Harvard Business Review*, 33 (March–April), 117–24.

Marx, K. and Engels, F. (1982), *On Religion* (Atlanta, CA: Scholars Press).

Maslow, A. (1971), *The Farther Reaches of Human Nature* (New York: The Viking Press).

Mellor, P.A. and Shilling, C. (1993), 'Modernity, Self-identity and the Sequestration of Death', *Sociology*, 27:3, 411–21.

Metzinger, T. (2003). *Being No One* (Cambridge, MA: MIT Press).

Mitroff, I.I. and Denton, E.A. (1999a), *A Spiritual Audit of Corporate America: A Hard Look at Spirituality, Religion, and Values in the Workplace* (San Francisco: Jossey Bass).

Mitroff, I.I., and Denton, E.A. (1999b), 'A Study of Spirituality in the Workplace', *Sloan Management Review*, 40:4, 83–92.

Palmer, S. (2006), *Toxic Childhood: How the Modern World is Damaging Our Children and What We Can Do About It* (London: Orion).

Polanyi, M. (1962), *Personal Knowledge* (London: Routledge & Keegan Paul).

Porter, M. (1980), *Competitive Strategy* (New York: Free Press).

Porter, M. (1985), *Competitive Advantage* (New York: Free Press).

Reason, P. and Rowan, J. (eds) (1981), *Human Inquiry: A Sourcebook of New Paradigm Research* (Chichester: Wiley).

Roof, W.C. (1999), *Spiritual Marketplace: Baby Boomers* (Ewing, NJ: Princeton University Press).

Roszak, T. (1969), *The Making of a Counter Culture* (New York: Doubleday & Co.).

Roszak, T. (1972), *Where the Wasteland Ends: Politics and Transcendence in Postindustrial Society* (London: Faber & Faber).

Schumacher, E.F. (1973), *Small is Beautiful: A Study of Economics as if People Mattered* (New York: Harper & Row).

Sievers, B. (1990), 'The Diabolization of Death: Some Thoughts on the Obsolescence of Mortality in Organization Theory and Practice', in J. Hassard and D. Pym (eds), *The Theory and Philosophy of Organizations: Critical Issues and New Perspectives* (London: Routledge).

Spretnak, C. (1999), *Resurgence of the Real: Body, Nature, and Place in a Hypermodern World* (New York: Routledge).

Taylor, C. (1989), *Sources of the Self: The Making of the Modern Identity* (Cambridge MA: Harvard University Press).

Varela, F., Thompson, E. and Rosch, E. (1993), *The Embodied Mind* (Cambridge, MA: MIT Press).

Wilhelm, R. and Baynes, C.F. (trans.) (1951), *I Ching, or the Book of Changes* (London: Routledge & Kegan Paul).

Williamson, O.E. (1990), 'The Firm as a Nexus of Treaties: An Introduction' in M. Aoki, B. Gustafsson and O.E. Williamson (eds), *The Firm as a Nexus of Treaties* (London: Sage Publications).

Willmott, H. (2000), 'Death: So what? Sociology, Sequestration and Emancipation', *Sociological Review*, 48:4, 649–66.

Whyte, D. and Reece, R. (2000), 'Preserving the Soul of Medicine and Physicians: A Talk with David Whyte', *Physician Executive*, 26:2, 14–19.

Zeller, T. Jr (2006), 'A Sense of Something Rotten on Aspen', *New York Times*, 155:53636, C3–C3.

Zizek, S. (2001), 'From Western Marxism to Western Buddhism: The Taoist Ethic and the Spirit of Global Capitalism', *Cabinet Magazine*, 2 at: http://www.cabinetmagazine.org/issues/2/ (accessed December 2005).

PART I

Issues

1

The Disappearance of the Spiritual Thinker

Pankaj Mishra

'I never knew a man', Graham Greene famously wrote in *The Quiet American* (1955), 'who had better motives for all the trouble he caused.' Since the disaster in Iraq, Greene's description of an idealistic American intellectual blundering through Vietnam seems increasingly prescient. People shaped entirely by book learning and enthralled by intellectual abstractions such as 'democracy' and 'nation-building' are already threatening to make the twenty-first century as bloody as the twentieth.

It is too easy to blame millenarian Christianity for the ideological fanaticism that led powerful individuals in the Bush administration to try to remake the reality of the Middle East. But many liberal intellectuals and human rights activists also supported the invasion of Iraq, justifying violence as a means to liberation for the Iraqi people. How did the best and the brightest – people from Ivy League universities, big corporations, Wall Street and the media – end up inflicting, despite their best intentions, violence and suffering on millions? Three decades after David Halberstam (1972) posed this question in his best-selling book on the origins of the Vietnam War, *The Best and the Brightest*, it continues to be urgently relevant: why does the modern intellectual – a person devoted as much professionally as temperamentally to the life of the mind – so often become what Albert Camus (1957) called 'the servant of hatred and oppression'? What is it about the intellectual life of the modern world that causes it to produce a kind of knowledge so conspicuously devoid of wisdom?

The Perils of Secular Fundamentalism

The power of secular ideas – and of the individuals espousing them – was first highlighted by the revolutions in Europe and America and the colonization of vast tracts of Asia and Africa, and then by Communist social engineering in Russia and China. These great and often bloody efforts to remake entire societies and cultures were led by intellectuals with passionately held conceptions of the good life; they possessed clear-cut theories of what state and society should mean; and in place of traditional religion, which they had already debunked, they were inspired by a new self-motivating religion – a belief in the power of 'history'.

It took two world wars, totalitarianism and the Holocaust for many European thinkers to see how the truly extraordinary violence of the twentieth century – what Camus (1951: 11) called the 'slave camps under the flag of freedom, massacres justified by philanthropy' – derived from a purely historical mode of reasoning, which made the unpredictable realm of human affairs appear as amenable to manipulation as a block of wood is to a carpenter.

Shocked, like many European intellectuals, by the mindless slaughter of the First World War, the French poet Paul Valéry dismissed as absurd the many books that had been written entitled 'the lesson of this, the teaching of that', which presumed to show the way to the future. The 'Thousand Year Reich', which collapsed after 12 years, ought to have buried the fantasy of human control over history. But advances in technological warfare strengthened the conceit, especially among the biggest victors of the Second World War, that they were 'history's actors' and, as a senior adviser to President Bush told the journalist Ron Suskind, 'when we act we create our own reality' (Suskind, 2004: 44).

Many British and American intellectuals today help the reality-makers draw 'lessons' for the present and future from the 'facts' of history. In his book *Surprise, Security, and the American Experience* (2004), the Yale historian John Lewis Gaddis claims that John Quincy Adams, in the early nineteenth century, first articulated the 'grand strategy' of pre-emption and unilateralism that President Bush has adopted. Gaddis believes that the methods that established American hegemony and that 'shaped our character as a people and nurtured our development as a nation' ought to be 'embedded within our national consciousness' (Gaddis, 2004: 31). In *Just War against Terror: The Burden of American Power in a Violent World* (2003), Jean Bethke Elshtain, the author of an estimable book on Jane Addams, invokes an even older tradition – Augustinian

Christianity – as a moral and philosophical justification for a forceful American engagement with the world.

History as an aid to the evolution of the human race seems to be most fully worked out by the respected Harvard historian Niall Ferguson. Writing in the *New York Times Magazine* a few weeks after the invasion of Iraq, Ferguson (2003) declared himself a 'fully paid-up member of the neo-imperialist gang', and asserted that the United States should own up to its imperial responsibilities and provide, in places like Afghanistan and Iraq, 'the sort of enlightened foreign administration once provided by self-confident Englishmen in jodhpurs and pith helmets'. In his recent book *Colossus: The Rise and Fall of the American Empire*, Ferguson argues that 'many parts of the world would benefit from a period of American rule' (2004: 2)

Delusion and Hubris in 'History-making'

It is hard to imagine now how this all began – how, in the nineteenth century, the concept of history acquired its significance and prestige. This was not history as the first great historians, Herodotus and Thucydides, had seen it: as a record of events worth remembering or commemorating. After a period of extraordinary dynamism in the nineteenth century, many people in Western Europe – not just Hegel and Marx – concluded that history was a way of charting humanity's progress to a higher state of evolution.

In its developed form, the ideology of history described a rational process whose specific laws could be known and mastered just as accurately as processes in the natural sciences. Backward natives in colonized societies could be persuaded or forced to duplicate this process; and the noble end of progress justified the sometimes dubious means – such as colonial wars and massacres.

This instrumental view of humanity, which communist regimes took to a new extreme with their bloody purges and gulags, could not be further from the Buddhist notion that only wholesome methods can lead to truly wholesome ends. It is in direct conflict with the notion of nirvana, the end of suffering – a goal many secular and modern intellectuals purport to share, but which can only be achieved through the extinction of attachment, hatred and delusion.

Indeed, no major traditions of Asia or Africa accommodate the notion that history is a meaningful narrative shaped by human beings. Time, in fact, is rarely conceptualized as linear progression in many Asian and African cultures; rather, it is custom and religion that circumscribe human interventions in the world. Buddhism, for instance, in its emphasis on compassion and interdependence, is innately inhospitable to the Promethean spirit of self-aggrandizement and conquest that has shaped the new 'historical' view of human prowess. This was partly true also for many European cultures until the modern era, when scientific and technological innovations began to foster the belief that our natural and social environment was to be subject to rational manipulation, and that history itself – no longer seen as a neutral, objective narrative – could be shaped by human will and action.

It was this faith in rational manipulation that powered the political, scientific and technological revolutions of the West in the nineteenth and twentieth centuries; it was also used to explain and justify Western domination of the world – a fact that gave conviction to such words as 'progress' and 'history' (as much as ideological buzzwords of the nineteenth century such as 'democracy' and 'globalization' are of the present moment).

The great material and technological success of the West, and the growth of mass literacy and higher education, produced its own model of *the secular thinker*: someone trained (usually in academia) in logical thinking and possessed of a great number of historical facts. No moral or spiritual distinction was considered necessary for this thinker; no more than technical expertise was asked of the scientists who helped create the nuclear weapons that could destroy the world many times over.

The Eclipse of Humane Wisdom

It is strange to note how quickly the figure of the spiritually-minded thinker disappeared from the mainstream of the modern West, to live on precariously in underdeveloped societies like India. In the West it was left to marginal religious figures such as Simone Weil, Reinhold Niebuhr and Thomas Merton to exercise a moral and spiritual intelligence untrammelled by the conviction that science or socialism or free trade or democracy were helping humankind march to a historically predetermined and glorious future. But then, as Hannah Arendt (1968: 8) wrote:

> *The nineteenth century's obsession with history and commitment to ideology still looms so large in the political thinking of our times that*

we are inclined to regard entirely free thinking, which employs neither history nor coercive logic as crutches, as having no authority over us.

This kind of free thinking was more likely among people not entirely shaped by Western modernity; its most distinguished exemplar was Mahatma Gandhi, a devout Hindu who used the ideals of the ethical and mindful life to challenge the prestige and influence of many purely materialistic Western notions about the nature and meaning of human life. Gandhi claimed that his Indian ancestors had done well to ignore history and seek wisdom in the *Mahabharata*, the epic account of a terrible war that is said to have occurred in India in the first century BCE. For, as Gandhi wrote in 1924, 'that which is permanent and therefore necessary eludes the historian of events. Truth transcends history' (Gandhi, 1998: 134–35).

Gandhi had little doubt about where this permanent and necessary truth of the *Mahabharata* lay, and it had little to do with affirming the greatness of extinct empires and civilizations. The truth lay in the *Mahabharata*'s depiction of the elemental human forces of greed and hatred: how they disguise themselves as self-righteousness and lead to a destructive war in which there are no victors, only survivors inheriting an immense wasteland. As Gandhi saw it, there was no clear-cut good or evil fighting for supremacy in the *Mahabharata*. The epic depicted a world full of ambiguities, where the battle between good and evil actually went on within individual souls and where human beings had to make their own moral choices and strive for mindfulness and virtue. Though unconcerned with facts, the *Mahabharata* taught the importance of an ethical life based on constant self-awareness. History, Gandhi (1998: 134) claimed, could not do this, certainly not 'history' as it is understood today, 'as an aid to the evolution of our race'.

Though not an intellectual, Gandhi had an instinctive underdog's suspicion of such grandiose Western words as 'progress' and 'history'. He knew that European empire-builders justified their worst excesses in Asia and Africa by invoking a particular history in which they were always in the avant-garde of humanity's march to a glorious future. He could sense that a pseudo-scientific history – one that justified foul means by positing noble ends and that could be used to retrospectively justify past crimes and legitimize present ones – had become the primary ideology of the world-conquering nations and empires of the West. It was an ideology that – as Albert Camus (1951: 11) wrote in *The Rebel* – 'can be used for anything, even for transforming murderers into judges'.

The Efficacy of Non-violence

Faced with increasingly bad news from Iraq and Afghanistan, such aspiring reality-makers as Ferguson appear to have faltered briefly before clamouring even more loudly for an assertion of American military might. 'Give violence a chance!' they seem to say. If violence cannot remake the Middle East, then it can at least deal with Islamic fascists and terrorists.

By a perversity peculiar to our times, it is the advocates of non-violent politics – of negotiation and dialogue – who face scepticism, if not outright derision. One of the commonplace rhetorical moves is to compare radical Islamism to German fascism and then ask, 'Could Gandhi have stopped Hitler?'. But then Gandhi or his ideas were not much in evidence at Versailles in 1918, where Western nations imposed humiliating terms on the defeated Axis powers, setting the stage for another world war. Non-violent principles of self-control, moral persuasion and dialogue are unlikely to repair overnight the vast devastation wrought by a form of politics that institutionalizes greed, hatred and violence.

It may be hard to conceive of non-violence as a viable force, especially as we appear to be in the midst of a worldwide upsurge of violence and cruelty. Nevertheless, the history of the contemporary world is full of examples of effective non-violent politics. The movements for national self-determination in colonized countries, the civil rights movement in the United States, the velvet revolutions in Russia and Eastern Europe, the end of apartheid in South Africa and the gradual spread of parliamentary democracy around the world – the great transformations of our time – have been essentially peaceful.

And there have been activists and thinkers in our own time, such as Gandhi, Martin Luther King Jr, Thich Nhat Hanh, Nelson Mandela, Aung San Suu Kyi and Václav Havel, who rejected politics as a zero-sum game (in which the other side's loss is seen as a gain) and adopted moral persuasion and conversion as means to political ends. As the Vietnamese monk Thich Nhat Hanh wrote to Martin Luther King after a spate of Buddhist self-immolations in Vietnam in 1965:

The monks who burned themselves did not aim at the death of the oppressors, but only at a change in their policy. Their enemies are not man. They are intolerance, fanaticism, dictatorship, cupidity, hatred and discrimination, which lie within the heart of man.

Imprisoned by the totalitarian regime of Czechoslovakia, Havel (1985: 69–70) echoed a Buddhist-like preoccupation with actions in the present moment when he warned that 'the less political policies are derived from a concrete and human "here and now", and the more they fix their sights on an abstract "someday", the more easily they can degenerate into new forms of human enslavement.' In his own political practice, Gandhi opposed any mode of politics that reduced human beings into passive means to a predetermined end – it was the burden of his complaint against history. He insisted that human beings were an end in themselves and that the here and now was more important than an illusory future.

This has always baffled or disappointed those who measure non-violent political action in terms of the regimes it changed. But, for Gandhi, non-violence was not merely another tactic – as terrorism often is – in a zero-sum game played against a political adversary. It was a whole way of being in the world, of relating truthfully to other people and one's own inner self: an individual project in which spiritual vigilance and strength created the basis for, and thus were inseparable from, political acts. Gandhi assumed that whatever regimes they lived under – democracy or dictatorship, capitalist or socialist – individuals always possessed a freedom of conscience. To live a political life was to be aware of that inner freedom to make moral choices in everyday life; it was to take upon one's own conscience the burden of political responsibility and action rather than placing it upon a political party or a government.

As Gandhi saw it, real political power arose from the cooperative action of such strongly self-aware individuals – the 'authentic, enduring power' of people whom, as Hannah Arendt (1951) presciently wrote in her analysis of the Prague Spring of 1968, a repressive regime or government could neither create nor suppress through the use of terror, and before whom it eventually surrendered.

Many of Gandhi's own colleagues often complained that he was delaying India's liberation from colonial rule. But Gandhi knew as intuitively as Havel (1986: 153) was to know later, that the task before him was not so much of achieving regime change as of resisting 'the irrational momentum of anonymous, impersonal, and inhuman power – the power of ideologies, systems, *apparat*, bureaucracy, artificial languages, and political slogans.'

This power, the unique creation of the political and economic systems of the modern world, pressed upon individuals everywhere – in the free as well as the unfree world. It was why Havel once thought that the Western cold warriors wishing to get rid of the totalitarian communist system he belonged to were like the 'ugly woman trying to get rid of her ugliness by smashing the mirror which reminds her of it'. 'Even if they won,' Havel wrote, 'the victors would emerge from a conflict inevitably resembling their defeated opponents far more than anyone today is willing to admit or able to imagine' (Havel, 1992: 263).

Intensifying Interdependence Trumps Political Wilfulness

The West did win the Cold War, in the wholly peaceful way that now makes its nuclear build-up appear even more insane, and now it claims to be fighting a new totalitarian enemy in the form of radical Islamists. The huge gulag archipelago which Havel once said that the West might build 'in the name of country, democracy, progress, and war discipline' does not appear likely now – at least not outside a few places in Iraq, Cuba and Afghanistan. But it is not hard to discern through the fog of a war built upon half-truths, in the continuing deceptions and self-deceptions of ideologues and technocrats, the contours of what Havel (1992: 260) called totalitarian power: 'a power grounded in an omnipresent ideological fiction which can rationalize anything without ever having to brush against the truth'.

However, this fiction is always likely to be exposed as such by the objective reality of the world. Certainly, any government or religious-political movement aiming to achieve 'full-spectrum dominance' through mostly violent means is not only morally null, but also doomed to fail. The humanity it seeks to remould has grown much more various and recalcitrant since the long day of the last empire waned. As Paul Valéry (1989: 114) warned, decades before the days of the Internet and *Al-Jazeera*:

> *The human mind is impotent before the political phenomena of our time [which] are accompanied and complicated by an unexampled change of scale, or rather by a change in the order of things. The world to which we, both men and nations, are beginning to belong is only similar to the world that was once familiar to us. The system of causes controlling the fate of every one of us, and now extending over the whole globe, makes it reverberate throughout at every shock; there are no more questions that can be settled by being settled at one point.*

Valéry (1989: 115) asserted (unknowingly underlining a profound truth of Buddhist philosophy) that in an interdependent world *'nothing can ever happen again without the whole world's taking a hand'* (Valéry's italics) and, for this reason, 'no one will ever be able to predict or circumscribe the almost immediate consequences of any undertaking whatever'.

Economic globalization has knit the world even tighter, and many people feel the interdependent nature of the world in their hearts. Yet many of the old secular ideologies – whether of the left or right – appear unable to phrase their longing for a knowledge that transcends personal and national self-interest and is not distinct from wisdom.

Many people have found in Buddhism – and in its suspicion of mental and intellectual abstractions – a practical way of resisting the 'power of ideologies, systems, *apparat,* bureaucracy, artificial languages, and political slogans', as Havel put it. But such is the hold of secular ideologies in the modern West that a mainstream intellectual invoking Buddhism would more often than not provoke the kind of derision reserved for anything vaguely religious or spiritual. It is a grim reflection on the life of the mind in the new century that, while apparently respectable intellectuals recycle selective historical 'facts' and line up to serve the manipulators of reality in the widespread *trahison des clercs*, a subtle moral philosophy such as Buddhism cannot speak its name in the public sphere.

References

Arendt, H. (1951), *The Origins of Totalitarianism* (New York: Harcourt, Brace).

Arendt, H. (1968), *Men in Dark Times* (New York: Harcourt, Brace & World).

Camus, A. (1951), *The Rebel: An Essay on Man and Revolt*, trans. A. Bower (London: Penguin).

Camus, A. (1957), Speech at the Nobel Banquet at the City Hall in Stockholm, 10 December 1957.

Elshtain, J.B (2003), *Just War against Terror: The Burden of American Power in a Violent World* (New York: Basic Books).

Ferguson, N. (2003), 'The Empire Slinks Back,' *New York Times Magazine*, 27 April 2003.

Ferguson, N. (2004), *Colossus: The Rise and Fall of the American Empire* (London and New York: Penguin).

Gaddis, J.L. (2004), *Surprise, Security, and the American Experience* (Cambridge, MA: Harvard University Press).

Gandhi, M. (1998), 'My Jail Experience – VI', in *The Collected Works of Mahatma Gandhi* (2nd edn), Vol. 28 (New Delhi: Indian Ministry of Information and Broadcasting). Originally published in *Young India*, 11 September 1924. Available at: http://www.gandhiserve.org/cwmg/VOL028.PDF.

Greene, G. (1955), *The Quiet American* (London: Heinemann).

Halberstam, D. (1972), *The Best and the Brightest* (New York: Random House).

Havel, V. (1986), *Living in Truth* (London and Boston, MA: Faber & Faber).

Havel, V. (1992), *Open Letters: Selected Writings, 1965–1990* (New York: Vintage Books).

Suskind, R. (2004), 'Faith, Certainty and the Presidency of George W. Bush', *New York Times Magazine*, 17 October 2004.

Valéry, P. (1989), *The Outlook for Intelligence*, trans. D. Folliot and J. Mathews (Princeton, NJ: Princeton University Press).

2

A Process Model for Management

Charles Birch and David Paul

> *We have to rethink what an organisation is, conceptually, and why it*
> *exists, for what and for whom. This is a task for a philosopher more than*
> *for a researcher, for philosophers pose questions which have yet to be asked*
> *and suggest answers which are often too new to be studied in action.*
>
> *Charles Handy (1997: 377)*

Two World-views

Behind managerial decisions and actions are assumptions about human nature, a philosophy of life and issues to do with meaning and purpose. A dominant model of the way the world works, which has been with us for 400 years, is the so-called Newtonian model. Newton envisaged the universe as clockwork, with laws that science was discovering. The machine became the model – the basis of what we now call mechanism or materialism – and its method is to subdivide the world into its smallest parts, which at one time were thought to be atoms. The essence of atomism is that these parts remain unchanged, no matter what particular whole they constitute, be it a star or a human being. Having divided the world into its smallest bits, you then try to build it up from the bits, and, of course, what you get is a machine. There is a hierarchy of such 'machines' that extend from the ultimate building-blocks (called the lower levels and once thought to be atoms) and the higher levels of organization, such as humans.

The principle of mechanism is to interpret the higher in terms of the lower – a process called reductionism. It really is a reducing of the human. The world so conceived consists of mindless, meaningless, self-contained building-blocks, uninfluenced in their nature by anything in their environment. Technically called substances, they resemble the bricks in a building which remain the same whether assembled into a house or a cathedral. We can call this view of a substance world a *declaration of independence.* An entity, be it a human or an atom, is completely independent in the sense described.

This is quite different from the alternative to the theory of mechanism, which has been called the theory of organism. The model here is the living organism rather than a lifeless machine. For example, cells form building-blocks for all living organisms. But each cell varies according to other cells around it. Some become muscle cells while others become nerve cells. In a cathedral the bricks are basically the same whether they are in the walls or the vaulted ceiling. An entity, be it a human being or an atom, is what it is by virtue of is relations to other entities. We can call this view a *declaration of interdependence.* The contrast between mechanism and organism or between independence and interdependence is critical; we discuss it more fully below.

Perhaps unconsciously, most people still live in a Newtonian mechanistic world of independent entities, despite the fact that modern physics has rejected mechanism as a principle for understanding the universe. The world of quantum physics is nothing like machinery. In this sense we are living at the end of an epoch whose chief architects were Newton, Descartes, Galileo and Locke.

What is the Importance of World-views for Management?

Dunphy and Stace (2002: 207) have pointed out that if we view the universe as a machine, we will build organizations on the basis of the machine metaphor: 'If we see ourselves as *deus ex machina*, we will create managers who see themselves as outside the organisation, pulling levers and pressing buttons to make things happen.' The result, they point out, is the traditional bureaucratic, mechanistic organization – a command-and-control model, with the once-familiar hierarchy of ten or more levels. Because of its emphasis on self-interest and lack of concern for its social responsibility, Bakan (2004) even argues that the corporation is a pathological institution.

What use is it to reject one philosophy for another? It is useful because understanding is useful. The great philosopher of process thought, Alfred North Whitehead, rejected exclusive mechanism for an organic view; he made the connection between thought and life even stronger when he said, 'As we think, we live' (Whitehead, 1938: 63). He went on to say that a philosophical outlook is the foundation of thought and life, since it moulds our civilization. The *organic* view gained its title because it displaces the machine metaphor with that of the living organism. We need to back the right metaphor so that we avoid being trapped into asking the wrong questions. Werner Heisenberg expressed this in his famous remark that we do not see nature as it is, but only as a consequence of the questions we put to it.

A non-materialist or organic philosophy has been available to the world of science since the rise of quantum physics. We call the particular version of it we advance in this chapter 'process philosophy'. It recognizes that advance in thought is no longer possible within the framework of a seventeenth-century cosmology of mechanism. Process philosophy is the main organic philosophy challenging mechanism or materialism.

What is Process Thought?

Process thought is a wide-ranging philosophy that addresses the nature of entities from protons to people. Protons stand for ultimate 'particles', which are probably quarks. The constitutive ideas of process philosophy have antecedents going back a long way in intellectual history, but its modern formulation stems from Whitehead, a mathematician and philosopher with a deep interest in science. He formulated a scientific world view opposed to materialism (see Birch and Cobb, 1981; Griffin, 1988; Griffin et al., 1993).

In contrast to mechanism, process thought does not see the world as made of substances; rather, it consists of particles which in themselves are self-sufficient and use forces such as gravitation to push each other around. Instead of material substances, process thought emphasizes events or happenings.

There are two kinds of ways in which entities such as protons or human beings interact – externally and internally. In the Newtonian or mechanistic world-view all relationships are external; for instance, when railway carriages are connected to the engine, the only difference to each carriage so related is that it is pushed or pulled by the engine. The carriage itself is not changed in any way. An internal relation has the opposite effect – it changes the entities being related. When two people fall in love it changes them internally, such that they become different people. They are different emotionally, in their sense of what is now important in their lives, and in the level of different hormones in their bodies. In the same way, people employed by an organization based on a mechanistic model differ from how they would manifest if working in an organization based on a human-relations model. For this reason, alternative names for process thought are pansubjectivism (Cobb) and panexperientialism (Griffin). This is not just academic theorizing: how we manage people in organizations impacts on competitive success. The five most successful firms in the United States from 1972 to 1992 were found to have similar approaches to managing their workforces – an aspect to which they gave top priority in their pursuit of commercial success (Pfeffer, 1994).

Consider further the distinction between external relations and internal relations. The newly-coupled railway carriage is now externally related to the engine, but still the same carriage. By contrast, an internal relation is one which constitutes the nature – even the existence – of something. Such relations cannot characterize substances, for the idea of a substance implies its independent existence, as in the notion of Newtonian atoms. Lovers are internally related to each other, and that makes a difference to each lover. Process thought turns the doctrine of mechanism on its head: instead of the higher entity (humans) being interpreted solely in terms of the lower (quarks or atoms), a new principle is invoked, namely that of interpreting the lower in terms of the higher. Quantum physicists know what this is all about – consider, for example, John Wheeler's rhetorical question, 'Here is a man so what must the universe be?'. The universe is of such a nature that it can produce humans. Ours is a humanizing universe, and that is a different universe from one which could not produce humans.

The unit events that compose the world, such as quarks, resemble living organisms in that they relate internally to their environments. To see the world as not simply made up of mechanisms, but of organisms, constitutes a radical break with the old view and draws our attention to the network of relations between people. We can interpret the human in terms of the cosmos, or we can interpret the cosmos in terms of the human. In the former case humans tend to become things, and meaning and value disappear. In the latter case, however, the way is open for an endless creative adventure.

Nikolai Berdyaev, a process thinker, believed that the primary commandment is to be creative and foster creativity in others. There is always a gap between what a human being is and what that human ought to become. Goethe acknowledged this in his warning that if we take someone as they are, we make them worse. If we take them as they ought to be, we help them to become it. And, as Robert Browning put it, 'Ah. But a man's reach should exceed his grasp. Or what's a heaven for?' Process thought challenges the belief that any order can be established beyond which there is no progress. That belief falsifies the meaning of perfection, which is not a final state, a terminus, but rather a way of progressing.

All individual entities, from atoms to people, are subjects in that they 'feel' their world and are changed in the process. Whitehead calls these events, from quarks to people, 'occasions of experience'. At the level of the human being they may be conscious, but there is also an unconscious subjective world of experience in the human. At the lower levels, such as the atomic one, the subjective element of their being is not conscious, but with a bit of imagination it can still be understood as experience or feeling. This unusual meaning of these terms goes to the heart of process thought. The concept could hardly have been given more emphasis than in Whitehead's (1978: 167) declaration that 'apart from the experiences of subjects there is nothing, nothing, nothing, bare nothingness'. Feeling endows entities such as quarks, atoms, molecules, cells and people with their particular intrinsic value, which is independent of any usefulness they might have (their instrumental value). In the mechanistic model these entities have no intrinsic value, only instrumental value – the mere usefulness of a thing. The intrinsic value of an entity is its value independent of its usefulness, which arises from its feeling.

What, then, is the nature of an experience? It has two aspects: feelings from the past, such as occur in memory, and feelings towards possible futures. As Whitehead (1938: 167) wrote, 'the present is the fringe of memory tinged with anticipation' and 'life is the enjoyment of emotion, derived from the past and aimed at the future'. Hence we need to have in store a rich memory and also a clear sense of direction and purpose – two ingredients of creativity. If 'memory' is a relation to the past and purpose implicated in order, then all actual entities have some degree of self-determination, even atoms and quarks. If we ourselves lack creativity, life becomes dull. There are two causes of evil in life, one is conflict (discord) and the other is boredom (triviality). Process thought makes a real difference to how we view our world – not only other people, but also the world of our companion animals and all of nature. As we shall see below, it also constitutes a powerful and practical philosophy for management.

In reality, what we have been discussing is that stream of entities (called actual entities) that stretches from quarks through atoms and cells, and much in between. These are all called organisms, some of which are traditionally called living (such as plants and humans) and some non-living (such as viruses and molecules), although there is no sharp boundary between living and the non-living. Biology is the study of large organisms; physics is the study of small organisms. But other things exist besides these organisms: rocks, tables and computers are not in the same category as organisms – they can be called aggregates of actual entities, for they have no internal relations. But they consist in their ultimate parts of actual entities such as quarks and atoms.

Many scientists and engineers are busy making robots, which are aggregates, hoping one day to construct one that will be conscious. We know of no aggregate that is conscious, and conscious beings that we do know took some 4 billion years to evolve. So the conscious robot is rather an unlikely prospect.

Some followers of process thought do not believe in a god. Others – probably most – are theists, including Whitehead, but their religion is a naturalistic, as opposed to supernaturalistic, one. Whitehead conceived of God as having both a primordial and a consequent nature. God's *primordial* nature is the store of possibilities or potentialities of the universe which are a constant lure to creation, including us humans. For process thought, persuasion is the energizing power in human affairs, since God cannot force human action: he can only influence it by the lure of persuasion. Hence the crucial significance of persuasion in history. The creation of a civilized order represents the victory of persuasion over force. There are future possibilities in life beckoning us, whether or not we call this the lure of God. We do not create values; rather, we appropriate them.

Moreover, the future is pregnant with as-yet unrealized possibilities. Soon after the Big Bang, the universe consisted of hydrogen atoms alone. But within that universe was the possibility of life, including human life. A universe that is capable of producing humans must be different from one that has no such possibility. Thus on the theistic view, God's primordial nature includes the potentialities of the universe. Most important here is the idea that entities, from quarks to people, exist in a constant process of development. Like the rest of the universe, we are in the process of being made.

The *consequent* nature of God, then, is the consequences for Him of the changing, evolving universe, since God experiences each new creation. Theistic process thought puts stress on God as the experiencer of all experience; He experiences both the good and the bad, the joys and the sufferings.

This twofold aspect of God's nature, as developed in process theism, overcomes the problem of evil in orthodox Christian belief. He cannot overcome suffering, but shares it with all of creation. God cannot remove suffering because He is all-powerful, so He works through persuasion rather than coercion. He persuades creation at each step towards a next step. In this way, God means love.

The truth or otherwise of these ideas is dependent on how the whole construct hangs together in making sense of our world. We have made no attempt to argue each point, but have simply set out the broad thrust of process thought as we understand it. This will hopefully provide a background for pursuing its implication for management.

General Implications of Process Thought for Management

Process thought attributes a unity to nature. In addition to the objective aspects of entities that science investigates, there is the subjective aspect of feelings that give intrinsic value. The existence of entities that have intrinsic value leads to the moral principle that it is unethical to treat these entities as the mere means to ends, and not as ends in themselves – a principle that has direct implications for the management of people, animal rights and respect for nature. There is no divide between humanity and nature, and unless managers and the people they manage give attention to the internal relations of one to another, the prospects for harmonious management are anything but creative and pleasant. Process thought calls for a management philosophy that is deeply rooted in human values; it sees every issue in terms of how it affects the quality of life.

Significantly, Whitehead – a professor of philosophy at Harvard University and its leading process philosopher – was invited to address the Harvard Graduate School of Business on its 25th anniversary. He stressed that the sharp distinction between institutions devoted to abstract knowledge, on the one hand, and those devoted to application and handicraft, on the other, is a mistake. He criticized 'much of the sweet simplicity of modern business policy which fastens its attention solely on one aspect of our complex human nature' (Whitehead, 1947: 165). In an address on the 300th anniversary of Harvard University, Whitehead (1947: 220) suggested that 'business requires for its understanding the whole complexity of human motives, and as yet has only been studied from the narrow ledge of economics'.

There are other narrow ledges created by the subdivision of knowledge into disciplines that train people to become experts. This has led to the creation of separate departments of knowledge and of experts who have difficulty in talking to one another. A task of the future is to create departments, colleges and universities without fixed boundaries. For teaching and research in management, this option would emphasize courses without fixed boundaries and ones that deliberately cross them, such as the philosophy of management and ethics – all constituting part of a core curriculum. The appropriate model for all courses is not the mechanistic model, but an organic one that respects the subjective aspects of entities as well as scientific objective knowledge, and that seeks a unity of knowledge. Once Babylon had its chance to produce a community of understanding, but instead produced the Tower of Babel. Are schools of business repeating Babylon's mistake by fostering disciplines whose experts are unable to communicate with one another? Or will they lead us into a future of creative relationships within their community of learning?

Theories of Management

Management has to do with running 'for-profit' organizations such as businesses, as well as non-profit organizations such as universities, charities and governments. There is no one theory of management and no one theory of the ideal organization. One definition of management theory is that it is 'concerned with a set of behaviours and thoughts of how a business could achieve its goals and objectives' (Nixon, 2003: 2). This view implies that any management theory addresses, first, the way in which management communicates with employees and, second, how tasks are to be defined and performed. Peter Drucker regards management as a central institution in society and suggests that there are very few differences between managing a business, diocese, hospital, university, symphony orchestra, research laboratory, trade union or government agency. In his view, management should not to be primarily concerned with power, but with responsibility. In a similar vein, Charles Handy is concerned with how companies manage their goals beyond the pursuit of profit, and develop into communities of human endeavour (Kennedy, 1991).

One mechanistic theory of management is the so-called *scientific management* of Frederick Taylor, according to which the organization is a machine. Scientific management became famous for having inspired Henry Ford to develop the assembly line for the production of the T-Model Ford motor car. Taylor was concerned that manual labour operated efficiently in the workplace. He thought in terms of finding 'the one best way' to perform tasks. He reasoned that this would bring an increase in both labour productivity and the organization's profitability; on Ford's assembly line human beings were essentially acting as robots. In the eventual evolution of the assembly line, mechanical robots did in fact come to replace many of the human operators. In recent times, computer scientist Mike Hammer's re-engineering carries the strong stamp of Taylor's scientific management. The most lasting indictment of Taylor's management theory was that it took the individual's pride and skill out of work (Kennedy, 1998).

The car manufacturer Volvo turned Taylorism on its head by replacing the assembly line with a series of teams of eight workers. Instead of each individual worker carrying out one monotonous operation, each team produced and tested a complete component: the workers switched jobs and so learned different skills. In this way Volvo created a human-centred approach to car assembly, so exemplifying the *human relations model* of management. Whereas Taylor focused on the nuts and bolts of an organization, the human relations model addressed the needs of the employee. People are emotional beings rather than economic ones, and organizations are cooperative social systems rather than mechanical ones. This model took account of diverse human needs and aspirations, including the need for meaning; it concentrates on such key values as morale, commitment, conflict resolution and consensus-building. Its proponents claimed that people work better if they are treated as people rather than as cogs in a machine. Its pioneer, Elton Mayo, began a series of experiments in 1927 with women workers in the Hawthorne plant of Western Electric in Chicago. His surprising finding was that, after working conditions were discussed with these women, they raised their performance whether or not any change was made – in this case, to the intensity of lighting in the workplace. What mattered was the attention from management; the women were responding to being considered worthy of the experiment and being given special attention. They responded to cooperative and creative relationships among their colleagues, and they performed better. Subsequently, the relation of workers to management gained recognition as a fundamental problem of large-scale industry (Kennedy, 1998). Self-managed teams and 'empowering' employees are now part of management wisdom.

The *sociotechnical model* of management was originally developed at the Tavistock Institute of Human Relations in London. It recognized that management should take into account both the human relations of endeavours and technology, which has to do with tools and machines. It also recognized the working group as the basic unit.

The model of management known as *total quality management* springs from both scientific management and the human relations movement (Kennedy, 1998). It recognizes that all processes are subject to loss of quality through variation. The levels of variation can be managed and quality raised. This process involves the persistent application of quality control to all aspects of the organization's activities, including customers and suppliers, and is credited with being a major ingredient in the success of postwar Japanese industry. It emphasizes continuous improvement monitored by statistical procedures called *kaizen* and the involvement of employees in decision-making at all levels (Burnes, 2004).

Sustainability is a model of management in which Dunphy and his collaborators include two components – ecological sustainability and human sustainability. By human sustainability is meant the quality of life of both the workforce and the community (Dunphy and Benveniste, 2000: 3). The meaning of ecological sustainability is discussed under that heading below. The quality of life in the workforce and the community is the subject of Birch and Paul's, *Life and Work* (2003).

Global management as yet hardly amounts to a theory. It presents substantial problems because of the many disciplines it covers, such as resource depletion, environmental deterioration, the greenhouse effect, the ozone hole, the population explosion, markets and poverty. The fragmentation of knowledge into disciplines makes it difficult for any one person to grasp global problems in their entirety. Furthermore, the problems cross national boundaries, so adding to the complexity of global management. There is no agreement as to how large the playing field should be: the Americans want it to be large, while the Chinese would probably want it smaller, with more social restraints. Nor is there agreement on how the playing field should be designed (Ehrlich and Ehrlich, 2004: 323). This complex of problems will not be solved by any one expert or any number of experts; it amounts to one aggregate problem and has to be tackled as such.

Process thought criticizes the fragmentation of knowledge into bounded disciplines when what we really need is to see knowledge as an undivided whole. 'For scientists to make substantial contributions to the battle for sustainability', Ehrlich and Ehrlich (2004: 261) suggest, 'there will need to be accelerating changes in the professional norms and ethics and in the ridiculously outdated structure of academic disciplines.' Multidisciplinary teams composed of experts are inadequate for the task, which demands instead interdisciplinary teams composed of people who focus not on their particular component of the problem, but collaboratively on the whole problem. A possible model that has been successful to date is the Intergovernmental Panel on Climate Change, which involves hundreds of scientists from nearly every nation and representing diverse disciplines. The need for an enlightened global management is critical as our natural and technological environments are changing so rapidly. The world population will grow by at least 2 billion people in the next half-century, and we are consuming natural capital and disrupting life-support systems at a rate the planet cannot support. Will 'all our pomp of yesterday' become 'one with Ninevah and Tyre'? So ask Ehrlich and Ehrlich (2004), in terms famously coined by Rudyard Kipling.

In these different models of management we can discern degrees of reliance on mechanistic man and varying degrees of humane concerns more consistent with a process model of management. Taylor based his scientific management on mechanical and economic man, thus turning employees into robots. The human relations model recognizes employees in humane terms. The sociotechnical model sees employees in human terms, but recognizes that they still depend on machines for many of their activities. This means that change in job design must go hand-in-hand with technological change if it is to be successful. The total quality management model in Japan came with an ethical imperative based on the Confucian principles of obedience to the family, total loyalty to one's superiors and reverence for education and self-development (Burnes, 2004).

Practical Implications of Process Thought for Management

The purpose of what follows is to raise aspects of management and ask in what ways process thought may throw light on them.

ORGANIZATIONAL CHANGE AS THE NORM

A traditional view holds that the normal state of management is established and changes little. Change, then, constitutes an interruption to the normal state of affairs – one perhaps brought about by some catastrophe or misadventure. It then attracts the title of 'transformational change', such as that which befell MLC Life Ltd in Australia when Lend Lease Corp took it over in 1983 and initiated a process of reshaping the mission, business strategies and management culture in general (Dunphy and Stace, 1992: 103).

By contrast, a radical implication of the process model is that change is the normal state of affairs, and stasis is abnormal (Chia and Tsoukas, 2003). The healthy entity, be it a living organism or an organization, is in a state of continuous change – rebuilding the road as you travel along it, or 'incremental change'. The Australian Macquarie Bank is an example of a highly successful organization characterized by incremental change (Dunphy and Stace, 1992). As one executive described it, 'we never stay still, but we don't change in quantum leaps' (Dunphy and Stace, 1992: 96). Incremental change is the way in which the Greek philosopher Heraclitus and process thought see the world, with the living organism as the model. While the organism may appear unchanged on the surface, below is constant change. Cells and their constituents are constantly being replaced; its cessation would mean the cessation of life itself. Any natural entity, from a quark to a human being, is moulded by events originating in the past and anticipating a future. It is less obvious in the quark or atom than in the human, yet change is the order of existence for both. Models of change inform thinking about change in areas such as management. Heraclitus described a telling model of change when he said that no-one steps into the same river (that is, the same water) twice, because the water is never the same from one moment to the next. He recognized that 'nothing is permanent except change'.

Process philosopher Alfred North Whitehead has said that human history exhibits great organizations as contrivances for progress and also for stunting humanity – a history of blessings and curses. 'The art of progress', he wrote, 'is to preserve order amid change, and to preserve change amid order' (Whitehead, 1978: 339). He added that the more prolonged the halt in some unrelieved system of order, the greater the crash of the dead society. Order is not sufficient by itself, but requires novelty with change. To live is to change.

DEMOCRACY IN THE WORKPLACE

An ideal of process thought would see each of us embraced by the whole community in which we find ourselves, and a democratic society gives us freedom to develop our talents and to foster that in others (Whitehead, 1938: 110). Jan Carlzon, the highly successful former CEO of Scandinavian Airlines System (SAS), attributed his success to two essential components: an overall vision that penetrated all levels of the organization and the decentralizing of decision-making so that every one of the 20,000 employees had some part in it. He compared his organization to a football team in which every player became his or her own boss during the game (Birch and Paul 2003: 23). The same could be said of the Brazilian manufacturing company Semco, where everyone gets a vote on all issues of importance (Semler, 1994). The analogy of a game holds with Semco also, for there is flexibility in a game that gives each player the chance to exercise individual skills and creativity. In the organization each individual can make a difference through small actions over time. Employees may resist democracy in the workplace, as Semler discovered, because a paternalistic hierarchy looks ordered, at least in part, whereas democracy can look like chaos (Trinca and Fox, 2004: 185).

TEAMWORK

Democracy works with fewer problems in small groups, such as a football club or a small business, but it can also be made to work in large organizations through the use of teams. Semco has a history of continuous democratic change promoted by many practices, one being its use of self-managing teams. Companies can get too big, so Semco has the policy of reducing its bureaucratic girth by dividing the workforce into units which might comprise a few dozen or hundreds. How small is small enough depends on the nature of the work, but it should probably be small enough for all members to be able to get to know each other. Alfred P. Sloan, head of General Motors from the early 1920s to the mid-1950s, also understood that corporations can become too big; he restructured this huge firm so that it became a federation of reasonably sized firms. He virtually invented today's decentralized, multidivisional corporation (Kennedy, 1991). Process thought emphasizes person-in-community, rather than individualism, and finds it best fostered in small groups rather than huge ones (Daly and Cobb, 1989).

ECONOMIC MAN

A metaphor for the dominant conception in economics is *homo oeconomicus*, economic man, which influences for-profit organizations in particular. Process thought recognizes the concept of economic man as an abstraction from that of the fully human person because it deals with humans as objects only, not as subjects. It presents employees as rational economic maximizers who seek merely to maximize the results of their labour – beings abstracted from all relationships with other people and the natural world. It exemplifies what Whitehead (1978: 7) calls the fallacy of misplaced concreteness, mistaking the abstraction for the real. Daly and Cobb (1989) devote the first chapter of their book, *For the Common Good*, to the fallacy of misplaced concreteness in economics, and portray economic man as an object that has only an external relation to the world. In other words, economic man is what is technically called a substance – an example of 'substantionalist' thought. Descartes conceived of a substance as any existent thing which requires nothing but itself to exist. As we have seen, process thought maintains that every entity, from quarks to people, is what it is by virtue of the internal relations it maintains with other entities. A human being is pre-eminently constituted by internal relations to the world, whereas a stone is a substance (though its constituent atoms are not).

Here we come to an important concept in process thought. Substance thinking conceives of natural entities, such as quarks and humans, as bits of matter that relate to other bits of matter externally. In the *homo oeconomicus* model, the 'atoms' are agents of economic activity. In process thought, by contrast, we conceive both the physicist's atoms and the human agents of economic activity as occasions of experience – that is, in terms of 'event-thinking'. Instead of thinking of employees in terms of economic man, process thought promotes the 'person-in-community' (Daly and Cobb, 1989), whose life includes feelings and values and meanings and anything that characterizes the humanness of people. To think in other terms is to demean the human; *homo oeconomicus* is not a real human being.

Economic theory builds on the concept of *homo oeconomicus* and has encouraged the quest for personal gain in the business world, often at the expense of humanness. It has encouraged the quest for a single 'bottom line', namely profits and extreme individualism. In reflecting on the central features of modern economics, Rees and Rodley (1995: 298) write: 'especially its individualism, acquisitiveness and elevation of the values of the market to a central social place will show they are at variance with the principles of humanity.' The concept of person-in-community has quite a different set of values: it is appropriate for a person to pursue a degree of self-interest, but also to honour the ethical ideal that people engage in other-regarding activities.

One of management's tasks is to find ways in which to foster person-in-community, and Pfeffer (1998) suggests a number of ways in which it can fulfil it. We have already mentioned one of them: organizing people into self-managed teams and decentralizing decision-making, so that employees can enjoy greater creativity and job satisfaction. Another way of fostering person-in-community is to share financial information and profits, in which case each worker becomes a part-owner of the organization. Yet another way is to reduce differences in status, symbolically through dress, labels and the organization of space and materially through reducing wage inequalities. But beyond these specific measures must be the shared conviction that people should be treated as real people with their own hopes, fears, joys and feelings, and not as objects to be manipulated. In other words, management needs to highlight internal relations. This understanding has enormous consequences.

DOWNSIZING

The economic man model has inspired downsizing – sacking staff in large numbers – which has been going on for more than a decade. It leaves behind a smaller workforce to do the work originally done by a much larger staff and supposedly serves the aim of increasing efficiency and survival in difficult times. The numbers involved can be huge: many corporations in Australia downsized severely in the 1990s and annually threw half a million employees out of their jobs. This process included 30,000 banking jobs and 50,000 manufacturing jobs downsized out of existence during the first half of the 1990s. In the Western world, the loss of a job, and the difficulty of finding work, has a profound effect on human lives. Furthermore, downsizing has deleterious effects on those remaining in the workforce. These include lower morale, more overtime and the fear of being next on the downsizing list (Birch and Paul, 2003: 102–3). But has downsizing achieved its stated goal? Alan Downs (1995) has found that it has not done so; he gives examples of impaired organizations whose situation was materially worsened, and whose mediocre financial benefits were bought at enormous human cost. He suggests solutions for reducing the human cost of adjustment without downsizing, such as reduced hours of work, making changes in vacation liability and payroll reduction.

The ethos of process thought affirms the intrinsic value of each individual, which is worthy of respect quite apart from the individual's instrumental value to the organization. Ironically, downsizing reduces to zero the instrumental value to the organization of the person who gets the sack. The experience also deeply affects the individual's self-esteem. But the downsized person still has intrinsic value. What should the organization do about that? Here, compassion is needed both in the way the sacking is done and the extent to which counselling is made available. But in the typical downsizing 'exercise', little attention is paid to anticipating its effects other than on the bottom line of profits. Similarly, some managerial faddists have promoted 're-engineering' as the new way of becoming efficient, with disastrous and unanticipated consequences.

THE SEARCH FOR MEANING IN THE WORKPLACE

In our approach to our work we might well ask: are we making a life, or a living? Many people work primarily to make a living; it adds little or nothing to the meaning of their lives. For some, job drudgery is hard to avoid, while, for others, work makes a major contribution to their lives and imbues them with meaning. 'A sense of meaning and purpose', Clive Hamilton (2003: 46) writes, 'is the single attitude most strongly associated with life-satisfaction'.

According to Trinca and Fox (2004), a surprising proportion of people now find meaning in their work, and voluntarily work long hours, typically in areas such as marketing and sales, financial services and jobs that focus on creation, innovation and knowledge. This phenomenon raises the question about what constitutes meaning in work and life. At one level, meaning in work conveys the sense that work is interesting, even exciting and creative. This insight is fine as far as it goes, but there are deeper levels of meaning that we should be plumbing, such as those raised by process thought.

The central question is: what is the meaning, the purpose and eventual value of lives, all of which come to an end in relatively few years? If no eventual value exists, then nothing we do, suffer or enjoy has any lasting importance. Yet we cannot live without a sense of significance. We assume that it is more important to save a human life than the life of a dog and to preserve our health than to enjoy some trifling luxury. But none of this makes sense unless there is such a thing as importance. The fact of mortality seems to make it problematic.

Our joys and sorrows are vivid realities although they soon pass away, except in so far as they may have brought joy and sorrow to others. Is there any future that receives our contribution? We may say that our contribution to life dies with us or, on the other hand, that there is a divine life able to appreciate and retain our lesser lives as enrichments of itself. Either we live for what transcends ourselves or we live as the other animals, blindly, with little, if any, conscious purpose. The Buddhists realized this long ago, but Western philosophers and theologians scarcely realize it even now. Whitehead is the outstanding exception; he sees the ultimate recipient of all realized value as God.

What makes life intrinsically valuable is its experience of values such as forgiveness, love, courage, generosity and caring. Intensity of experience contrasts with monotonous regularity that inhibits intensity. 'Be ye perfect' is an injunction from the New Testament. It does not mean that there is a goal of perfection beyond which we can go no further. Perfection is not a static end-point; rather, it is a dynamic *process*. 'Be ye perfect' does not mean 'be ye immutable' – it indicates a process of becoming. It applies as much to

God's experience as it does to that of humans. In theistic process thought, all value generated accumulates in the divine experience.[1] The implication for management is the injunction to create work that is fulfilling and creative and has a spiritual component

DOWNSHIFTING

What can you do if your work lacks meaning and is not fulfilling? You can downshift! A surprisingly large number of people in the Western world are responding in a very practical way to the need for more meaning in their lives. In 2003 the Australia Institute published the results of a survey which shows that nearly a quarter of all Australian adults (from those in their thirties to fifties) had downshifted. They had made a voluntary decision to change their lives in ways that reduced their incomes and spending, because they had come to realize that their way of life and work was diminishing their humanity. Australia is not alone in experiencing this phenomenon; people have also been switching to less demanding and less stressful jobs in the UK, the rest of Europe and the USA. The people who do this are called downshifters (Breakspear and Hamilton, 2004). What follows comes from the Australian studies, but replicates what is happening in the USA and elsewhere.

Downshifters adopt a number of strategies. They may reduce their hours of work, change to a lower-paying job, change careers, take on voluntary work such as in non-government organizations, or stop work altogether. They do this for a combination of reasons. First comes the desire for a more balanced life in which home and family play a bigger role. Second is a clash between personal values and those of the workplace: many react against unbridled profit-seeking, and leave prestigious jobs in law, banking and business to work in the non-profit sector. Third (related to the first two) is the search for more fulfilling lives. Downshifters want congruence between what they do at work and what they feel themselves to be. A fourth reason for downshifting is ill-health, often caused by work-related stress over a long period of time.

All downshifters become much less preoccupied with money, and some move from city to the country. All of them look for some way of making life more fulfilling, and many of them respond to environmental degradation and want to tread more lightly on the earth. Some opt for communal living.

---

1   Much of the argument in this section is inspired by an unpublished paper, 'The Meaning of Mankind', by the process philosopher Charles Hartshorne.

For some, downshifting involves providing a practical solution to the need for more fulfilment and meaning in life, just as process thought would predict. It does not follow, of course, that downshifting is the way for everyone who is searching for meaning and fulfilment. But the phenomenon bears witness to a break with a mechanistic past and an embrace of humanistic values such as those prized by process thought.

ECOLOGICAL SUSTAINABILITY

The concept and practice of economic man, with its emphasis on economic growth, lead inevitably to today's ecological crisis in the form of resource depletion and pollution. We should look after nature for two reasons. One is that nature looks after us; the other (which is less emphasized except in process thought) is that creatures other than humans also have intrinsic value. They experience, they have needs and other feelings. For economic man, the natural world of plants and animals has no value in itself and exists only to be exploited by human beings. Contrary to economic doctrine, we are not the only pebbles of value on the cosmic beach, and we share the world with many other creatures. This truth has practical and ethical consequences.

The way in which we live on the earth today has many consequences: topsoil disappears at the rate of one football field each second; arable land is covered with concrete at the rate of three football fields each minute; forests disappear at the rate of four football fields each minute; and species disappear at the rate of 100 a day. Add to this the greenhouse effect and the hole in the ozone layer and it becomes obvious that our present treatment of the earth is unsustainable in the long run. The earth has a limited carrying capacity for people beyond which it can no longer sustain our present impact, which began at the dawn of agriculture 10,000 years ago. The second great impact came with the Industrial Revolution from about 1850. Ehrlich and Ehrlich (2004: 85) conclude, after a very careful analysis of all factors involved, that the earth has a carrying capacity of about 2 billion people, which is less than one-third of today's global population.

The impact of humans on the environment is best conceived as a product of three components: the number of people; the average person's consumption of resources; and the negative environmental impact of the technologies used to produce the goods consumed. For an ecologically sustainable future, global policy must attend to reducing each of these components.

What has all this to do with management? As Dunphy, Griffiths and Benn (2003: 3) emphasize, '[c]orporations are the fundamental cells of modern economic life and their phenomenal success in transforming the earth's resources into wealth has shaped the physical and social world in which we live'. Corporations have contributed to these problems and therefore have a responsibility to be part of the answer. Hence Dunphy and his collaborators' programme on sustainability for organizations: they present a clear challenge to managers at all levels. Under the rubric of sustainability, they include what they call human sustainability – 'sustaining and renewing the quality of life of the work force and the community' (Dunphy and Beneviste, 2000: 3). A 'declaration of sustainability' (for the corporate world) is the subtitle of Paul Hawken's (1994) *The Ecology of Commerce*, which analyses in detail what is ecologically unsustainable in the world of corporations and presents some equally detailed 'green' solutions.

In process thought, two ethical imperatives follow: the conservation of resources, including the pollution-absorbing capacity of the earth; and the recognition that all living creatures have intrinsic value independent of any usefulness they may have for us or other creatures. The latter point includes their right to live on the earth with us. The process model thus calls for a new ecological economics that includes both people and nature (see Daly and Cobb, 1989).

TAKING RISKS

If we are prepared to be adventurous and forward-looking, we have to be prepared to take risks, and therefore to make mistakes, because any experimentation involves the possibility of making mistakes. The great inventor Thomas Edison said, 'I have never failed. I've just found 10,000 ways that don't work [in developing the first electric light bulb]' (quoted in Jay, 2001: 53). And Henry Ford said, 'Failure is only the opportunity to begin again more intelligently.' The inventor and successful businessman, Edwin Land, suggested that we should '[w]ork only on problems that are manifestly important and seem to be nearly impossible to solve' (quoted in Jay, 2001: 102). He drew this wisdom from a life of adventure and risk which included the invention and sale of cameras at the cutting edge. Edison and Land were both scientists and businessmen who knew that business, as well as science, involved taking risks. Those with high self-esteem are more likely to take intelligent risks than those less inclined to trust themselves. Hence the organization of the future will expect to make mistakes and experience failures in managing change – it is an essential part of its learning process.

Process philosopher Charles Hartshorne (1948: 136) argues that great risk and great opportunity seem to go together. This is no mere accident, since great opportunity arises only in the presence of great sensitivity and great intensity. Given only lesser sensitivity and lesser intensity there is little chance of any great opportunity being grasped. According to Louis Pasteur, chance discovery favours only the mind that is prepared; thought comes before observation. In a similar vein, Charles Darwin claimed never to have gone into the field without some hypothesis in mind. He didn't go into the Amazonian jungle just to collect facts about plants and animals; he went there with a hypothesis about the origins of species that led him to ask particular questions about nature.

We can be too tame and harmless, just as we can be too wild and dangerous. There is a golden mean somewhere between risk and opportunity which those endowed with sensitivity and intensity may discover, while others flounder around. 'If we didn't make mistakes,' said Hartshorne's teacher, A.N. Whitehead, 'we wouldn't make anything' (quoted in Anshen, 1986: 8).

POWER AND LEADERSHIP

The art of life is, first, to be alive; second, to be alive in a satisfactory way; and third, to acquire an increase in satisfaction. All this is central to the view of life in process thought (Whitehead, 1929: 8). If those who live did not prize life, death would soon triumph. Yet the urge to live involves so much more than mere survival, not only for human beings but for other creatures as well; beyond survival there is enjoyment, love, creative activity and goal-setting. So whence comes all the suffering, destruction, cruelty and injustice we do to one another individually, in our institutions, nationally and internationally? This question has puzzled human beings across the ages, and there are no simple answers. Yet it behoves us to face this question, otherwise we can have an overoptimistic view of human nature.

Reinhold Niebuhr has cast some light on this question in his book, *The Children of Light and the Children of Darkness* (1944). 'Children of darkness' is the scriptural designation for those who know no law beyond their self-interest; they are wise, though evil, because they understand the power of self-interest. Jack Lang, a former premier of New South Wales, was fond of saying that the only certainty in the race of life was self-interest. It was the only horse you could be sure was trying. The children of light are those who believe that self-interest should be brought under the discipline of a higher law, but they are foolish when they underestimate the power of self-interest. Niebuhr takes up his argument from the recognition that we have an urge to live. We desire to fulfil the potentialities of life and not merely to maintain its existence, so the will to live transmutes into the will to self-realization. But it also transmutes into the will to power, or the desire for power and glory.

The person who has achieved power seeks to gain security against the perils that surround power by enhancing their power. The will to power inevitably justifies itself in terms of the morally more acceptable will to realize our true nature. Even what appear to be the altruistic acts of good people are alloyed with some degree of self-interest. No level of human moral or social achievement is free from the taint of self-love, such that corruption of ideals is a much more persistent factor in human affairs than any simple moralistic code tends to admit. Some world problems arise from ignorant and wicked people, such as fascists and their demonic fury; however, much evil is done, Niebuhr argues, not so much by evil people, but by good people who do not know themselves.

Great power is relatively new in the organization of human societies. Hunter-gatherer societies, for instance, were relatively egalitarian. The agricultural revolution some 10,000 years ago gave rise to stratified societies that led to massive inequalities in access to power. This exists in our societies today, in the hierarchical organization of business with its plethora of experts (Ehrlich and Ehrlich, 2004: 240). Power of the sort described characterizes a substantial number of organizations studied in Australia and New Zealand (McCarthy, 2004).

The exercise of power in institutions can create a sense of powerlessness in others. On the other hand, by empowering others, leaders do not decrease their influence, but instead enhance it for the benefit of the whole organization.

Conclusion and Summary

There are basically two philosophical models of organizations, and therefore two basic models of management – the mechanistic and the organic models. In the former case, the organization is modelled on the machine; in the latter case the organization resembles a living organism. The mechanistic model of management prescribes a command-and-control order, but in the organic model persuasion takes the place of control and power exercised through a hierarchy. It recognizes a degree of freedom in every life, together with the capacity for self-determination. The Frederick Taylor's so-called scientific management, with its assembly line of employees acting as robots, is an example of the mechanistic model, while the human-relations model exemplifies an organic model of management. Other models combine elements of the two.

The particular philosophical model of organism described in this chapter is known as process thought. It received this name because it replaces the concept of substances as the basic units of the universe and every entity in it with those of events or processes. Thus its seminal philosopher, A.N. Whitehead, called his Gifford Lectures 'Process and Reality'. The living organism is the central metaphor of the process model (Birch and Cobb, 1981). Consider a living organism with which we are familiar, ourselves: we may look like a machine to the outsider, but as living organisms we are different from machines in the following ways:

1.   A machine remains the same from day to day except in so far as it wears out. By contrast, the living organism is constantly changing in every moment. No cell in the body is the same as it was an hour ago, and the cells which compose bodies are constantly being replaced. The 'me' still exists and is identifiable, but it is a different 'me' every hour and every day. Change is the essence of life, and in process thought this applies to the organization. Change in the organization is the normal state of affairs – stasis is abnormal.

2.   In the mechanistic model the entities that make up the machine are nuts and bolts, or what are technically called substances. By definition, a substance exists independently of its environment. A billiard ball is a billiard ball is a billiard ball is a billiard ball on whatever billiard table it is hit by whatever player, since it has only external relations. But an organism is quite unlike a billiard ball in that it has internal relations which change it. We experience this principle for ourselves through friendships and any relationship that involves feeling our world: such is the subjective side of life, which does not exist for the machine. Our feelings change us and constitute our being, contrary to the mechanistic concept of

economic man which detracts from the human because it abstracts from the human; it leads to social tragedies such as those caused by downsizing.

People-in-community is an organic concept: in the process model of organizations, people's quality of life in the organization and in the society it touches is of prime importance. This aspect of process thought extends to all living creatures and beyond, to the foundation building-blocks of the universe, such as quarks. The real nature of a quark may not matter to business executives except in so far as they want a comprehensive understanding of the world – one that penetrates to a deeper meaning that perhaps only the philosophical mind seeks. The deeper the model, the greater is the understanding.

3. Mechanism interprets the higher (such as the human) in terms of the lower (such as quarks). It reduces the world down to its supposed basic building-blocks, which are the atoms of classical physics. This manoeuvre is called reductionism: it reduces the real world to its supposed building-blocks and then tries to build the world up again from the building-blocks, so in the end you get a machine. It so happens that physicists no longer believe in the building-blocks as substances – the so-called fundamental particles of physics do not resemble machines at all. So they are strictly no longer called particles.

Process thought turns mechanism on its head and, in addition to giving some place to mechanism (the heart is a pump), it also interprets the lower (quarks) in terms of the higher (humans). What we find at the level of the human are internal relations and subjectivity. There is no dualism between mind and matter, but a unity all the way down from humans to quarks. It may seem strange to use the same language for quarks as for humans – feelings or experience – but these words point to something similar all the way down, namely internal relations. We occupy a feeling universe rather than a mechanical universe. Subjectivity has two elements: feelings from the past, such as memory; and feelings towards a possible future, which is purpose. What has this to do with organizations and management? It has ethical consequences.

4.   The mechanistic model has nothing to say about ethical responsibilities, but, in process thought, ethical consequences flow from postulating internal relations or feelings all the way down from humans to quarks – consequences which have to do with our valuation of the environment. We need to look after nature because nature looks after us: it provides us with resources, life-support systems and natural pollution control. Organizations are responsible for much of the deterioration of the environment; hence they have a responsibility to care for it. Moreover, living organisms have feelings, which give them an intrinsic value beside their instrumental one. Intrinsic value is quite independent of their instrumental value, so we should care when our activity on the earth causes suffering and loss. Theories of management that address sustainability seek to bring ecological sustainability into the programme of management as widely as possible. It recognizes the value of life-support systems and the intrinsic value of individual living organisms, as well as our corresponding responsibilities.

5.   Exponents of the mechanistic model do not usually ask what is the meaning of their lives. If they do pose the question, the answer is: none. Many young people in organizations worry about the gap between their quality of life in the organization and the meanings in life they aspire to. Organizations should respond to these concerns; they are seeing many of their best people leaving them by downshifting and in other ways.

There are different levels of meaning that people aspire to. At the deepest level, process thought leads one to ask what is the eventual value of lives, given that they all come to an end. We may either believe that our contribution to life dies with us or that there is a divine life able to retain our lesser lives as enrichments. The theistic form of process thought leads in that direction, but whatever value we place on life, organizations should give encouragement to the values that enrich life and give it meaning.

6.   Widespread injustice and destruction should lead process thought to a realism that does not have an overoptimistic view of human nature. In particular, organizations need to be aware of the roots of

power which easily take control in a mechanistic organization. Each of us experiences an urge to live: we desire to fulfil life's possibilities for us, rather than simply maintain life's existence. The will to live transmutes into the will to self-realization, but also into the will to power or the desire for power and glory, sometimes at whatever cost, such that even apparently altruistic acts are alloyed with inordinate self-interest. The hierarchical organization of business in particular can lead to great inequalities of power, and power tends to take control. We can guard against this trend by reducing the levels in the hierarchy, by introducing more democracy in the workplace, and by organizing work in small groups. By empowering others in these and other ways leaders do not decrease their influence, but rather enhance it for the benefit of all. In this way, the role of power and coercion is replaced in process thought by persuasion or love. The paradox is that there is power in persuasion and love which, in the end, is the only power that matters: its achievements are the only ones that last.

On the basis of process thought we have indicated particular lines of action for management. Other managers who have never heard of process thought, let alone practised it, may well reach similar conclusions – for instance, ones concerning incremental growth or a conservation ethic. What, then, is the particular merit of process thought? There is merit in having an overall philosophy that can be applied to all situations – one that helps to overcome inconsistencies and promotes a sense of significance around the issues at stake. This is particularly true when the overall philosophy has a religious dimension that is naturalistic and is committed to humane values. Whitehead (1957: xiv) emphasizes the importance of a philosophy that attempts to embrace the whole of experience:

> ... the movement of historical, and philosophical criticism of detached questions, which on the whole has dominated the last two centuries, has done its work, and requires to be supplemented by a more sustained effort of constructive thought ... the importance of philosophy lies in its sustained effort to make schemes explicit, and thereby capable of criticism and improvement.

References

Anshen, R.N. (1986), *Biography of an Idea* (New York: Moyer Bell).

Bakan, J. (2004), *The Corporation: The Pathological Pursuit of Profit and Power* (London: Constable).

Birch, C. and Cobb, J.B. (1981), *The Liberation of Life* (Cambridge: Cambridge University Press).

Birch, C. and Paul, D. (2003), *Life and Work* (Sydney: University of New South Wales Press).

Breakspear, C. and Hamilton, C. (2004), *Getting a Life: Understanding the Downshifting Phenomenon in Australia*, Discussion Paper 62 (Canberra: The Australia Institute).

Burnes, B. (2004), *Managing Change: A Strategic Approach to Organisational Dynamics* (Sydney: Prentice Hall).

Chia, R. and Tsoukas, H. (2003), 'Everything Flows and Nothing Abides: A Rhizomic Model of Organisational Change, Transformation and Action', *Process Studies*, 32:2, 196–224.

Daly, H.E. and Cobb, J.B. (1989), *For the Common Good* (Boston, MA: Beacon Press).

Downs, A. (1995), *Corporate Executions* (New York: Amacom).

Dunphy, D. and Stace, D. (1992), *Under New Management: Australian Organisations in Transition* (Sydney: McGraw Hill).

Dunphy, D. and Benveniste, J. (2000), 'An Introduction to the Sustainable Corporation', in D. Dunphy, J. Benveniste, A. Griffiths. and P. Sutton. (eds), *Sustainability: The Corporate Strategy of the 21st Century* (Sydney: Allen & Unwin).

Dunphy, D. and Stace, D. (2002), 'Changing Forms of Organisation and Management', in R. Callus and R.D. Lansbury (eds), *Working Futures: The Changing Nature of Work and Employment Relations in Australia* (Sydney: Federation Press).

Dunphy, D., Griffiths, A. and Benn, S. (2003), *Organisational Change for Corporate Sustainability* (London: Routledge).

Ehrlich, P.R. and Ehrlich, A.H. (2004), *One with Nineveh: Politics, Consumption and the Human Future* (Washington: Island Press).

Griffin, D.R. (ed.) (1988), *The Reenchantment of Science* (Albany, NY: State University of New York Press).

Griffin, D.R., Cobb, J.B., Ford, M.P., Gunter, P.A.Y. and Ochs, P. (1993), *Founders of Constructive Postmodern Philosophy* (Albany, NY: State University of New York Press).

Hamilton, C. (2003), *Growth Fetish* (Sydney: Allen and Unwin).

Handy, C. (1997), 'Unimagined Futures' in F. Hesselbein, M. Goldsmith and R. Beckhard (eds), *Organization of the Future* (San Fransisco: Jossey-Bass).

Hartshorne, C. (1948), *The Divine Relativity* (New Haven, CT: Yale University Press).

Hawken, P. (1994), *The Ecology of Commerce: A Declaration of Sustainability* (New York: HarperBusiness).

Jay, R. (2001), *Winning Minds* (Oxford: Capstone).

Kennedy, C. (1991), *Instant Management* (New York: William Morrow).

Kennedy, C. (1998), 'Guide to the Management Gurus', *Director*, 51:10, 52–57.

McCarthy, S. (2004), *The Culture-Performance Connection*, (Sydney: Human Synergistics New Zealand and Australia).

Niebuhr, R. (1944), *The Children of Light and the Children of Darkness* (New York: Charles Scribner's Sons).

Nixon, L. (2003), 'Management Theories: An Historical Perspective', *Business Date*, 11:4, 5–8.

Pfeffer, J. (1994), 'Competitive Advantage through People', *California Management Review*, 36:2, 9–28.

Pfeffer, J. (1998), 'Seven Practices of Successful Organizations', *California Management Review*, 40:4, 80–96.

Rees, S. and Rodley, G. (1995), *The Human Costs of Managerialism: Advocating the Recovery of Humanity* (Sydney: Pluto Press).

Semler, R. (1993), *Maverick! The Success Story behind the World's Most Unusual Workplace* (London: Arrow).

Stace, D. and Dunphy, D. (1996), *Beyond the Boundaries: Leading and Re-creating the Successful Enterprise* (Sydney: McGraw Hill).

Trinca, H. and Fox, C. (2004), *Better than Sex: How a Whole Generation Got Hooked on Work* (Sydney: Random House).

Whitehead, A.N. (1929), *The Function of Reason* (Boston, MA: Beacon Press).

Whitehead, A.N. (1938), *Modes of Thought* (New York: Free Press).

Whitehead, A.N. (1978), *Process and Reality* (corrected edn), ed. D.R. Griffin and D.W. Sherbourne (New York: Free Press).

Whitehead, A.N. (1947), *Essays in Science and Philosophy* (New York: Philosophical Library). First published in the *Harvard Business Review* in 1933.

3

Business and Society

Winton Higgins

The current management and industrial-relations literature often assumes that changes in market operations since the 1970s have been so radical as to present economic activity today as an entirely new ballgame. Whatever economic insights we might have gained before, say, the 1980s, have now been rendered obsolete by the coming of the neo-liberal political ascendancy, globalization, new information and communication technologies and other recent wonders which advocates of this view breathlessly reel off. Fundamentalist conclusions about the vanity of all political and social interventions appear to flow quite naturally from this assumption.

In this chapter, I want to bring recent changes back to their true proportion. Unfashionably, I will start with George Santayana's truth that those who do not learn from history will be forced to relive it. For around four centuries, since the issue first began to make itself felt, leading minds in the West have grappled with the relationship between private enterprise, on the one hand, and, on the other, the kind of society that supports it. In particular, generations of Western thinkers have wondered how this relationship can be sustained in the long term. Throughout this period there have been business fundamentalists and utopians who have believed that business will automatically (or with God's beneficence) sustain a good economy and a good society, and that their relationship is thus entirely unproblematic. For instance, the fundamentalist slogan of the 1980s proclaimed that 'greed is good!' – both economically and socially good.

More sophisticated and sober thinkers have remained unconvinced. They have worked to produce cogent accounts of the often vexed relationship between business and society, and to contribute to policy formation on this basis. This new age of business fundamentalism calls for a quick review of the story so far. On that basis we can look at how some older insights still apply to the relationship between business and society now.

Business and Community in Early Modernity

A 'new ballgame' did slowly emerge in Western Europe around the sixteenth century and attracted serious analytical attention in the following century. In its economic aspects, this new ballgame later came to be known as capitalism, and, still later, various euphemisms were invented such as the currently recycled one, 'the free enterprise system'. In its social and cultural aspects the new ballgame came to be known as *modernity*. The seventeenth-century analysts, above all Thomas Hobbes (1588–1679), showed considerable vision in how they understood the change and began to mint some important terms in which to couch the pertinent questions about it.

The most immediate change, of course, was the expansion of markets and the growth of production for trade at the expense of production for local use, or economic self-sufficiency. This change brought strangers, diverse cultures and remote communities into contact with each other for the first time, while undermining the old, inward-looking solidarities that had sustained communal governance and cohesion. These older solidarities had underwritten trust and organized economic redistribution from their economically active members to their non-productive members (the very young and the aged, those without a livelihood for other reasons, and those fulfilling social, political, administrative and religious tasks). How were these vital social underpinnings – trust and redistribution – to be guaranteed in the new large-scale and impersonal world of 'commercial society'?

Some of the terms tossed around – and, indeed, form part of our core vocabulary – in the present-day debate about 'where we're headed' were invented at this time in answer to this question. Take 'civility', 'civil society' and 'civilization', for instance. 'Civility' was an entirely new form of trust that emerged to facilitate the working of commercial society. In its original, most basic meaning, civility denotes a code of conduct, including truth-telling and promise-keeping, that allows me to strike a deal with another trader who lives a long way away and who looks and speaks differently to me. Normally, I would distrust such a person, but when I know that they will be held to the same set of rules as I am, I can feel more relaxed about clinching the deal. Civility and the wealth creation it facilitates, Hobbes famously argued in his 1651 classic, *Leviathan*, depends on a powerful sovereign state which reliably and impartially imposes the same set of rules on everyone, so creating trust (Hobbes, 1996[1651]). Civility extends to the inviolability of the person and of their property, as well as to the enforcement of contractual obligations, which are also essential for markets to function at all. *Only a good society based on these principles can support a good economy.*

A *civil society*, as the name implies, is one based on civility, but the term came to be developed much more in the eighteenth century. What was then emerging in modern commercial societies was a peculiar form of governance. The Hobbesian state still hovered over this brave new world as the condition of its existence. Within society and economy, people were organizing their own economic and social associations – joint-stock companies, stock exchanges, interest groups (including religious ones), occupational groups, parliamentary parties, political and recreational clubs and so on. It was this freedom and habit of self-organization that came to define what we mean by civil society. It included – but could by no means be reduced to – market economy. And it was the combination of this new kind of society and the high standard of living its leading class came to enjoy that was encompassed by the term 'civilization'.

How was the relationship between this powerful state and this self-organizing society to be understood? The two can seem contradictory, and indeed are presented simplistically as being contradictory by free-market fundamentalists today. In the eighteenth century, Baron Charles de Montesquieu (1689–1755) tackled this question head-on in his 1748 classic, *The Spirit of the Laws* (Montesquieu, 1989[1748]). He drew a contrast between despotic states, on the one hand, and 'moderate' or constitutional states, on the other. We might have assumed – and many still do so today – that despotisms are far more powerful than moderate states. Not so, Montesquieu tells us. Despotisms depend on terror and have no roots embedded in society; when their threats no longer convince, they blow over in the next strong oppositional wind. But constitutional states have both representative assemblies and regulatory functions, starting with the rule of law. Civil society is thus represented in the constitutional state, and the constitutional state is a constant regulatory presence in civil society. So the moderate state is in fact by far the stronger of the two, and this is because state and society mutually reinforce one another. Each is the precondition of the other's existence.

A quick glance at the history of the modern West confirms Montesquieu's insight: seemingly all-powerful dictatorships have arisen only to collapse just as quickly, while the apparently 'weak' constitutional states endure and grow richer (Krygier, 1996).

Montesquieu also draws a distinction between the public forms of deliberation appropriate to the state and the private forms of calculation appropriate to business. Because he built into his picture of the constitutional state all sorts of public processes, such as representative assemblies and open interactions between functionally differentiated parts of the state, his model is often referred to as the *deliberative state*. Its golden rule derives, in fact, from ancient Athens: what concerns the public must be publicly debated and transacted. Later, with the coming of democracy, the deliberative state became its vital foundation.

Many of these lessons were missing or understated when, in 1776, Adam Smith (1723–90) published *The Wealth of Nations* (1996[1776]), which is still a bible of sorts for business fundamentalists today. Although Smith was a more subtle thinker than his present-day followers would have us believe, he did hold to a curiously theological view of the 'invisible hand' of the market: private actions in pursuit of personal gain, he claimed, activated it, whereupon it would somehow miraculously – and automatically – turn out to satisfy the public interest as well. Smith's market theology pioneered the idea that 'greed is good'. Like so many business fundamentalists today, Smith had a 'gee-whizz' attitude to the then new-fangled market economy and saw it as a revolutionary answer to all socio-economic problems. If this view were true, then the legitimate ambit of state regulation and intervention would be restricted to protecting persons and their property (including contractual rights) in aid of effective market transactions; the state would then be demoted to a mere nightwatchman. There would be no role for the deliberative state as the vehicle of democratic self-rule. This shrunken view of the public interest, of state functions and, later, of democracy itself came to be encapsulated in the ideal of the *nightwatchman state* – the utopia pursued not only by today's neo-liberals, but also by all economic liberals from their first appearance in early nineteenth-century Britain.

Business and Community in the Industrial Age

Smith's market theology was soon challenged. Early in the nineteenth century the German political philosopher Georg Hegel (1770–1831) adopted Montesquieu's insights about the relationship between civil society and the constitutional state as he voiced concerns about how capitalist society was developing. Significantly, he was the first major thinker to observe the beginnings of the Industrial Revolution and its social effects. Individuals and groups absorbed in the pursuit of their mutually antagonistic interests in the private economy and civil society were ill-equipped to take a societal view or understand the public interest, Hegel argued in *The Philosophy of Right* (1990[1821]). Left to their own devices, private interests would tear society apart and so destroy the social underpinnings of their self-centred economic activity as well. A bad society cannot sustain a good economy. Quite simply, commercial society had a strong self-destructive impulse. For Hegel, a symptom of this was what he called the 'social exile' of the working class and other groups. In other words, the capitalist system tended to polarize society between those who were benefiting from the steep rise in productivity, on the one hand, and those excluded by the private economy's defective distribution system, on the other. This polarization could have dire consequences for all concerned.

Under these circumstances, Hegel suggested, the constitutional state had a lot more to do than simply act as a nightwatchman. It had to assert itself as the expression of the moral unity of society, reconstituting a sense of solidarity around shared values in the much the same way as the now superseded premodern communities had done. This entailed the assertion of a public interest, which included economic regulation and redistribution in the interest of macro-economic and macro-social coordination and solidarity. By such means the state could include in the 'common wealth' those groups whom unregulated market mechanisms would otherwise socially 'exile' – that is, marginalize and impoverish.

Although he is seldom given the credit for it, Hegel foreshadowed twentieth-century social-democratic thinking and the post-Second World War concept of the mixed economy. In the latter, private enterprise is 'mixed' with significant levels of state coordination and public enterprise to compensate for market failure, especially the market's inability to reliably serve the public interest (Higgins, 1988).

From the 1870s to the end of the 1920s a school of British analysts, the 'new liberals', began to revisit these issues (Freeden, 1978, 1986). Although they had different starting-points from Hegel's, they came to similar conclusions, which they applied and elaborated in greater detail. Quite a few of the new liberals were active politicians, economists and policy-makers at a time when industrialization was well advanced in their native country, the pioneer of the Industrial Revolution. Their analysis of the missed opportunities and social and environmental distortions of industrialization, as unregulated market mechanisms shaped it, led them to propose a public-policy programme that fits neatly into Hegel's prescriptions. Their growing focus on industrialization gave their work a relevance that endures into our own time.

The new liberals celebrated industrialization as such. For them, as for other enthusiasts of modernity, it had the potential to generate enough wealth to abolish poverty, to produce the infrastructure needed for a dramatic increase in access to good housing, public recreational and cultural facilities, and quality education and health care. In the workplace, machines could take over the most brutalizing tasks, progressively overcoming drudgery and reducing the hours of work. More and more people would have access to intellectually challenging occupations instead of being stuck in monotonous, back-breaking jobs.

But all this was precisely what was *not* happening in Britain's 'successful' industrialization. Instead, 'two nations' with drastically different living and working conditions and prospects emerged, just as Hegel had feared. While the middle class enjoyed the affluence of Victorian Britain, the 'exiled' working class knew only grinding poverty, social and economic insecurity, appalling working conditions (including long hours, occupational disease and accidents), bad housing in squalid urban neighbourhoods and dreadful standards of public health. Not only had the moral potential of industrialization not been realized, but free-market principles were killing – if also disguising the decline of – British industry itself (Tomlinson, 1981). The profits of industry were finding their way into the mighty financial houses of the City of London, which considered investment overseas more profitable than reinvestment in domestic industry, thus preventing the further modernization and rationalization of existing industry and investment in new technologies. Finally, the form of industrialization in Britain was devastating the environment. In noting these problems in the world's first example of industrialization, under the aegis of Smith's 'invisible hand', the new liberals were discovering the rationale for modern state intervention and for industry policy in particular.

At play here were two enduring and contrasting conceptions of efficiency, one of the most central values for all moderns, including for us in the twenty-first century. All definitions of efficiency are social products; none is free from ideological and value assumptions. Free-market economics recognizes one single measure of efficiency – profits returning to private hands within the shortest possible timeframe (as measured most commonly by return-on-investment calculations). For the new liberals, by contrast, industrial development should be considered efficient only if it can sustain itself over time and serve the 'social utility' of a raised standard of living and better quality of life for the populace as a whole, including higher housing, health and education standards, a constantly improving quality of work life and an undamaged environment. Their definition thus incorporated what are now called *social responsibility* and *sustainability.*

Free-market industrialization failed on each and every one of these criteria of efficiency. Some individuals grew fabulously rich (thus satisfying the single free-market criterion of efficiency), but the great majority active in industry remained impoverished, and were indeed thrown into new forms of impoverishment, including relative deprivation and environmental jeopardy. The price of private affluence was public squalor. One of the last prominent members of this school, John Maynard Keynes (1883–1946), demonstrated that what is rational at the level of the firm – such as disinvesting and laying off workers in a recession – can produce massive irrationalities (above all, severe depressions) at the macro-economic and macro-social level (Keynes, 1936). Like efficiency, rationality is not a given. Rather, it means different things to different social interests and at different levels of analysis.

New-liberal thought came in two waves. Before the First World War it concentrated on policy initiatives to achieve the moral and macro-social aspects of efficient industrialization. In this period it sought some redistribution of the profits of industry towards the provision of social security, public education and health, and slum clearance (Freeden, 1978). In the 1920s its contributors focused much more on ways whereby public authorities could take responsibility for national manufacturing performance by providing for the recapitalization of industry (to thwart the financiers' tendency to invest elsewhere, in non-productive placements) and the public coordination of the continuous restructuring (Freeden, 1986) that every national manufacturing sector must provide for. Today one can extrapolate from the new liberals' last great product, the famous Yellow Book (Liberal Industrial Inquiry, 1928), most of the principles on which a rational industry policy would rely today, and we will return to them in the next section.

While the new liberals focused on policy, they had very little success in having their policies adopted in the 1920s because they were associated with the British Liberal Party, then in steep electoral decline for unrelated reasons. In rough and ready ways, most countries involved in the twentieth century's 'total wars', above all Britain, brushed aside free-market steering of industry and developed industry policies when industrial efficiency meant the difference between losing or winning the war. They sometimes did so by imposing tight social criteria on the distribution of food and health resources, which saw the living standards of the working class actually improve despite the overall strain on national resources, as during the First World War (Marwick, 1991).

However, it is postwar Japan that provides the most advanced peacetime example of industrial policy. The rise of the Japanese industrial phoenix out of the ashes of devastation and defeat in the Second World War attracted the attention of foreign analysts only slowly. What was obvious to the most casual observer was that Japan husbanded its manufacturing sector as a matter of national (that is, public) priority, but it did so without compromising its private-enterprise system. In flat contradiction of free-market fundamentalists, Japan showed that private enterprise was perfectly compatible with indicative – and sometimes even mandatory – public planning. Its public-policy regime enabled its industrialists to target the key manufactures in postwar trade (cars, white goods, light engineering, process technology, electronics and, later, information technology). In this way Japan could outcompete those countries – above all the USA – that had pioneered the technological development of these products (Johnson, 1984).

Postwar Western European social democracy presents a more holistic approach to bringing business into a constructive relationship with the community. Up to the 1980s Sweden constituted the most developed example. While respecting the prerogatives of business in principle, the Swedish government required it to achieve certain popularly supported national goals for social development. These included sustained full employment, a steadily rising standard of living for all, reduction in inequality, universal access to quality free education and health, and continuous improvements in the quality of work life. To the extent that business contributed to these national goals, it would be left to its own devices. To the extent that it could not or would not do so, the state would step in to lead, coordinate and regulate socio-economic development (Higgins and Apple, 1983). Interestingly, the Swedish social democrats inherited much of the theory underpinning their policy regime from the British new liberals (Higgins, 1988).

Throughout this development, business fundamentalists never ceased to decry it as 'dictatorship' or 'serfdom', as the most important ideologue of the time, Friedrich von Hayek (1944), called it. They thus tried to enlist the horror the postwar generation felt towards fascism and communism in order to push a sectional interest that sought to subvert the vital link between a strong state, on the one hand, and a strong and free civil society, on the other. In short, these fundamentalists reissued the utopia of the nightwatchman state.

Apart from its other irrationalities, all this economic–liberal invective missed Montesquieu's fundamental distinction between despotic and constitutional states. The political parties which implemented social-democratic reforms were the very parties that a little earlier had introduced democracy, particularly universal suffrage (often in the teeth of liberal and conservative opposition) – the finishing touch to the kind of constitutional state Montesquieu extolled. In the fully developed deliberative state that thus emerged in countries like Sweden, business took a leading role in forming public policy and in the constant debate surrounding this process. It had nothing imposed on it by an alien, despotic power at all.

Indeed, in all the postwar Western mixed economies and welfare states, an enriched civil society emerged. Strong states nurtured free and cohesive civil societies. In striving to overcome 'social exile' they made an egalitarian inclusiveness the hallmark of modern Western civilization and of the enhanced dignity of citizenship it bestowed. Comparative studies of national economic performance show that business tended to prosper under this new dispensation (Dow, 1993; Parker, 1997: 270). The fundamentalists' constant refrain that public intervention cripples business simply does not fit the evidence.

Market Failure and Industry Policy

In the 1970s business fundamentalists added a new myth to their collection – 'post-industrial society'. According to this myth, we in Western countries can observe the decline of our national manufacturing sectors with equanimity, even satisfaction, because the wealth of the most developed nations will henceforth depend on trade in 'invisibles', such as services and capital flows, particularly expertise and 'information'. Only poor countries will actually have to make things. A moment's reflection will reveal how silly this idea is. To a large extent we continue to measure our personal and communal affluence in material commodities, such as cars, household appliances and public amenities of many kinds (including hi-tech hospital and defence equipment) *and in the rate at which we upgrade them*. Even computers, those powerhouses of 'information', are made up of components that have to be manufactured and assembled.

The truth is, if we neglect our national manufacturing effort, we jeopardize both our standard of living and our future policy choices – our ability to choose our lines of national socio-economic development. We become relatively less affluent as a community, more bedevilled by the social exile of unemployment, poverty, relative deprivation and deregulated 'junk jobs', especially the spiritual wasteland of menial service industries that don't enrich and develop their incumbents. The community thus has an immediate legitimate interest in how well business manages the manufacturing sector.

Yet another line of fundamentalism suggests, of course, that the community can no longer influence its own economic destiny because globalization has now eroded the state's sovereignty (and thereby the efficacy of democratic self-rule) over each country's development. This issue lies outside the limits of the present chapter, but it suffices to say that the simplistic version of the globalization thesis in question has come under formidable challenge (see Parker, 1996; Weiss, 1998). Once again, then, we find that historical experience has not magically become irrelevant.

Why can't we simply leave our industrial future in the hands of private businesses and their preferred unregulated markets? Recent economic history shows a marked rearrangement of the international division of labour in manufacturing, especially with China's rising proportion of world industrial output. But a clear pattern of winners and losers persists in international competition in the trade in manufactures. If we go back to review the conditions of industrial success since the Industrial Revolution, we also see recurring contingencies that determine success or failure. These conditions are specific to manufacturing as a particular kind of economic activity and are therefore missed in fundamentalist broad-brush theories designed to explain all forms of economic activity as reducible to financial calculations and flows. First, technologies are interdependent. Railways depended on developments in both steam and metallurgical technology; power generation depended on progress in steam, metallurgical and electrical technology; and today numerically controlled and automated process technology depends on linking information technology to mechanical engineering technology. Markets often fail to link the technologies in question (Rosenberg, 1982), and such linkages are typically the focus of successful industry policy, as in the Japanese case.

Second, like other forms of life, industries go through a life cycle, at either end of which financial markets habitually fail to provide the large inputs of external finance they need. In their infancy, industries tend to apply either process or product technologies that are commercially untried, and their markets are uncertain. Investors face high risks and can expect rewards only in the long term. At the other end of the life cycle, mature industries often face the choice between going under or radically restructuring in a process of 'de-maturation', which also requires a major input of capital with uncertain prospects for investors. From the community's point of view, innovation and restructuring are essential to the viability of a national manufacturing base, yet the market does not support these processes (Ewer, Higgins and Stevens, 1987: ch. 4). It is essential, then, that the community develops institutions that compensate for this clear type of market failure.

Third, even more clearly, each industrialized society has an interest in seeing that the constant and inevitable restructuring process, involving cutbacks and closures, does not impact unfairly on the local communities and individuals directly affected. Such a pattern leads once again to social exile and to significant political opposition to restructuring as such, no matter how economically well motivated. Spiritually speaking, our well-being as communal beings depends on a sense of justice – of living in a moral universe – which the sudden devastation of whole working communities violates. Once again, bad societies – such as ones that leave equity issues like this unaddressed – cannot sustain good economies in the long run. Industrial and labour-market policies can neutralize the social effects of restructuring, while a developed welfare state can ensure that, if all else fails, the individuals affected by restructuring do not face a drastic disruption of their way of life (Castles, 1988). This kind of public policy, which provides for certain essential industrial mechanisms to play themselves out without social harm, exemplifies the way in which business and community can work together. Failure to do so leads to both industrial decline and social breakdown.

In sum, as Williams, Williams and Thomas (1983; see also Streeck, 1997) argue, intelligent public policy settings and the new institutions they put in place can lead firms into making morally, socially and macro-economically responsible decisions over time. The forms of calculation that underpin decision-making in any firm depend on the institutional environment it is responding to. Like it or not, every business is embedded in a particular institutional setting, of which markets are only one component. But if the community does not set up supportive institutions and policies, then firms will respond only to the market. And it constantly constrains firms to look only to short-term, purely financial outcomes and to defend its own inward-looking interest to the detriment of society, the national economy and the individuals whose lives it touches.

Business and Society Today

Since the mid-1970s, a particular economic–liberal ideology and rationality of government – neo-liberalism – has been in the ascendancy in Western countries, especially the English-speaking ones (Higgins and Tamm Hallström, 2007). As with all its fundamentalist predecessors reviewed here, it asserts that greed is good: all we need is unfettered proprietorial prerogatives and unregulated markets. In the fundamentalists' age-old doctrine, these supposed boons will produce good economy, and that will automatically sustain a good society. Neo-liberalism inspired and organized economic globalization, which the USA and UK pushed under the leadership of Reagan and Thatcher. Three decades later, neo-liberals celebrate globalization – much as Adam Smith venerated the free market – as if it were the work of a beneficent Providence rather than achievement of their own political project. The latter crystallized in policies pushed through GATT (later the World Trade Organization), the World Bank, the International Monetary Fund and the other powerful, ideologically-driven actors that have fostered the globalization of markets and denigrated national development strategies with Mrs Thatcher's catchcry 'There is no alternative!'. As Rachel Parker (1997: ch. 7), among many others, has shown, there has indeed always been an alternative, and those countries which took it achieved better industrial, economic and social outcomes.

The present period in the globalized world can be compared to British industrialization during the ascendancy of economic liberalism from the 1840s. In his classic study of this 'great transformation' under economic–liberal auspices, Karl Polanyi (1944) pointed out that the programme to destroy the social institutions that compensated for the market's social failures led to a social catastrophe of immiseration, inhuman working conditions, a breakdown of public health and urban decay. Tomlinson (1981) showed that it also led to the world's first striking example of industrial decline. If we don't want to relive this history we have to learn from it.

Unfortunately, the reliving has already begun, and because global interdependence has indeed intensified, the social, environmental and moral damage inexorably spreads across the world. Unrestrained market operations have led to exacerbated north–south conflicts, although enthusiasts for the 'war on terror' desperately deny that the terrorist threat has its roots in the predictable fruit of global deregulation – the subversion of non-Western ways of life and the growing maldistribution of wealth, income and life-chances between developed and developing countries (Dow and Higgins, 2003; Harvey, 2005). The plundering spirit in which private corporations and their neo-liberal champions in government have conducted north–south trade constitutes one of the most spectacular failures of corporate social responsibility in recent times.

In those countries with the most pronounced neo-liberal policy regimes today, we see the telltale signs of social decay in rapidly growing inequality, relative deprivation, social exclusion, criminality, suicide and addiction. As David Harvey (2005) argues, neo-liberal policies have enormously widened the gap between rich and poor in those countries where such policies have been pursued in near-pure form – countries in which one has to go back many decades to find comparable extremes of inequality and social exclusion. The free-market response to the consequent social breakdown has taken the form of spawning private armies of security guards and gated suburbs – those ghettoes of the worried wealthy. The latter demographic also increasingly turns to exclusive private solutions to education and health care, at the same time as they support governments that divert resources away from the public provision of these amenities. The withdrawal of their resources from public health and education further undermine citizen entitlements and exacerbate social inequity. Market-driven developments like these intensify, rather than alleviate, social breakdown. With civility itself now under pressure, how long can business expect to prosper in bad societies?

The eminent German industrial-relations specialist, Wolfgang Streeck (1997), has reissued the challenge, notwithstanding the neo-liberal ascendancy and tales of globalization, to impose 'beneficial constraints' on business in its own interest and in that of society as a whole. The constraints he refers to, such as thwarting low-wage policies and labour-market deregulation, safeguard the legitimate, democratically-chosen goals of social equity and a humane work life. But more than that, reforms like these make industry more efficient. By creating trust in business circles through the nationwide enforcement of minimum standards, the community can remove the temptation for the individual firm to seek a short-term advantage in the degradation of its own labour force. In the long term, a well-paid, secure workforce with opportunities for skill and career enhancement is going to be far more productive than one reduced to factory fodder on a deregulated labour market, as the German case shows. Once again, a good society supports a good economy. But, as we saw in the beginning, business cannot achieve these good results if it is left to its own resources. Collective preferences have to emerge out of democratic deliberation, to be implemented by supporting social institutions.

Conclusion

Those who sit at the helm of business, or who intend to do so, would do well to avoid being beguiled by fundamentalist appeals to their own sectional interests.

In practice, business fundamentalism supports policy regimes that may serve the short-term financial interests of business, but always at the expense of its long-term ones. Economic activity occurs in a definite social context and in a particular institutional setting. In the last resort, business has good pragmatic reasons for defending and enhancing a good society – for shouldering its social responsibility – rather than foolishly treating the social ramifications of its actions as irrelevant. In the long run, only good societies sustain good economies.

The interest business has in maintaining the good society in fact extends into the moral values expressed in Western civilization's signature institutions of civil society and democracy. After 30 years of the neo-liberal ascendancy, both these values are now under threat. Naomi Klein (2007) has recently unfurled the spectacular example of what she calls 'disaster capitalism' – the vast (and vastly profitable) business of hi-tech snooping on private citizens that the US Department of Homeland Security simply outsources to private corporations with virtually no political accountability or financial transparency. This case exemplifies not only the squandering of public resources, but also the subversion of both democracy and citizenship through excluding the public from knowledge of, and influence over, public affairs.

The currently growing socio-economic polarization and social exclusion are morally abhorrent. They also destabilize both political arrangements and the safety of individuals and property – *civility*, to give this condition its original name – that business needs in order to be heard in public affairs and to function in the marketplace. Business fundamentalism is undemocratic in striving to reduce the ambit of public affairs, of effective, deliberative self-rule in a democratic society. Business leaders would do well to eschew it in favour of a more sophisticated view which locates them in a supportive social framework and as citizens of an enviable – but always vulnerable – democratic order.

References

Castles, F. (1988), *Australian Public Policy and Economic Vulnerability: A Comparative and Historical Perspective* (Sydney: Allen & Unwin).

Dow, G. (1993), 'What Do We Know About Social Democracy?', *Economic and Industrial Democracy*, 14:1, 11–48.

Dow, G. and Higgins, W. (2003), 'What Have We Done Wrong? The Responsibilities of the Rich', *Australian Journal of Politics and History*, 49:3, 380–97.

Ewer, P., Higgins, W. and Stevens, A. (1987) *Unions and the Future of Australian Manufacturing* (Sydney: Allen & Unwin).

Freeden, M. (1978), *The New Liberalism: An Ideology of Social Reform* (Oxford: Clarendon).

Freeden, M. (1986), *Liberalism Divided: A Study in British Political Thought* (Oxford: Clarendon).

Harvey, D. (2005), *A Brief History of Neoliberalism* (Oxford: Oxford University Press).

Hayek, F. von (1944), *The Road to Serfdom* (London: Routledge & Kegan Paul).

Hegel, G.W.F. (1991[1821]), *Elements of the Philosophy of Right* (Cambridge: Cambridge University Press).

Higgins, W. (1988), 'Swedish Social Democracy and the New Democratic Socialism' in D. Sainsbury (ed.), *Democracy, State and Justice: Critical Perspectives and New Interpretations* (Stockholm: Almkvist & Wiksell).

Higgins, W. and Apple, N. (1983), 'How Limited is Reformism?', *Theory and Society*, 12:5, 603–30.

Higgins, W. and Tamm Hallström, K. (2007), 'Standardization, Globalization and Rationalities of Government', *Organization*, 14:5, 685–704.

Hobbes, T. (1996[1651]), *Leviathan* (Cambridge: Cambridge University Press).

Johnson, C. (1984), 'The Industrial Policy Debate Re-examined', *California Management Review*, 27: 1, 71–89.

Keynes, J.M. (1936), *The General Theory of Employment, Interest and Money* (London: Macmillan).

Klein, N. (2007), *The Shock Doctrine: The Rise of Disaster Capitalism* (London: Allen Lane).

Krygier, M. (1996), 'The Sources of Civil Society', *Quadrant*, 40:10, 12–22, 40:11, 26–32.

Liberal Industrial Inquiry (1928), *Britain's Industrial Future* (Report) (London: Ernest Benn).

Marwick, A. (1991), *The Deluge: British Society and the First World War* (2nd edn), (London: Macmillan).

Montesquieu, C. de (1989[1748]), *The Spirit of the Laws* (Cambridge: Cambridge University Press).

Parker, R. (1996), 'Industry Policy: Possibilities in a Changing International Economy', *Journal of Australian Political Economy*, 37, 49–67.

Parker, R. (1997), 'The Indeterminacy of Globalization: A Comparative Analysis of Industry Policy and Economic Performance in 15 OECD Countries', PhD thesis (Department of Government, University of Queensland).

Polanyi, K. (1944), *The Great Transformation: The Political and Economic Origins of our Time* (Boston, MA: Beacon Press).

Rosenberg, N. (1982), *Inside the Black Box: Technology and Economics* (New York: Cambridge University Press).

Smith, A. (1996[1776]), *An Inquiry into the Nature and the Causes of the Wealth of Nations* (Oxford: Clarendon).

Streeck, W. (1997), 'Beneficial Constraints: On the Economic Limits of Rational Voluntarism' in J.R. Hollingsworth and R. Boyer (eds), *Contemporary Capitalism: The Embeddedness of Institutions* (Cambridge: Cambridge University Press).

Tomlinson, J. (1981), *Problems in British Economic Policy 1870–1945* (London: Methuen).

Weiss, L. (1998), *The Myth of the Powerless State: Governing the Economy in a Global Era* (Cambridge: Polity Press).

Williams, K., Williams, J. and Thomas, D. (1983), *Why are the British Bad at Manufacturing?* (London: Routledge & Kegan Paul).

4

The Technological Project as the Spiritual Quest of Modernity

Nicholas Capaldi

René Descartes conceptualized the technological project in his *Discourse on Method*, in which he proclaimed that what we seek is to make ourselves the 'masters and possessors of nature'.[1] Instead of seeing nature as an organic process to which we as individuals conform, Descartes proclaimed the modern vision of controlling nature for human benefit. It is the same project that Bacon had in mind when he observed that knowledge is power.

The technological project is not just a new way of engaging with the world. It is also a new way of understanding ourselves. Modern science, and the technological project that emerges from it, is different from classical science, which focused on careful observation. For example, an agricultural economy needs an accurate calendar, and observational astronomy informs such a calendar. By contrast, modern science requires two very different activities in addition to observation: modelling of what we hypothesize is the hidden structure of the world (for instance, the molecular theory of gases, atomic theory and germ theory); and experimentation – the deliberate manipulation of the world to test for results or to confirm hypotheses. Both the formulation of hypotheses and experimental design require inner-directed, autonomous individuals cooperating to produce innovative ideas (scientific and technical thinking) for understanding and controlling natural processes. Descartes' *Discourse on Method* provides and advocates a method, a self-imposed form of inner discipline, for promoting this kind of independent thinking. We do not look for an external structure or pattern; rather, we formulate models. As Kant

---

1   The so-called Industrial Revolution is but a later example of the technological project. The more fundamental idea is the notion of transforming the world. See Descartes (1968), Bacon (1995, nos 13, 16–17) and Weinberger (1980).

was to put it later, in what he called the 'Copernican revolution in philosophy', structure is something we project on to the world, not something given to us in experience.

There are two points that we need to make about the technological project. First, it is intimately connected with modern market economies; it operates most efficiently in this kind of economic order. A free-market economy is a system for the exchange of goods and services wherein there is no central allocation of these commodities, and they are privately owned (that is, they are private property). A market economy provides two advantages for the pursuit of the technological project. First, it promotes competition: since resources are privately owned, and there is no central command over what people should be doing with those resources, owners of resources are free to experiment and devise novel ways of using them. By definition, innovation resists planning. To the extent that property is privately owned and not centrally controlled, and to the extent that a free-market economy is competitive, there is a greater possibility for innovation. Markets also reward successful innovators and entrepreneurs. Finally, since labour is itself now a commodity, imaginative and creative inner-directed individuals can not only sell their services to the highest bidder, but they can also redefine business enterprises.

The second advantage of a market economy, as identified by Adam Smith in the *Wealth of Nations*, is that it encourages innovation. It is innovative because the division of labour leads to specialization, and specialization leads to innovation – in labour-saving devices, for example – as well as to greater productivity. All of this has been confirmed by the implosion of the Soviet Union and the nascent capitalism of China. The organization of modern economic life cannot be understood apart from its relationship to the technological project.

The second point to be noted about the technological project is that its major protagonist, Descartes, saw and proclaimed the spiritual dimension of this project. Its underlying idea holds that the physical world has a hidden structure which can be discovered by physical science; once we discover that structure, we can manipulate it to produce the results we want. In order for us to be able to speak intelligibly about manipulating the structure there must be some sense in which we are outside it. Since our bodies clearly belong to the physical world, our minds (souls) must in some significant sense be outside it. Descartes enunciated a dualism of mind and body, and clearly alluded to the religious and spiritual significance of the mind. It is through our mind that we come to know God and God's creation of a world that is at once intelligible and hospitable to humanity. As Locke would put it, we are made in God's image as a creator, and we mimic that creativity in the reconstruction of nature. It is a point later replicated in Kant's recognition that we can only know ourselves noumenally, and that the noumenal self presupposes God, freedom and immortality.

Kant (and later Hegel) clarified one additional feature of the technological project. Although initially expressed as the conquest of nature, as the imposition of human order on nature, the technological project is ultimately to be understood as the expression of human freedom. We come to know who and what we are through the externalization of our freedom. In this very important sense, the technological project is the spiritual quest of modernity and only incidentally the pursuit of material comfort.

Descartes' and Kant's critics rejected this view by maintaining a physical monism in which the mind was the brain, and in which the whole self was part of the great physical machine that constitutes the physical world. In the eyes of many of the critics, there is nothing but the physical world. The problem with this critique of Descartes lies in its rendering of the technological project as unintelligible. In order for us to impose our values on the physical world, we would first have to identify our values. If our values are themselves merely the product of earlier physical forces, then our values are themselves manipulable. If our values do not enjoy an independent status, then it no longer makes sense for us to manipulate the world. How or why should we manipulate it? How would we decide which values to use as a frame of reference?

In their response, the critics maintained that we could prove the existence of God by observing the order of the world, which contained a guide to the values we ought to pursue. In short, they posited a dualism in which an upper-level teleology floated serenely upon a lower-level mechanism. Ultimately forced to abandon the idea that they could prove the existence of God by observation of the world's order (Hume), they settled for a presumed miraculous teleology/mechanism dualism – 'miraculous' in that there was no foundation for it.

The Enlightenment Project[2]

For the past 200 years, a particular intellectual vision – the technological project – has dominated the modern industrial and technologically advanced countries

---

2   For a fuller account see Capaldi (1998).

of the world. By contrast, the enlightenment project is the attempt to define, explain and deal with the human predicament through science. This project appealed to an autonomous human reason freed of any higher authority and it deployed science as its privileged tool. In this sense, the enlightenment project is the attempt to define and explain the human predicament through science, as well as to achieve mastery over it through the use of a social technology.

The enlightenment project constituted the critical response to the technological project.[3] It presupposes that physical science presents the whole truth about everything; that there can be a social–scientific account of the human social world that mirrors the account of the physical world; and that, just as there is a technology to manipulate the physical world for human betterment, so there can be a social technology to solve all human problems. This project originated in France in the eighteenth century with the *philosophes*. The most influential among them were Diderot, d'Alembert, La Mettrie, Condillac, Helvetius, d'Holbach, Turgot, Condorcet, Cabanis and Voltaire.

Isaiah Berlin (1993: 27–28) characterizes the enlightenment project in these terms:

> *There were certain beliefs that were more or less common to the entire party of progress and civilization, and this is what makes it proper to speak of it as a single movement. These were, in effect, the conviction that the world, or nature, was a single whole, subject to a single set of laws, in principle discoverable by the intelligence of man; that the laws which governed inanimate nature were in principle the same as those which governed plants, animals and sentient beings; that man was capable of improvement; that there existed certain objectively recognizable human goals which all men, rightly so described, sought after, namely, happiness, knowledge, justice, liberty, and what was somewhat vaguely described but well understood as virtue; that these goals were common to all men as such, were not unattainable, nor incompatible, and that human misery, vice and folly were mainly due to ignorance either of what these goals consisted in or of the means of attaining them – ignorance due in turn to insufficient knowledge of the laws of nature ... Consequently, the discovery of general laws that governed human behaviour, their clear and logical integration into scientific systems – of psychology, sociology, economics, political science and the like (though they did not*

---

3   The term 'enlightenment' is a much broader term. Here I intend to identify one particular intellectually prominent movement that began in the eighteenth century.

use these names) – and the determination of their proper place in the great corpus of knowledge that covered all discoverable facts, would, by replacing the chaotic amalgam of guesswork, tradition, superstition, prejudice, dogma, fantasy and 'interested error' that hitherto did service as human knowledge and human wisdom (and of which by far the chief protector and instigator was the Church), create a new, sane, rational, happy, just and self-perpetuating human society, which, having arrived at the peak of attainable perfection, would preserve itself against all hostile influences, save perhaps those of nature.[4]

The enlightenment project continued in the nineteenth century with the positivism of Comte and Marx, and in the twentieth century it is known as positivism, behaviourism, analytic philosophy and cognitive science. It is represented in all versions of social science that have been reduced to recreational mathematics.

The enlightenment dream of a technological utopia is the common inheritance of liberals, socialists and Marxists (Becker, 1932: ch. 4). Classical liberal ideologues espouse the standard and dominant rational economic view of the world, which rests on the following propositions:

1.   Values are epiphenomena of a materialist substructure.

2.   The relevant explanatory constituents of the substructure are physiological drives.

3.   The supposed fundamental drives in the substructure are neither culture-specific nor consciousness-specific, but are physiological (for instance, seeking pleasure) and therefore universal.

4.   The fundamental drives also seek some kind of homeostasis or maximization that permits negotiation or the overruling specific rules (utilitarianism).

---

4   Randall (1962: 862) identifies the intellectual origins of the project as follows: 'Voltaire and his successors took over and used four main bodies of English ideas. First, there was Newtonian science, which was developed in France into a thoroughgoing materialism. Secondly, there was natural religion, or Deism, which the French pushed to atheism. Thirdly, there was Locke and British empiricism, which became theoretically a thoroughgoing sensationalism, and practically the omnipotence of the environment. Finally, there were British political institutions as interpreted by Locke, the apologist for 1688, which became the basis of the political theories of the Revolution.'

5.   The foregoing conception leads to a political conception of ethics
      based on external social sanctions instead of morality (which
      involves the inner sanction of autonomous agents).

6.   This substructure allows for a social technology in which cognition
      can control volition, because it does not depend on a perspective;
      it is a structure that reveals our basic and universal drives so that
      we respond automatically (causally) to any information about this
      structure.

Whereas classical liberals stress presocial rights, modern liberal ideologues,
socialists and Marxists add a cultural (that is, social and historical) dimension to
our understanding of this substructure – a social epistemology. Society defines
or constitutes individual good, so that individuals only fulfil themselves within
social institutions.

These views are all replicated in modern theories of management (see Hoopes,
2003). Orthodox Marxism, for example, can be considered a management
theory found in centrally planned economies in which scientific experts plan
all economic activity. Motivation of the workers is enhanced by the workers'
presumed recognition that they are also the (collective) owners of the means of
production, an arrangement which should automatically eliminate exploitation
and alienation. The failures of Marxism no longer need to be rehearsed.

    Scientific management is represented in classical liberal models beginning
with Frederick Taylor. Taylor's work is reminiscent of Bentham's Panopticon
design for a prison! Elton Mayo extended scientific management in a slightly
more sophisticated form by drawing attention to the more subtle psychological
needs that managers had to take into account. But his therapeutic management
was still scientific management from the top by experts.

    A wide variety of current management theories reflect the modern liberal
and socialist model. W. Edwards Deming's quality movement is a form of
communitarianism allegedly to be found in Japan. But feudalism constitutes
a form of communitarianism as well, and Deming failed to see the feudal
hierarchy in Japanese management. Peter Drucker is perhaps the most
famous management guru to advocate that management interpret modern
corporations as self-governing communities, perhaps indistinguishable from
non-profit organizations. Democratization movements in management theory
essentially attempt to replicate democratic socialism within the firm. Some

recent attempts to introduce spirituality into the workplace are no more than the use of theological terminology to advance a social-democratic model of the workplace by clergy and others who have lost any real direct and daily sense of the transcendent.[5] Most of the major Protestant theologians of the twentieth century, including Barth, Bultmann, Jaspers and Tillich, caved in to positivism and turned to faith alone as a justification of Christianity.[6] The 'death of God' movement in the 1960s marks for Protestantism the onset of a post-Christian era characterized by a kind of religious atheism, or even what Louis Dupré has called a form of humanism beyond atheism.[7]

In their ideological versions, both the classical and modern liberal perspectives fail because they do not capture the spiritual dimension of human life. The former tends to be reductionist; the latter is so focused on a group common good that it has reconceived human beings as if they were solely political beings. Various cultural manifestations, such as the prevalence of the use of drugs and the virtual reality of modern technology as entertainment, reflect both an escape from the present world and the search for a different reality. We seem to have solved what economists call the production problem – that is, providing for everyone's physical well-being – but just as work becomes less necessary, it also becomes even less fulfilling. Secular life no longer seems intrinsically valuable.

The Collapse of the Enlightenment Project

The intellectual credibility of the enlightenment project was completely undermined during the last half of the twentieth century. In his attack on the 'two dogmas of empiricism', Quine (1953) undermined traditional empiricism by asserting that there is nothing independent of different conceptual schemes (ontological relativism) and that different conceptual schemes are alternative readings of experience. The significance of Kuhn's *The Structure of Scientific Revolutions* is that it used the history of science to further discredit the original positivist conception of scientific theories as experimentally verifiable or

---

5   See, for example, Williams (2003). While I cannot argue this thesis at length here, I would suggest that this is especially problematic for Catholics in general and Jesuits in particular. Specifically, there has been a tendency with Thomistically trained theologians to emphasize reason to such an extent that issues of faith appear only at the highest metaphysical level instead of in our daily lives. One might argue that the entire enlightenment project was medieval Thomism without the theology.
6   Jaspers (1931); Bultmann and Tillich were influenced by Heidegger's *Being and Time*.
7   See Vahanian (1960) and Robinson (1963); see also the works of Thomas Altizer and Paul Van Buren.

deniable. As he showed, scientists operate with paradigms, understood as a framework of background assumptions, which structures the way in which experiments are interpreted. After Kuhn's work came Feyerabend's more radical views; in *Against Method* he extended Kuhn's thesis to argue that paradigms were more than just frameworks within science. Paradigms constituted the entire cultural pretheoretical context within which theoretical science operated. Science could not, therefore, serve as the arbiter among competing paradigms or pretheoretical contexts. The enlightenment project now lingers on, but only as an act of faith, a sort of scientific fideism made all the more militant by the awareness of its lack of a fundamental rational foundation.

Religion is intellectually discredited only if the enlightenment project succeeds; but if that project has failed, then religion has not been discredited. The enlightenment project rests on the view that physical science constitutes the whole truth about everything and the ground of its own intelligibility. This project has failed because science does not have the intellectual virtues claimed for it and is not self-certifying. Science cannot provide a naturalistic account. All those who recognize that the project has failed may be called postmodern, although how they respond to the recognition of the failure varies widely. Religion does not fail, because it has been judged by delegitimated criteria.

More important are the implications of the collapse. Science presupposes the human frame of reference, and any attempt to render the human framework itself intelligible, requires a hermeneutical account. Many philosophers understand the need for the hermeneutical account; however, they revert – as many postmodern deconstructionists do – to the social–scientific version of the hermeneutical account. What do I mean by this? Faced with the prospect of competition between narratives, adherents of one narrative will offer a hidden-structure account of what motivates adherents of the competing narratives in an attempt to delegitimate them. (Freudians and Marxists do this all the time.) In the old days we would have said this is the *ad hominem* fallacy, or the genetic fallacy. This mode of attack is illegitimate because, once scientism is discredited, social scientism is also discredited. Social scientism is no more valid than scientism as such, and would itself require reference to the human framework. The challenge posed by the collapse of the enlightenment project consists in coming to terms with the human framework and realizing that it cannot be done in a naturalistic fashion. How we understand ourselves is fundamental and cannot be reduced to how we understand the world. It's just the reverse.

Implications of the Collapse: Making Room for the Sacred

Philosophy and religion present us with two different narratives. Philosophy is monistic and naturalistic: the world is fully intelligible in its own terms. Philosophy is rationalistic (everything is in principle able to be conceptualized); impersonal (the ultimate principles of intelligibility have no direct reference to or concern for human welfare); and secularly Pelagian (despite the impersonality, humanity can solve its problems on its own). By contrast, religion is dualistic (we can only make sense of the world by appeal to something supernatural); mysterious (there is an ultimate mystery at the heart of the universe, a preconceptual domain that is beyond capture in conceptual form); personal, at least in its Abrahamic versions (the supernatural preconceptual ground of our own existence is an entity who cares for us); and involves grace (humanity needs divine aid in order to deal with the human predicament).[8]

Voegelin (1952) has astutely described the progression from the philosophical to the religious perspective. The preconceptual ground has three 'truths' which emerged chronologically. First, the *cosmological* truth found in all ancient civilizations portrays a given society's institutions as a reflection of the order observable in the visible heavens.[9] This form of representation lacks self-critical capacity and thus tends to induce fatalism, thereby encouraging tyrannical or authoritarian regimes. It expresses itself in myth. Second, the *anthropological* truth reflects the classical Greeks' discovery of the psyche or soul (which Voegelin defines as the 'sensorium of transcendence'). It attempts an attunement with an invisible order of right judgement beyond the visible order of the heavens (Socrates' and Plato's theory of the forms). Platonic philosophy discovers the continuity between the order of reality and the order of the soul in each human being, so that the human being is the microcosm of the order of reality, and the order of reality is the macro-anthropos, or the human being writ large. This is the experiential heart of Greek philosophy, embodied in Socrates. Third, the *soteriological* truth reflects the experience of human beings who open their psyches to the unveiling of the unseen measure in time by a God who reaches out to humans through grace (monotheistic Christianity). It expresses itself in revelation.

---

8   In contrast with the Abrahamic notion of God, are Hinduism, which has a very different notion of deity; Buddhism, which is godless; Confucianism, whose ultimate meaning is ambiguous; and Taoism, in which the universe has no personal relations with humans. In the Abrahamic view, God created the world with a clear purpose; whereas Hinduism, Buddhism, Confucianism and Taoism conceive of the world as having no ultimate purpose.

9   Note the similarities and differences with Jaspers' (1931) notion of the 'axial age' between 800 and 200 BCE as the origin of most major religions.

Classical philosophy failed and lost the battle with religion partly because it had degenerated into a labyrinth of puzzles. Voegelin asserts that Christian revelation completes the unfolding of the dimensions of truth and, in this sense, surpasses Greek philosophy. However, each of the three truths remains a genuine part of human experience. Historically, soteriological truth operates as a necessary presupposition of our thought. Modern philosophy in the form of the enlightenment project has similarly failed because it, too, has degenerated into a labyrinth of puzzles and a rationalization for private political agendas.

Implications for Organizational Life

The growing disenchantment with all schemes of social engineering opens up the possibility of a rediscovery of, and reorientation to, religion, and the spiritual dimension of human existence.

RECAPTURING THE SPIRITUAL

We shall have to accept that there are many dimensions to human experience (intellectual, moral–practical, aesthetic, religious and so on). We need to recognize the religious dimension, its difference from the others, and the need to make a place for it. Specifically, the religious dimension is not a form of agency; rather, it is best understood as a form of 'listening'. We need to allow much to happen *to* and perhaps eventually *through* us (Erickson, 1999: 267). This is especially difficult for Westerners because we have put such stress on moral and political action, especially in the technological project. However, the project's ultimate goal is not action per se, but the rediscovery of ourselves. The appeal of non-Western or non-Abrahamic religious traditions is precisely their greater emphasis on 'listening'.

We can no longer characterize 'disbelief' as the failure of religion to meet certain rational criteria, because those very criteria (of the scientism of the enlightenment project) have themselves been delegitimated. Nor can we characterize disbelief as the knowledge that there is no ultimate human meaning; no-one is in a position to 'know' this, and any 'meaning' that there could be has to be 'human' in some sense – that is the implication of the Copernican revolution. Disbelief can only be a moral choice and not a miscalculation. It is a moral choice that reflects a kind of resentment towards a universe that is not amenable to a wholly philosophical mind, especially one that eschews mystery and ritual.

END OF HOLISM

The demise of the enlightenment project does not mean a return to pre-enlightenment views. The notion of a single, comprehensive and all-encompassing religion that directly informs every other institution in the way that medieval Christendom supposedly did is simply not viable. That alleged unity was based on a philosophical interpretation of religion. If religion is granted its own autonomy there is no way in which a totalizing rational scheme can capture that religion or structure the rest of the world. We are not going to be able to draw authoritative and consensual conclusions about economic and political life from religion. At best we might agree on some procedural norms, but we will not be able to establish substantive norms. Reintroducing spirituality in management cannot mean establishing a new religion in the workplace.

PLURALISM

Religion, when shorn of its pretentious rationalism, inevitably generates a world within which there will be a plurality of religions. Within each religion there may or may not be a priestly or authoritative class or specific rituals. What is important is not establishing the authority of one of these religions, but providing a space for each. Public policies will not be determined by discursive argument within committees composed of representatives of all points of view. Public policy will have to reflect the need for universal procedural norms, but a diversity of substantive norms.

WORKPLACE

The structure of the workplace should no longer be determined by management theories that are variations on the enlightenment project. Nevertheless, the organization of firms will inevitably reflect the fact that firms are enterprise associations, which means that they have a collective goal requiring an authoritarian structure.[10] But the project means that we operate within a knowledge economy requiring the presence of autonomous people, and that is what saves us.

---

10   Michael Oakeshott (1996) articulates the distinction between a civil association and an enterprise association. If the larger society is a civil association (that is, it lacks a collective common good), then an indefinite number of institutions within it may act as enterprise associations, as long as entrance and exit are voluntary.

Such people are connected to the firm by a contractual relationship. Hence the nexus of contracts view is not incompatible with spirituality. Rather than thinking of themselves as members of an organization, these individuals will think of themselves as beings with their own agendas, including spirituality – beings that have contracted to serve the ends of an enterprise not because these ends are theirs, but because the enterprise is a common means to diverse ends. Firms will be more than willing to accommodate a large variety of idiosyncratic practices precisely because the technological project cannot proceed without this kind of individual. For example, instead of national holidays (defined politically or quasi-religiously) we will get personal days off. Rather than finding meaning in an organization, the autonomous individual uses the organization as a means to create a life that is independent of the organization. Just as there is no holistic way of capturing all of human experience or reducing all of it to one form, so there is no reason to think that every engagement in every form of life has to have the same meaning for everyone.

Depending on one's spiritual view, there will be certain forms of activity, economic and otherwise, from which individuals may abstain. There will be different rituals associated with common activities, including economic ones, which will give that work different meanings to diverse individuals. In this sense the transcendent and the personal can penetrate organizational life, but not as company policy. Perhaps what we need is not a firm's mission statement, but individuals who have their own mission statements.

References

Bacon, F. (1995), *Essays* (Amherst, NY: Prometheus Books).
Becker, C.L. (1932), *The Heavenly City of the Eighteenth Century Philosophers* (New Haven, CT: Yale University Press).
Berlin, I. (1993), *The Magus of the North: J.G. Hamann and the Origins of Modern Irrationalism* (London: John Murray/Fontana).
Capaldi, N. (1998), *The Enlightenment Project in the Analytic Conversation* (Dordrecht: Kluwer).
Descartes, R. (1968), *Discourse on Method and the Meditations* (London: Penguin).
Erickson, S. (1999), *The Coming Age of Thresholding* (Dordrecht: Springer).
Feyerabend, P. (1975), *Against Method* (London: Verso).
Hoopes, J. (2003), *False Prophets* (Cambridge, MA: Perseus).
Jaspers, K. (1931), *Philosophie* (Berlin: H. Springer)

Kuhn, T.S. (1962), *The Structure of Scientific Revolutions* (Chicago: University of Chicago Press).

Oakeshott, Michael (1996), *On Human Conduct* (Oxford: Clarendon).

Quine, W.V.O (1953), *From a Logical Point of View* (Cambridge, MA: Harvard University Press).

Randall, J.H. (1962), *The Career of Philosophy* (New York: Columbia University Press).

Robinson, J.A.T (1963), *Honest to God* (Philadelphia: Westminster Press).

Vahanian, G. (1960), *The Death of God: The Culture of our Post-Christian Era* (New York: George Braziller).

Voegelin, E. (1952) *The New Science of Politics* (Chicago: University of Chicago Press).

Weinberger, J. (ed.) (1980), *The Great Instauration and New Atlantis* (Arlington Heights, IL.: AHM Publishing Corporation).

Williams, O.F. (ed.) (2003), *Business, Religion and Spirituality* (Notre Dame, IN: University of Notre Dame Press).

5

The Three Poisons, Institutionalized

David R. Loy

Shakyamuni, the historical Buddha, lived at least 2,400 years ago. Buddhism began as an Iron Age religion, and all its teachings are premodern. So can Buddhism really help us understand and respond to contemporary social problems such as economic globalization and biotechnology, war and terrorism (and the war on terrorism), climate change and other ecological crises?

What the Buddha did understand is human *dukkha*: how it works, what causes it and how to end it. *Dukkha* is usually translated as 'suffering', but the point of *dukkha* is that even those who are wealthy and healthy experience a basic dissatisfaction, a dis-ease, which continually festers. That we find life unsatisfactory, one damn problem after another, is not accidental: it is in the nature of our unawakened minds always to be bothered about something.

According to early Buddhism there are three types of *dukkha*. Everything we usually identify as physical and mental suffering – including being separated from those we want to be with and stuck with those we don't want to be with (the Buddha had a sense of humour!) – is included in the first type of *dukkha*. The second type of *dukkha* arises from impermanence: the realization that, although I might be enjoying an ice-cream cone right now, it will soon be finished. The best example is our awareness of death, which haunts our appreciation of life. Knowing that death is inevitable casts a shadow that usually hinders our ability to live fully now.

The third type of *dukkha* is more subtle; it arises from 'conditioned states', which is a reference to the important Buddhist doctrine of 'not-self' (*anatta*). My deepest frustration comes from my sense of being a self that is separate from others and from the world I inhabit. This sense of separation is illusory – in fact, it is our most dangerous delusion. A modern way of expressing this truth is that the ego-self has no reality of its own because it is a psychosocial–linguistic construct. This allows for the possibility of a deconstruction and a reconstruction, which is what the spiritual path is about. We are prompted to undertake such a spiritual quest because our lack of reality is normally experienced as an uncomfortable hole or emptiness at our very core. Being a construct, the sense of self is ungrounded and therefore inherently insecure. We *feel* this problem as a sense of inadequacy, of *lack,* which is a source of continual frustration because it is never resolved.

By way of compensation for this constant sense of lack and inadequacy, we usually spend our lives trying to accomplish things that (we think) will make us more real. But no matter how hard I try, my anxious sense-of-self can never become a *real* self. The tendency is to identify with, and become attached to, something *in* the world in the belief that it can make me feel whole and complete: 'If I can get enough money … if I become famous or powerful … if I find the right lover …' and so forth. None of these attempts succeeds, however, because the basic problem is spiritual and thus requires a spiritual solution: I need to realize the true nature of the emptiness at my core, which transforms that core and enables me to stop clinging. Until I understand this truth, I will continue to act and react out of an unacknowledged sense of lack – that is, in egocentric (and perhaps even evil) ways. By continuing to act in this way, I reinforce my self-seeking behaviours, my negative habits – a process Buddhism elucidates in its doctrine of karma. The latter literally means 'action', including speech-acts, but it refers in particular to the intention behind each such action, and its positive or negative consequences.

Collective Selves and Institutionalizing the Roots of Evil

But what about *collective* selves? Don't we also have a group sense of separation between ourselves 'inside' and the rest of the world 'outside'? We Americans (Japanese, Chinese and so on) *here* are different from other people *over there*. Our country (culture, religion and so on) is better than their country and so forth. This realization has an uncomfortable implication. If my individual sense of self is the basic source of my *dukkha*, because I can never feel secure enough, what about collective senses of self? Are there such things as collective *dukkha* and collective karma?

In fact, many of our social problems can be traced back to such a group ego, when we identify with our own gender, race, ethnic group, nation, religion and other collectivities, and discriminate between our group and another group. It is ironic that institutionalized religion often reinforces this discrimination, because religion at its best encourages us to subvert such problematic dualisms between self and other. For example, Buddhist non-discrimination does not involve privileging *us* over *them*, because selflessness provides the foundation for Buddhist social action too. In some ways, however, our present situation has become quite different from that of Shakyamuni Buddha. Today we have not only much more powerful scientific technologies, but also much more powerful social institutions.

From a Buddhist perspective, the problem with modern institutions is that they tend to take on a life of their own as new types of collective ego. Consider, for example, how a big corporation works. Even if CEOs of transnational corporations would like to exercise social responsibility, they are limited by the expectations of stockholders. If their sensitivity to environmental concerns threatens profits, they are likely to lose their jobs. Large corporations are new forms of *impersonal* collective self, which excel at preserving themselves and increasing their power, quite apart from the personal motivations of the individuals who serve them. In this way, amorality thrives. In *The Doubter's Companion: A Dictionary of Aggressive Common Sense*, John Ralston Saul defines 'amorality' as a byproduct of modern organizations:

> *Amorality: A quality admired and rewarded in modern organizations, where it is referred to through metaphors such as professionalism and efficiency. Amorality is corporatist wisdom. It is one of the terms which highlight the confusion in society between what is officially taught as a value and what is actually rewarded by the structure.*
>
> *Immorality is doing wrong of our own volition. Amorality is doing it because a structure or an organization expects us to do it. Amorality is thus worse than immorality because it involves denying our responsibility and therefore our existence as anything more than an animal.*
>
> (Saul, 1994: 22–23)

There is another Buddhist principle that can help us understand this connection between collective selves and collective *dukkha*: the three unwholesome motivations – also known as the three poisons – greed, ill-will and delusion. As already noted, the Buddhist understanding of karma emphasizes the role of intentions, because one's sense of self is composed largely of habitual intentions and the habitual actions that follow from them. Instead of emphasizing the duality between good and evil, Buddhism distinguishes between wholesome and unwholesome (*kusala* versus *akusalamula*) tendencies. Negative motivations reinforce the sense of separation between self and others. That is why they need to be transformed into their more wholesome and non-dual counterparts: greed into generosity, ill-will into loving kindness, and delusion into wisdom.

This point brings us to perhaps the most important question for socially engaged Buddhism: do the three poisons also operate at the collective level? If there are collective selves, does that mean there are also collective greed, collective ill-will and collective delusion? To ask the question in this way is to realize the answer. Our present economic system institutionalizes greed, our militarism institutionalizes ill-will, and our corporate media institutionalize delusion. To repeat, the problem is not only that the three poisons operate collectively, but that they have taken on a life of their own. Today it is crucial for us to wake up and face the implications of these three institutional poisons.

INSTITUTIONALIZED GREED

Despite all its benefits, our economic system institutionalizes greed in at least two ways: it inculcates and enforces the truisms that corporations are never profitable enough and people never consume enough. To increase profits, we must be conditioned into finding the meaning of our lives in buying and consuming.

Consider how the stock market works. It tends to function as an ethical 'black hole' that dilutes responsibility for the actual consequences of the collective greed that now fuels economic growth. On the one side of that hole, investors want increasing returns in the form of dividends and higher share prices. That's all that most of them care about, or need to care about – not because investors are bad people, but because the system discourages any other kind of responsibility. On the other side of that black hole, however, this generalized expectation translates into an impersonal, but constant, pressure on corporate managers to maximize profitability and growth, preferably in the short run. The globalization of corporate capitalism means that this emphasis on profitability and growth is becoming increasingly important as the engine of the world's economic activity. Everything else, including the environment and the quality of life, tends to become subordinated to this anonymous demand for ever more profit and growth, a goal that can never be satisfied. The biosphere is broken down into a grab-bag of 'resources', while human individuals are reduced to a mass of 'human resources'.

The generative idea of capitalism is capital: using money to make more money. The other side of capital investment is debt. A capitalist economy is one that runs on debt and requires a society that tolerates large amounts of indebtedness. But the debt is always bigger than the original loan, since those who invest expect to get more back than their original investment. This is another way of understanding the general pressure for continuous growth and expansion – because that is the only way to repay the accumulating debt. The result is a collective future-orientation: the present is never good enough; the future will (or *must*) be better.

Who is responsible for the pressure for growth? The system has attained a life of its own. We all participate in this process, as workers, employers, managers, consumers, investors and pensioners, with little if any personal sense of moral responsibility for what happens. Such awareness has been diffused so completely that it is lost in the impersonal anonymity of the corporate economic system. In other words, greed has been thoroughly institutionalized.

INSTITUTIONALIZED ILL-WILL

Many examples of this phenomenon spring to mind, such as racism, undocumented immigrants and our system of law and order. But the 'best' example, by far, is the plague of militarism. The United States has been a militarized society since the Second World War, and its militarization has been intensifying. During the twentieth century at least 105 million people, and perhaps as many as 170 million, were killed in war – most of them non-combatants. Global military expenditures, including the arms trade, amounted to the world's largest expenditure in 2005: over a trillion dollars, about half of that spent by the United States alone. To put this in perspective, the United Nations as a whole spends about $10 billion a year.

From a Buddhist perspective, the 'war on terror' appears as an Abrahamic civil war. Despite being on opposite sides, George W. Bush and Osama bin Laden share a similar understanding about the struggle between good and evil, and the need for good to destroy evil by any means necessary. Ironically, however, one of the main causes of evil has been the attempt to get rid of evil. Hitler, Stalin and Mao were all attempting to purify humanity by eliminating what they claimed were its negative elements (Jews, kulaks, landlords). Are we following in their footsteps?

More recently, the second Iraq War, conceived and sold on the basis of lies and propaganda, has obviously been a disaster, at the same time as 'the war on terror' has been making all of us less secure, because every 'terrorist' we kill or torture leaves many grieving relatives and outraged friends to swell the ranks of future 'terrorists'. Terrorism cannot be destroyed militarily because it is a tactic, not an enemy. Just as war is the terrorism of the rich, terrorism is the war of the poor and disempowered. We must find other ways to address its root causes.

The basic problem with war is that, whether we are 'the good guys' or 'the bad guys', it promotes and rationalizes the very worst part of ourselves: it encourages us to kill and brutalize other human beings. In doing these things to others, though, we also do them to ourselves. At base, the principle of karma is very simple: to brutalize another is to brutalize myself – that is, to become the kind of person who brutalizes. This is the sort of behaviour people would not sink to by themselves, except for a very small number who attract our heaviest social retribution. In war, however, such behaviour is encouraged. No matter what the circumstances, belligerents always justify their waging war as collective self-defence. We all accept the right and necessity to defend ourselves, don't we? If someone invades my home and attacks me, I have the right to hurt them in self-defence, even kill them if necessary. War is always passed off as collective self-defence, and, as we know all too well today, collective defence can be used to rationalize anything, including torture and what is euphemistically called 'preventive war' (that is, aggression) – war waged, paradoxically enough, to preserve the peace.

The latter paradox supports another. National self-defence requires the United States to maintain at least 737 (the official number in 2005) overseas military installations in 135 countries. It turns out that, in order to defend itself, this nation-state needs to dominate the rest of the world. While it insists that other nations not allied to it must desist from developing nuclear weapons, it itself spends almost $18 billion a year to maintain and develop its own stockpile, which now comprises weapons equivalent to about 150,000 Hiroshima-size bombs. And since 1997 the United States has conducted 23 'subcritical' nuclear tests to develop ever more destructive nuclear weapons. Deployment of as little as 2 or 3 per cent of those bombs would end civilization as we know it! No matter how hard we try, no matter how many weapons we have, it seems like we can never feel secure enough.

Needless to say, the huge defence budgets proliferate supply contracts for many corporations, which thereby generate huge profits, attract investment and satisfy shareholders' expectations for optimal returns on their investments. In this co-dependent institutionalized relationship between the military and the capitalist systems there is no point at which moral responsibility becomes an issue, either for the millions of individuals employed in it or for the collective entities that institutionalize it.

In sum, the huge 'military–industrial complex' (President Dwight D. Eisenhower's ominous but felicitous term for it) institutionalizes ill-will. Our collective negativity has once again taken on a life of its own, with a self-reinforcing logic likely to destroy us all if we don't find a way to subvert it.

INSTITUTIONALIZED DELUSION

'The Buddha' literally means 'the awakened one', which implies that the rest of us are unawakened until we complete the personal transformation that he achieved. We live in a dream-like world. Each of us lives inside an individual bubble of self-referential delusions which distort our perceptions and expectations. Buddhist practitioners are familiar with this problem. Moreover, we also dwell in collectivities enclosed by much bigger bubbles that largely determine how we, as members of these collectivities, understand the world and ourselves. The institutions most responsible for moulding our collective sense of self and collective outlook are the media, which have become our 'group nervous system'. Genuine democracy requires an independent and activist press, to expose abuse and articulate political issues. In the process of becoming mega-corporations, however, the major media have abandoned all but the pretence of objectivity and fair-mindedness.

Since they are profit-making institutions whose bottom line relies on advertising revenue, their main concern is to do whatever maximizes profits. It is never in their own interest to question the grip of consumerism or the supremacy of the profit motive over any other considerations. We will never see a major network television series about a happy family that decides to 'downshift' – to live more simply so they can have more time together. Thanks to clever advertisements, my son can learn to crave Nike shoes and Gap shirts without ever wondering about how they are made. I can satisfy my coffee and chocolate cravings without knowing about the social conditions of the farmers who grow those commodities for me and without any awareness of what is happening to the biosphere: global warming, disappearing rainforests, species extinction and so forth.

An important role of genuine education is to stimulate people to question the many of the things we take for granted as being part of the natural order – immutable and thus acceptable – are in fact conditioned (and therefore can be changed). The world doesn't need to be the way it is; there are other possibilities. The present role of the media is to foreclose most of those possibilities by confining public awareness and discussion within narrow limits. With few exceptions, the world's developed (or 'economized') societies are now dominated by a power elite composed of the government and large corporations, including the major media. People move seamlessly from each of these institutions to another, because there is little difference in their world-views or their goals (which are primarily economic expansion). Politics remains 'the shadow cast by big business over society', as John Dewey once put it. The role of the media in this unholy alliance is to 'normalize' this situation, so that we accept it and continue to perform our required roles, especially the frenzied production and consumption without limit that keeps the economy growing.

It is important to realize that we are not simply being manipulated by a clever group of people who benefit from that manipulation. Rather, we are being manipulated in a self-deluded way by a group of people who think they benefit from it – because they buy into the root delusion that their ego-selves are separate from other people. They, too, are victims of their own propaganda, caught up in the larger webs of collective illusion that include virtually all of us. (As Karl Kraus put it, 'How do wars begin? Politicians tell lies to journalists, then believe what they read in the newspapers'.) According to Buddhism, *samsara* is not only a world of suffering, it is just as much a world of delusion, because delusions are at the root of our suffering. That includes collective fantasies, such as the necessity of consumerism and perpetual economic growth, and collective repressions, such as denial of global climate change.

Realizing the nature of these three institutional poisons is just as important as any personal realization we might have as a result of spiritual practice. In fact, any individual awakening we may have on our meditation cushions remains incomplete until it is supplemented by such a 'social awakening'. Usually, we think of expanded consciousness in individual terms, but today we must burst the bubble of group delusion in order to attain greater understanding of dualistic social, economic and ecological realities.

If this parallel between individual *dukkha* and collective *dukkha* holds, it is difficult to avoid the conclusion that the great social, economic and ecological crises of our day are also *spiritual* challenges, which therefore call for a response that must also have a spiritual component.

A Buddhist Solution?

So much for an outline of how Buddhism might frame the institutionalized problems we face. What can Buddhism say about the solution to them? We can envision the solution to social *dukkha* as a society that does not institutionalize greed, ill-will or delusion. In their place, what might be called a dharmic society would have institutions encouraging generosity and compassion, grounded in a wisdom that recognizes our interconnectedness. (In the Buddhist tradition the doctrine is called the dharma, so a dharmic society would be one that cultivates the key Buddhist values of generosity, compassion and clear understanding.)

So far, so good, but that approach does not take us very far. Is a reformed capitalism consistent with a dharmic society or do we need altogether different kinds of economic institutions? How can our world demilitarize? Can representative democracy be revitalized by stricter controls on campaigns and lobbying or do we need a more participatory and decentralized political system? Should newspapers and television stations be non-profit or be more carefully regulated? Can the United Nations be transformed into the kind of international organization the world needs or does an emerging global community call for something different?

I do not think that Buddhism has the answers to these questions. Nor, I suspect, does anyone or anything else. There is no magic formula to be invoked. The solutions are not to be found; rather, they are to be worked out together. This is a challenging task but not an insuperable one, if men and women of good will can find ways to work together, without the deformations of pressure groups defending special privileges and vested interests. Needless to say, that is not an easy condition to achieve, and it reminds us of the transformative role of personal spirituality which works precisely to develop men and women of good will. Yet Buddhist principles can contribute to the development of solutions. In conclusion, I set out three examples.

THE IMPORTANCE OF A PERSONAL SPIRITUAL PRACTICE

The basis of Buddhist social engagement is the need to work on oneself as well as on the social system. Why have so many revolutions and reform movements ended up merely replacing one gang of oppressors with another? If we have not begun to transform our own greed, ill-will and delusion, our efforts to address their institutionalized forms are likely to be useless, or worse. If I do not struggle with the greed inside myself, it is quite likely that, when I gain power, I too will be inclined to take advantage of the situation to serve my own interests. If I do not acknowledge the ill-will in my own heart as my own problem, I am likely to project my anger on to those who obstruct my purposes. If I am unaware that my own sense of duality is a dangerous delusion, I will understand the problem of social change as the need for me to dominate the socio-political order. Add a conviction of my good intentions, along with my superior understanding of the situation, and one has a recipe for tyranny and social, as well as personal, disaster. History is littered with examples.

COMMITMENT TO NON-VIOLENCE

A non-violent approach is implied by our realization of non-duality, which overcomes the dichotomies between self and other, and between 'us' and 'them', even in situations of conflict. Non-duality also implies that means and ends cannot be separated and that peace is not only the goal – it must also be the way. We ourselves must be the peace we want to create. A spiritual awakening reduces our sense of duality from those who have power over us. Gandhi, for example, always treated the British authorities in India with respect. He never tried to dehumanize them, which is one reason why he was successful. The Buddhist emphasis on delusion provides an important guideline here: the nastier another person is, the more he or she is acting out of ignorance and *dukkha*. The basic problem is delusion, not evil. If so, the basic solution must involve wisdom and insight, rather than good attempting to destroy evil (only to discover that it is looking in a mirror).

AWAKENING TOGETHER

Social engagement is not about sacrificing our own happiness to help unfortunate others who are suffering. That just reinforces a self-defeating (and self-exhausting) dualism between us and them. Rather, we join together to improve the situation for all of us. As Lila Watson, an Australian aboriginal activist once put it, 'If you have come here to help me, you are wasting your time. But if you have come because your liberation is tied up with mine, then let us work together'. The point of the Bodhisattva path (the altruistic ideal that inspires spiritual practice in Mahayana Buddhism) is that none of us can be fully awakened until everyone else is too. The critical world situation today means that sometimes Bodhisattvas need to manifest their compassion in more politically engaged ways.

To sum up, what is distinctively Buddhist about socially engaged Buddhism? It is the emphasis on the social *dukkha* promoted by group-selves as well as by ego-selves – the three collective poisons of institutionalized greed, institutionalized ill-will and institutionalized delusion – and on the importance of personal spiritual practice and commitment to non-violence, plus the realization that ending our own *dukkha* requires us to address the *dukkha* of everyone else as well, because we are not separate from each other.

Today's power elites and institutions have shown themselves incapable of addressing the various crises that now threaten humanity and the future of the biosphere. It has become obvious that those elites are themselves a large part of the problem and that the solutions will need to come from somewhere else. Perhaps a socially awakened Buddhism can play a role in that transformation. If, however, Buddhists cannot or will not participate in this transformation, then perhaps Buddhism is not the spiritual path that the world needs today.

References

Saul, J.R. (1994), *The Doubter's Companion: A Dictionary of Aggressive Common Sense* (New York: The Free Press).

6

The Relational Firm: A Buddhist and Feminist Analysis

Julie Nelson

And, the Venerable Nâgasena said to Milinda the king …'How then did you come, on foot, or in a chariot?'

'I did not come, Sir, on foot. I came in a carriage.'

'Then if you came, Sire, in a carriage, explain to me what that is. Is it the pole that is the chariot?'

'I did not say that.'

'Is it the axle that is the chariot?'

'Certainly not.'

'Is it the wheels, or the framework, or the ropes, or the yoke, or the spokes of the wheels, or the goad that are the chariot?'

And to all these he still answered no.

'Then is it all these parts of it that are the chariot?'

'No, Sir.'

'But is there anything outside them that is the chariot?'

And still he answered no.

'Then thus, ask as I may, I can discover no chariot. Chariot is a mere empty sound. What then is the chariot you say you came in? It is a falsehood that your Majesty has spoken an untruth! There is no such thing as a chariot!'

…

And Milinda the king replied to Nâgasena, and said: 'I have spoken no untruth, reverend Sir. It is on account of its having all these things — the pole, and the axle, the wheels, and the framework, the ropes, the yoke, the spokes, and the goad — that it comes under the generally understood term,, the designation in common use, of "chariot".'

'Very good! Your Majesty has rightly grasped the meaning of "chariot".'

The Questions of King Milinda (1890, Book II, Ch. 1, pp. 43-44)

If we look at the world we live in with any degree of wisdom and compassion, we cannot help but notice the severe problems of poverty, oppression and environmental deterioration that burden our current economic systems, which are characterized by increasing globalization and dominance by large corporations. Not surprisingly, many put the blame for these ills on for-profit business firms, especially large ones, which are placed in the role of villain in discussions of ethics and economics. Commercial interests, it is argued, directly oppose human interests. That competitive market pressures force firms to maximize profits at whatever cost to human and other life is commonly asserted as a scientific fact. Another kind of economics – perhaps a 'small is beautiful' or 'Buddhist' economics *à la* E.F. Schumacher (1973) of small-scale technologies and cooperative, egalitarian and small-scale enterprises – is thus often prescribed as the only way of bringing compassion and justice to this sorry world.

While such advocacy seems plausible, and enough verifiable instances of corporate irresponsibility have occurred to keep grist in the mill, I want to argue here that this way of thinking is fundamentally misleading and unhelpful. The logical structure of this story requires that the phenomena in question be split dualistically into categories of 'good' and 'bad', and that substantive entities we call 'for-profit firms' attract the 'bad' category. Such a way of thinking, I will suggest, breaches basic tenets of Buddhist philosophy.

The ancient Buddhist text quoted above demonstrates the interdependent, relational, non-substantive nature of things we commonly consider to be stand-alone objects. A chariot is not the solid, mechanical entity we perceive with our senses, nor is it identical with its axle or wheels. We must release our too-easy conception of the chariot if we are to understand the interdependent nature of reality. Can we in like manner let go of the idea of a substantive 'firm' identical with the interests of its shareholders? I will argue that we can better understand it relationally and that such an understanding considerably widens the space for wise and compassionate social action on economic problems. Feminist analysis forms part of the argument, because many of the obstacles to achieving a truly relational understanding of anything are vividly illustrated by

– and are perhaps strongly historically, psychologically and spiritually rooted in – problems in gender relations.

Relational versus Substantivist Ontologies

Deep ecology and Buddhism share a thoroughly relational ontology – that is, a theory of the nature of being or existence. In both deep ecology and Buddhist philosophy what really *exist* are relations and processes, unfolding out of a common substrate through time. When we believe we perceive 'some*thing*' – such as a chair, a chariot or a distinct human self – what we are in fact perceiving is our own organizing concept or abstraction. As the chariot example illustrates, things exist in a state of dependence on the relations which constitute them.

Also common to both philosophies is an abiding sense that the diversity and elaboration of these relations and processes has *value*. The intrinsic worth of this relationality, and the responsiveness of humans to this worth through gratitude, compassion and care, form the basis for a notion of ethics as something which permeates the very ground of being.

Buddhist thinking also warns us against simplistic identification with either 'self' or 'non-self'. To put it another way, we need to avoid being stuck in seeing 'form' without 'emptiness', or its opposite – 'emptiness' without 'form' (either there is a solid chariot or none at all). According to Buddhist teachings, attachment to either side of such dualistic categories underpins a great deal of unenlightened thought and action. Buddhist ontology proposes a middle way that avoids both sides of such dualisms.

On the other hand, of course, most modern Western thought is based on a substantivist ontology. The latter rejects the idea of a profoundly valuable (and ethical) substrate in favour of a 'tough-minded' just-taking-things-as-they-are – where what they 'are' being presumed to be solid things-in-themselves. Substantivist ontology sees relations as secondary, as simply the way that pre-existing 'stuff' forms patterns with, or bounces off, other stuff. Since the rise of modern science, the physical world has been conceived of as an ethically neutral clockwork, driven by the 'laws' of physics. Some modern thinkers try to take a thoroughly reductionist approach in which they see all issues of ethics, aesthetics and emotions as simply the epiphenomena of indifferent processes of evolution. But most of us cannot live in such a completely valueless world. And so we resort to dualistic thinking in which we take comfort in a distinct and important realm of ethics and value, while acknowledging that basic material and social structures may be heartless and mechanical.

Mechanical Theories of the Firm

It is from the dominant substantivist ontology that we get the notion of 'the firm' as a non-relational and amoral entity. In this framework, business firms appear as pre-existing entities, each complete unto itself, each presumably just maximizing profits. This view leads to the further assumption that the pressures from a pre-existing, impersonal and amoral competitive marketplace constrain and regulate the profit-maximizing actions of firms. Profit maximization and 'the logic of the market' then appear as inexorable characteristics of an underlying solid and mechanical reality. Values – if they are thought to be important at all – are presumed to operate in some other, less material realm.

People across a wide ideological spectrum hold to this belief. To take one significant example, mainstream neo-classical economists embrace it strongly; they positively extol a lack of attention to ethics. As a profession, we economists still hold to Adam Smith's apparently clever and counterintuitive insight that the impersonal workings of the market's 'invisible hand' will make individual self-interest work for the social good.[1] People will communicate what they value through market prices, neo-classical theory asserts, and the pressures of competition will cause the economy to work efficiently to the benefit of all. The conservative economist Milton Friedman (1982: 133) highlighted this conception of firms as asocial, amoral, discrete and mechanical entities in his famous pronouncement: 'Few trends could so thoroughly undermine the very foundations of our free society as the acceptance by corporate officials of a social responsibility other than to make as much money for their stockholders as possible'.

Yet *most* of this conception *also* finds acceptance from those who see for-profit firms in a consistently negative light, and who propose replacing for-profit firms by completely different modes of economic organization. This camp, too, asserts that firms must maximize profits and are driven by market forces. The difference comes at the end of the story, when the anti-capitalists judge the outcomes as bad, rather than good. Market prices do not reflect the

---

1   There is, of course, much controversy about what Smith actually meant. He certainly split ethics from economics to a far lesser degree than his present-day disciples. Here I am addressing his most far-reaching and popularly known assertion.

values of people with no money to spend or the value of the environment, such writers point out. The pressures of competition lead to a hunt for ever-cheaper workforces, to the detriment of communities and workers. Just like neo-classical economists, these writers depict the economy as cold and mechanical, only now the machine is called 'the global capitalist system' and perceived as an immense, impersonal and malevolent force. In *The New Social Face of Buddhism*, for example, Ken Jones (2003: 161–62) describes 'global, free market capitalism' as a structure or system driven by 'the logic of the market'. This, he argues, must be 'dismantled'. Ecological writer Barbara Kingsolver (2002: 13) describes commerce as 'simply an engine with no objective but to feed itself'. Sometimes those who condemn the social and ecological results of current economic functioning assume that someone – usually 'elites', 'corporate elites' or 'capitalists' – 'control' the machine. They generally propose solutions that involve replacing the controllers, or breaking the big machine down into little ones with local controls, or both.

This position is poor social science and is at odds with relational ontology. It is poor social science because an Enlightenment-era machine metaphor for the nature of reality – which has since been largely discredited in the physical sciences – has been allowed to colour and constrain our perceptions of our own experience in the world. It is at odds with a Buddhist, relational ontology because it obstructs acceptance of the way things are. By this I do not mean at all that Buddhist thought prescribes simple resignation and indifference in the face of economic injustice; on the contrary, compassion and wisdom should lead to action. But the mechanical analysis suggests that the putatively unalterable economic world in which we live must be somehow radically transcended so that we can jump into some other economic world to find justice. It does *not* see the phenomenal economic world currently around us in Buddhist terms, as arising in dependence on conditions that themselves are in constant flux and permeated with value, but rather as something fixed and cold.[2] The mechanistic view does *not* see the possibility of living with equanimity in the here and now, but rather seems to prescribe a path of cultivated aversion and striving so that we might, after some future revolution or massive structural change, make the leap from our current unacceptable world into another.

---

2   While Jones (2003) later lapses into mechanical metaphors, as quoted above, at one point earlier in his book he describes the dependent nature of economic systems and the illusion of their solidity well: 'Yet the objectification of society is no more than objectification. For example, the "market economy" is a set of subjectively agreed meanings, a game that has historically evolved. But "market forces" and the "laws of economics" are experienced as forces of nature … so that their ultimate origins in mentality are forgotten' (Jones, 2003: 53–54).

The 'small is beautiful' prescriptions, to the extent that they include an outright rejection of for-profit business as possibly human- and world-serving institutions, suffer just as much as neo-classical economics does from a failure to think relationally about firms and economies. As a practical matter, by condemning modern business firms and corporations as hopelessly corrupt, the proponents of this view make themselves largely irrelevant to most people in the work-a-day world. The latter, unlike utopian thinkers, tend to live wherever they happen to be. They also, very importantly, let contemporary business firms off the hook, ethically speaking. Since disbanding would seem to be the only prescribed ethical act for many companies, no possibility for here-and-now moral action seems to be open to them. On a more philosophical note, such thinkers are operating *within* dualistic thinking, rather than overcoming it, when they set up an image of a local, cooperative, egalitarian and altruistic economy as a counterpoint to a global, corporate, hierarchical and greedy capitalism. When we try to go beyond reified concepts and tired dualisms, I believe that some insights from feminist scholarship can help us to lever open – and keep open – new ways of thinking.

Non-relationality

Thinking relationally requires breaking many deeply entrenched habits of thought. At the deepest level, relationality challenges our own understanding of what we mean by 'myself'. Non-relationality – our usual model of perceiving reality – is related to the false belief that we ourselves are 'stuff'. If we fundamentally *are* things (egos, selves) then we have to *do* something with this 'stuff'.

Two main possibilities are then open to us. On the one hand, we may feel a need to defend this ego or self – to establish, aggrandize and gratify it. While in modern life both men and women may entertain the image of a discrete and concrete self, the characteristics of activity, status, individuality, heroism and self-creation that are valorized in this option have historically and psychologically been associated with masculinity. Feminist theologian Catherine Keller (1986) calls this the conception of the 'separative self'.

On the other hand, one may be just as attached to getting rid of one's (imagined substantive) 'self'. We find intolerable our distinctness, our reality and the responsibility it might imply. How much more comforting it can be to put our 'selves' in the hands of a heavenly father, husband, teacher or guru

– some authority who will lead us through the thicket of confusing reality and choices. We see salvation in giving of ourselves all the way, tuning in to a life force that is not our own, repressing our uniqueness, taking orders. While in modern life both men and women may engage in a project of becoming 'selfless', this agenda valorizes what have historically and psychologically been feminine-associated characteristics of passivity, humility, selflessness, powerlessness and self-effacement. Keller calls this conception 'the soluble self'. For example, women in many Western cultures used to be completely 'soluble' legal persons who dissolved, for all purposes related to the law, into their husbands upon marriage. In mythological terms, the image of the soluble self appears in stories of humans giving themselves over to the direction of higher authorities, thus finding salvation in submission and sacrifice.

These two conceptions, the separative self and the soluble self, are complementary. From the separative-self side of the substantialist view, the only alternative to active self-building that can be imagined is a pit of nothingness and the vertigo of an infinite fall. Mythology depicts the void as a threatening, maternally-imaged (matter, mother) passive chaos (Keller, 1986; Epstein, 1998: 86–87). Similarly, if we start from the soluble-self pole, the only imaginable alternative to passive self-effacement is a 'selfish' inappropriate usurpation of power that is not one's own.

This separative–soluble dualism is what I mean by a non-relational understanding of the world. In neither case is there an I–Thou relationship (Buber, 1958). In each case there is only room for one 'I' – either the heroic self or the higher authority to which the no-self attaches. To borrow some of theologian Martin Buber's phrases, the model of the separative self avoids dealing with relations to the world because in it 'the world [is] embedded in the I, and … there is really no world at all', while the soluble-self model avoids it by imagining 'the I … embedded in the world, and there is really no I at all' (Buber, 1958: 71–72). The non-relational view of the world imposes this dualism on everything: it simply cannot accommodate the possibility of authentic relation, because it is locked into 'stuff'.

Many cultural and intellectual projects exemplify this dualism. When some commentators look at religions cross-culturally, for example, they often posit the existence of a 'Western' individualist orientation and an opposing 'Eastern' submission to community. They often perceive Buddhism itself through this lens. Since it rejects the 'Western' notion of individualism, then – the commentator concludes – it must partake of a supposed 'Eastern' dissolution of individualism.

Deep ecology often receives the same treatment: the commentator concludes that since it doesn't perceive 'man' as the ruler of nature, it must advocate an image of 'man' as dissolved into, and ruled by, nature. There is simply no room for real relationships, no means of authentic and mutual connection, between distinct 'stuffs'.

In fact, the insight that gender-laden categories of thought play important roles in ontological projects, both historically and psychologically, sheds light on an important source of misunderstanding and resistance about deep ecology and Buddhist thought. These schools do not merely pose an intellectual challenge at an impersonal and philosophical level to Western modernist thinkers and feelers; they pose a threat to the very notion of selfhood that such an individual has learned to take for granted. While an understanding of relationality in fact promises freedom, we should be aware that many people who filter our words through a substantivist understanding will often instead perceive it as representing a loss of control – as impotence and emasculation.

Yet the 'small is beautiful' argument also uses such dualistic thought to the extent that it presents problems of economic domination as *primarily* a matter of scale. If the problems and the solution really were a matter of scale – if simply forming small, face-to-face, non-profit economic structures would itself remedy problems of injustice and exploitation – then we should see evidence of this in the actual history and practice of such institutions. But consider, for example, marriage and the nuclear family, a small-scale institution *par excellence*. People often assume that rational self-interest rules in business, while altruism rules in the home. If small is beautiful, then the family, intimate in size and supposedly based on love and affection (as opposed to profit and exchange), should offer the greatest fulfilment. And yet – rosy images of altruism in the literature to the contrary – feminists have pointed out that abuses, relations of domination and oppression, and the prevalence of physical and psychological violence too often characterize actual family life. The reality does not fit the stereotype. A truly relational and Buddhist understanding of our social world requires that such habitual preconceptions be set aside.

From Non-relationality to Relationality

A radically individual and active person exemplifies the separative self at the non-relational, autonomous extreme. A radically selfless and passive person similarly typifies the soluble self in being overly connected and extremely dependent. If we limit ourselves to these two possibilities, then the only possible relations among persons (see Nelson, 2003; Nelson and England, 2002) are:

1. *Separative–separative (arms-length).* When separative selves interact with other separative selves, such interactions must be purely external. The action of one party cannot have any effect on the other's inviolable constitution.

2. *Soluble–soluble (merger).* When soluble selves interact with other soluble selves, the relation must be one of complete merger. The individuals must completely meld into one unit.

3. *Separative–soluble (domination).* When a separative self interacts with one or more soluble selves, the result is a strict hierarchy. The soluble selves take orders from and support (albeit invisibly) the separative self, who is perceived as autonomous, active and in control.

Market relations, for example, are often thought of as separative–separative. The idea of the family as a harmonious unit relies on a soluble–soluble understanding. The traditional patriarchal idea of marriage relies on a separative–soluble image of husband–wife relations. The dominant conception of the human-nature relation is separative–soluble, in which we humans perceive ourselves as agents over and against the passive materiality of a valueless and unconscious physical world.[3] Examples related to the theory of the firm will be given in the next section.

Yet a relational approach encourages us to go further – to find ways of analytically approaching relations in which more than one self (understood contingently) can be present at the same time. Feminist scholars (for instance, England, 2003; Mackenzie and Stoljar, 2000) have suggested alternative models. I have developed a model I call *individuals-in-relation* (Nelson, 1996). That is, while the separative concept recognizes human individuality without recognizing relation, and the soluble recognizes relation without recognizing individuality, the image of individuals-in-relation recognizes that people are *both* individually unique and socially constituted. In equivalent Buddhist terms, this aggregate of relational processes we think of as 'myself' is neither 'self' nor 'non-self', but rather a unique karmic result of co-dependent origination.

---

3   Many of my examples deal with human relations, but have obvious extensions to relations of humans with non-human sentient beings, and with the rest of the natural world in general.

With recognition of individuals-in-relation, a fourth relational possibility opens up:

4.   *Mutuality.* When individuals-in-relation treat each other with respect and consideration, the relation supports the positive formative process of each.

In relations of mutuality, people have mutual respect and mutual constitutive influence. The concept can also be extended to the idea of humans as co-constituted with a creative and value-imbued natural world.

Within this category, two variants can be distinguished. The first is:

4a   *Symmetric mutuality*: mutuality between similarly-situated persons. This kind of relationship underpins, for example, the model of cooperative, democratic and radically egalitarian economic enterprises in which worker-owners share work and responsibilities. When people are conceived of as *equals* it is not too difficult to imagine that these might be relations of mutual respect.

The second possibility, however, is perhaps more challenging to understand and accept:

4b   *Asymmetric mutuality*: mutuality in relations characterized by unequal power, status, ability or resources.

At first, this may seem an impossibility: we are accustomed to thinking of *either* a horizontal relation of citizens in a democracy *or* a vertical relation of hierarchy and domination. The idea of *asymmetric* mutuality suggests that respect and consideration can exist even within relations of inequality of resources or power.

The relation of a parent and child, for example, is quite obviously one of inequality in power. Feminist scholars have taken the lead in discussing both the *abuse* of power within families (in systems of parental or patriarchal domination) and the *use* of power in care-giving work. Historically, women have done most of the latter, within families and in low-paid work caring for children, the sick and the elderly. Scholars of economics and politics have treated care-giving work as trivial and as part of 'nature' rather than as a critical part of what it means to be human. The point that is often missed is that relations of inequality can be characterized not only by *power over*, but also by *power to*. Without the respectful use of the power *to* give birth, *to* nurture, *to* teach and *to* heal, human life could not continue.

The insights of relationality, I argue, extend even to big, human-made and materially-oriented institutions such as corporations and economies. These entities often appear – even to some relationalist scholars – as somehow too big, too hard and too 'structural' to fall within the relationalist purview. Relationality may be everywhere, it seems, except in a corporate boardroom! Yet relationalist insights can be extended to how we talk about these things and to the role that each one of us plays as an individual nexus in a web of intricate material and social relations. Extended to the theory of the firm, a recognition of the possibility of *symmetric* mutuality opens our thinking to ways in which co-workers, for example, might treat each other with respect. The recognition of *asymmetric* mutuality further opens up the possibility of thinking about relations of respect among people with different levels of power and different roles. Not all workers in an enterprise have equal abilities in leadership, inventiveness or finance. Can enterprises be structured in ways that take advantage of individuals' different qualities of *power to*, while still retaining a fundamental attitude of mutuality?

What is a 'Firm'?

Separative–soluble thinking has strongly influenced ideas about the behaviour of firms, at two levels. First, looking at firms from the point of view of the larger economy and environment, it is clear that a business is often thought to be:

- *separative*, inasmuch as a firm is seen as profoundly individual – a unit clearly distinguishable from its natural and social environments; and

- *soluble*, inasmuch as the 'dictates' of law or competitive market pressures are often portrayed as inexorably forcing it to move in certain directions, implicitly denying the firm any real agency or autonomy.

Furthermore, if we look at what is assumed to go on *inside* the firm, we see that the relations among various actors, such as shareholders, managers and workers, are often thought to be:

- *separative–separative*, when people who make up the firm are themselves considered to be self-interested, autonomous agents; or

- *soluble–soluble*, when all are assumed to be united in pursuit of a common goal (usually the maximization of value to shareholders); or

- *separative–soluble*, when organizational issues are expressed simply as problems of designing the appropriate hierarchies of control.

What is clearly missing in all of these variations is any notion that firms might be active, connected and evolving organizations, or that they, or the people within them, have the capacity to act in engaged, meaningful and responsible ways.

As mentioned above, conventional economists and many writers in the humanities seem to limit their thinking about firms to the separative–soluble options. Other researchers and scholars, however, have developed very different models of business behaviour. Looking at actual conduct within and among firms – without the presupposition that these must represent only coldly impersonal, merged or hierarchical interactions – many have found evidence of rather rich and complex economic phenomena. Each of the above-listed characterizations of firms can be challenged, using insights in bodies of literature from philosophy, feminist theory, religion, economics, economic sociology, business ethics and organization theory. We can take each characteristic, one by one (for a fuller treatment see Nelson, 2003).

IS THE FIRM SEPARATIVE – A WELL-DEFINED, AUTONOMOUS UNIT?

As already noted, the firm, envisioned as separative, is defined as a distinct organizational entity which has the sole purpose of maximizing profits for the shareholders. 'It' is merely an organizational extension of the will of its owners and therefore acts to maximize returns. However, the responsibilities of corporations to parties other than their shareholders came under scrutiny in the 1930s. It surged again in the 1980s, framed in the terminology of 'shareholders' and 'stakeholders', following a formulation of the problem by the influential business administration scholar R. Edward Freeman (1984). He questioned whether it is the sole purpose of a corporation to generate profits for its shareholders, or whether its actions should also take into account the interests of others who have a stake in the firm. Suppliers, customers, creditors and local communities, for example, may have made accommodations on the assumption that the corporation will continue as a going concern. In fact, '[t]he modern trend in state law is to view the corporation as a "nexus of contracts"' (Adams and Matheson, 2000: 1096).

Taking into account the relations that make up a corporation leads to a model of the firm as a social organization, and a complex and dynamic one at that. The firm isn't something that just 'is', and then acts; it is made up of the actions and interrelations of managers, workers, shareholders, customers, suppliers, local communities, activists, legislators and regulators. In short, a firm comprises individuals-in-relation. A firm is also profoundly intertwined with the sustenance and change of the natural environment. Movements towards 'green investing' recognize that the same is true of firms; they, too, have a physical constitution, as well as a reciprocal relationship with the natural world. Firms are not independent of the influence of natural disasters, ecological degradation or improvement, and their actions in turn affect the ecological balance.

IS THE FIRM 'SOLUBLE' – DRIVEN BY LEGAL MANDATES?

Alongside the model of the firm as a free, unencumbered rational actor, we find theories which deny firms significant independent choices. Firms are often thought of as so tightly constrained by the legal obligations to their shareholders, for example, that they simply have no discretion to take into account ethical, stakeholder or environmental considerations. Perhaps the most cited legal case concerning corporations' obligations is *Dodge* v. *Ford*, decided in Michigan in 1919, in which the court decided that if Henry Ford wanted to pursue goals other than maximization of returns to shareholders, 'he should do it with his own money, not the corporation's' (quoted in Dimma, 1997: 33). Although frequently cited as the legal underpinning of corporate capitalism, this case constitutes, however, only one, outdated, snapshot of a long-running legal controversy. In the United States, corporations are granted charters by the 50 states, and the states have the authority to specify what can be required in return. In clear contradiction to the usual interpretation of the *Ford* case, legal scholars note that, in contemporary law, 'each state implicitly recognizes that a broader group of interests may be considered' and '*no* state corporation code in existence specifies that the directors of a corporation owe a fiduciary duty *solely* to the shareholders' (Adams and Matheson, 2000: 1088, emphasis added). Further, in 32 states, 'constituency statutes presently exist which explicitly transform the obligations of corporate directors by expanding the groups to which boards of directors are accountable' (Adams and Matheson. 2000: 1085). Nor are ethical considerations always considered out of bounds: according to the American Law Institute (1994: 80), 'corporate decisions are not infrequently made on the basis of ethical considerations even when doing so would not enhance corporate profit or shareholder gain. Such behaviour is not only appropriate, but desirable.'

IS THE FIRM 'SOLUBLE' – DRIVEN BY MARKET FORCES?

A further argument may, however, arise. The market, it is often claimed, exerts inexorable pressures that will keep firms in line with unyielding economic laws. Competitive pressures and the increasing globalization of financial, input and product markets will simply force out of business any corporation that might want to pay attention to anything other than wealth maximization. Economists Bengt Holstrom and Steven N. Kaplan (2001), for example, claim that market discipline will drive firms back into shareholder-interest-only governance. In the light of such market pressures, David Korten, a critic of corporate capitalism, sees no hope for corporate social responsibility (1995: 212–13). Evidence suggests, however, that running with some 'slack', rather than at the competitive razor's edge, may be normal for many organizations, and that acting on ethical and social concerns may even increase long-term profitability. For example, the idea that competition mechanically determines a 'market wage' is undermined by research suggesting that wages for the same job in the same geographic area may vary by 20 per cent or more, with the variation depending on, among other things, the firm's financial health and concern with worker morale (Krueger, 2001). Business scholars James Collins and Jerry Porras (1994: 8) reported in their influential book, *Built to Last: Successful Habits of Visionary Companies*, that '"maximizing shareholder wealth" or "profit maximization"' was *not* 'the dominant driving force or primary objective' of the 'visionary' companies they studied. Yet these companies were all leaders in their fields, in existence for at least 50 years. As David Packard (of Hewlett-Packard) once said, '[p]rofit … is not the proper end and aim of management – it is what makes all of the proper ends and aims possible'. The proper aim was in fact to 'make a contribution to society' (quoted in Collins and Porras, 1994: 56). It would be more realistic to replace the notion of an all-powerful market, to which 'soluble' firms can only submit, with an image of markets (as well as firms and individuals) as webs of relationships.

ARE MANAGERS AND WORKERS 'SOLUBLE–SOLUBLE' – DRIVEN ONLY BY THE INTERESTS OF THE FIRM AS A WHOLE?

In basic neo-classical theory, this is the case. When the firm is thought of as just a unit, it is simply presumed that all parts of it will work smoothly towards the goal of profit maximization. Managers and workers alike are assumed to cease to have independent interests of their own once they have signed their contracts. Although few economists would seriously defend this view any more, in practice it still serves as the base for much teaching and research. In popular writing the easy assumption that corporations are evil tends to erase the individuals who actually populate corporations from the relevant moral universe. Yet non-'soluble' actions – from the individually greedy actions of top executives at Enron and WorldCom at one extreme to the often personally costly but socially beneficial actions of whistleblowers at the other – provide ample evidence that not all actions within a business are undertaken simply in the interest of shareholders.

ARE MANAGERS AND WORKERS SEPARATIVE – AUTONOMOUS AGENTS? OR SEPARATIVE–SOLUBLE – CONTROLLED BY HIERARCHIES?

At the other extreme to solubility, managers and workers are sometimes treated as though each were a separative agent, interested only in his or her own economic gain and tied to the firm only by arms-length agreements. How to get managers and workers to act in the interests of the shareholders is treated in some subdisciplines of economics as a technical problem of writing a clever enough contract, so that actions that maximize profits will also be in the self-interest of the (presumably) opportunistic agents. Another variant of non-relational modelling sees firms as structures directed from the top, in separative–soluble relations of hierarchical control from shareholder to manager, and manager to worker.

These limitations on possible relationships to either arms-length contract or hierarchical control rule out the idea that values, group identity, mutuality, non-hierarchical structures or ethics – *not* merely derived as some variant of self-interest – could play a role within and among contemporary business organizations. Both symmetrical and asymmetrical mutuality are ruled out. Yet the evidence on employee behaviour suggests otherwise. Real human beings do not simply leave their needs for social relations, their values, their loyalties and their creativity at the workplace door. Economic sociologists Karin Knorr Cetina and Urs Bruegger (2002), for example, have examined foreign-exchange trading. Even here, in what would seem to be a classic case of an impersonal auction market, the traders created 'virtual societies' in which trust, reputation and social repartee were integral to carrying on economic transactions. As Collins and Porras (1994: 228, emphasis in original) reported:

> People still have a fundamental human need to belong to something they can feel proud of. They have a fundamental need for guiding values and sense of purpose ... a fundamental need for connection with other people ... [E]mployees will demand operating autonomy while also demanding that the organization they're connected to stand for something.

While many social scientists and intellectuals seem to have missed these positive signs, many managers and researchers in organizational behaviour share the insight that people work better when they are supported, empowered and allowed to draw on their own creativity than when they are consistently treated as potential shirkers who have to be brought under control.

Conclusion

Understanding business firms as relational entities – as vital and co-constituted with their social and natural environments, rather than as mechanical cogs in a globalized market machine – puts issues of ethics and economics in a new light. Instead of working from a dualistic social theory that counterposes harsh, mechanical corporations with idealized, altruistically-run community enterprises, a thoroughly relational understanding stays closer to experience. Our habitual metaphors and dualisms are laid aside, allowing us to take a fresh look at economic reality.

Nothing in this essay should be taken to imply that we can relax our ethical vigilance towards global corporations and simply assume that, as a group, they are generally benign or harmless. This is too often not the case. But what I hope to inspire is a certain scepticism about 'us–them' thinking that consigns the contemporary business world – a world in which we are all deeply intertwined, as consumers if not necessarily as employees – to an irredeemably 'bad' category.

We cannot prejudge the ethical merit of organizations simply by their size or by their supposed purpose (for-profit or non-profit) written into their articles of incorporation. Organizations must be evaluated on *what they do*. For example, small purportedly 'loving' families too often harbour domestic violence. Small non-profit hospitals too often exploit their own workers for the sake of keeping costs in line. On the other hand, large for-profit corporations have at times taken actions that demonstrate that they can be good workplaces and responsible members of social and environmental communities when given the chance, and especially when encouraged in these directions by consumer, shareholder and political activism.

'But they will be *driven to* do nasty things by the profit motive!' a sceptic might reply. Is such a statement actually based on clear observation, or is it based rather on belief and dusty theories of social science, on substantivist and mechanical ontologies? Even if businesses do, indeed, become increasingly destructive in the future, would this be proof of such a statement? Or would such a result be just a self-fulfilling prophecy? If we believe corporations *must* act irresponsibly, and if business leaders themselves believe that they have no scope for ethical action, such an outcome could be the natural result not of 'the way the world works', but of our own beliefs.

While not in the least denying the severity of contemporary social and environmental problems or the roots of many of the problems in attachment and ignorance, this essay challenges the idea that Buddhist thinking necessarily prescribes replacement of for-profit businesses with systems of small-scale and cooperative enterprises as the cure for economic suffering. It challenges this because it challenges the common image of business firms and markets as mechanical, mindless structures. 'The firm' and 'the market' are no more substantive entities than are chariots – the example in the classic Buddhist text that opened this essay. Like all else, they exist through interrelationships.

References

Adams, E.S. and Matheson, J.H. (2000), 'A Statutory Model for Corporate Constituency Concerns', *Emory Law Journal*, 49, 1085–135.

American Law Institute (1994), 'Principles of Corporate Governance: Analysis and Recommendations', excerpted in *Managerial Duties and Business Law*, Harvard Business School publication No. 9-395-244, July 1995.

Buber, M. (1958), *I and Thou* (New York: Scribner's).

Collins, J.C. and Porras, J.I. (1994), *Built to Last: Successful Habits of Visionary Companies* (New York: HarperBusiness).

Dimma, W.A. (1997), 'Putting Shareholders First', *Ivey Business Quarterly*, 62:1, 33.

England, P. (2003), 'Separative and Soluble Selves: Dichotomous Thinking in Economics' in M.A. Ferber and J.A. Nelson (eds), *Feminist Economics Today: Beyond Economic Man* (Chicago: University of Chicago Press).

Epstein, M. (1998), *Going to Pieces Without Falling Apart: A Buddhist Perspective on Wholeness* (New York: Broadway Books).

Freeman, R.E. (1984), *Strategic Management: A Stakeholder Approach* (Boston, MA: Pittman).

Friedman, M. (1982), *Capitalism and Freedom* (Chicago: University of Chicago Press).

Gilligan, C. (1982), *In a Different Voice: Psychological Theory and Women's Development* (Cambridge, MA: Harvard University Press).

Holstrom, B. and Kaplan S.N. (2001), 'Corporate Governance and Merger Activity in the United States', *Journal of Economic Perspectives*, 15, 121–44.

Jones, K. (2003), *The New Social Face of Buddhism: A Call to Action* (Boston, MA: Wisdom Publications).

Keller, C. (1986), *From a Broken Web: Separation, Sexism, and Self* (Boston, MA: Beacon Press).

Kingsolver, B. (2002), *Small Wonders* (New York: HarperCollins Publishers).

Knorr Cetina, K. and Bruegger, U. (2002), 'Global Microstructures: The Virtual Societies of Financial Markets', *American Journal of Sociology*, 107:4, 905–50.

Korten, D. (1995), *When Corporations Rule the World* (West Hartford, CT: Kumarian/Berrett-Koehler Press).

Krueger, A.B. (2001), 'Economic Scene', *New York Times*, 26 April.

Mackenzie, C. and Stoljar, N. (eds) (2000), *Relational Autonomy: Feminist Perspectives on Autonomy, Agency, and the Social Self* (New York: Oxford University Press).

Nelson, J.A. (1996), *Feminism, Objectivity, and Economics* (London: Routledge).

Nelson, J.A. (2003), 'Separative and Soluble Firms: Androcentric Bias and Business Ethics' in M.A. Ferber and J.A. Nelson (eds), *Feminist Economics Today: Beyond Economic Man* (Chicago: University of Chicago Press).

Nelson, J.A. and England, P. (2002), 'Feminist Philosophies of Love and Work', *Hypatia: A Journal of Feminist Philosophy*, 17:2, 1–18.

The Questions of King Milinda (1890), trans. T.W. Rhys Davids, Part I of II, Vol. XXXV of *The Sacred Books of the East*, at: http://www.sacred-texts.com/bud/milinda.htm (accessed 23 November 2008).

Schumacher, E.F. (1973), *Small is Beautiful: Economics as if People Mattered* (New York: Harper & Row).

PART II

Pathways for Change

7

The Organizational Whisperer: What Animal and Human Behaviour Can Teach Us About Producing Healthy People and Integral Organizations

Ian I. Mitroff, Terri D. Egan, C. Murat Alpaslan and Sandy E. Green

Over the years the following idea came to be the cornerstone of my thinking, so much so that it became like a mantra, and one proven by experience to be true: 'A good trainer can hear a horse speak to him. A great trainer can hear him whisper'

Roberts (1997: 46, italics in original)

In dog training, most people conceive of obedience simply as something the dog does in response to his handler: the dog is the one who is obedient or not. This is only half of what real obedience is. 'Obedience' comes from the Latin word oboedire *which in turn is cognate to* ob-audier, *meaning 'to listen, to hear'; by extension, this always implies* acting on *what is heard. Contrary to popular thought, obedience is as much your responsibility as it is your dog's – even more so, since you are responsible for shaping your dog's behaviour to fit your living circumstances. The problem with many dog owners is that they fail to listen and respond to the real needs of their dog; unknowingly, they are disobedient,*

The Monks of New Skate (1991: 136)

I ... wanted to stop and simply observe the horses. There was something compelling about seeing them as a family, the alpha male or breeding stallion circling and lifting his tail, stepping out with a high, proud action, and acknowledging our presence. It made me want to melt into the background and see what could be seen, without subjecting them to our interference. It was almost as if I wanted to be a horse myself, so thoroughly had I taken their side. These horses were not only [their] brothers and sisters, they were mine, too. I wanted to understand them, and I was more than ever certain that I knew less than I thought I did.

Roberts (1997: 9)

The need for an integrally informed approach to organizational behaviour, leadership and transformation couldn't be greater than it is at the present time. An integrally informed approach to research, such as the one outlined in Ken Wilber's AQAL (All-Quadrant-All-Levels) model, must address at least four dimensions of human consciousness. It must also recognize and address different developmental lines and levels in each quadrant (see Table 7.1). Furthermore, it must give equal recognition and legitimacy to all four dimensions. No single dimension or quadrant should be privileged over the other.

In sharp contrast, conventional scholarly research on organizational behaviour, leadership and transformation focuses predominantly on the 'exterior' quadrants (it, its). This is due to its overemphasis on the 'true'. In turn, this overemphasis arises from the reduction of 'the real, the scientific and the true' to the external quadrants, or what is exclusively observable. In short, conventional scholarly research not only underemphasizes the importance of 'interiors' (I, we), but also devalues them altogether.

In this essay we emphasize the importance of focusing on interior quadrants. We do so in the context of humankind's long history of relating to its animal companions. This relationship illuminates the nature of the interior quadrants more clearly and perhaps more strongly than any other phenomenon. A mutually developed sense of 'we' and 'us', or a sense of values shared by human beings and animals, may be difficult to imagine. But a mutual understanding of the interior quadrants between humans and animals is possible. Indeed, some of humankind's greatest teachers have been its animal companions; the quotes above provide some support for this view. We draw on a growing body of knowledge labelled 'whispering': a particular approach to working with animals that offers insights that can help transform organizational life. One of our purposes is to show that if animals' interior dimensions can be

	INTERIOR	EXTERIOR
INDIVIDUAL	**I** • Thinking • Feelings • Values The Beautiful	**IT** • Behaviours • Actions The True
COLLECTIVE	**WE** • Culture • Shared Values The Good	**ITS** • Organizational Processes and Systems The True

Table 7.1   The four quadrants of the integrally informed approach

acknowledged and treated with respect, human beings' interiors can and must be acknowledged and treated with even more respect.

Our use of the term 'organizational whisperer' is more than just a metaphor or catchy phrase – it reflects a fundamental shift in how we understand and treat people and organizations. It represents a profound shift from a near-exclusive focus on the exterior quadrants to an integrally informed one that embraces *both* the exterior *and* the interior quadrants. We offer lessons culled from the literature on whispering and from our own experiences in applying the lessons of whisperers to our animal companions and, more importantly, to ourselves.

We need to make clear that, throughout this essay, we are *not* suggesting that people and animals are identical. They clearly are not: what applies to animals does not directly apply to people. What we are suggesting is that people can learn much about themselves through their interactions with their most intimate 'companions'.

A New Role

Years ago, people began to discover the value of using horses and dogs in psychotherapy. They have also discovered the value of using animals in helping people to connect deeply with themselves and with others (von Rust McCormick and McCormick, 1997). The time is long overdue for us to use what we have learned to help people better understand themselves in the setting where they spend most of their waking life – that is, at work. This essay is about a role or function that is in the process of emerging. It is also about viewing organizations in an integrally informed way. One of our main purposes is to outline this new way of conceiving and running organizations.

While there is currently no single organization we can point to as a role model, individual managers and executives are practising selected aspects of this new function that we label 'organizational whispering'. One of the principal goals of this essay is to outline a way of bringing these selective strands together into an integrated whole. In this way, we hope that more and more academics, managers and executives, as well as their organizations, will appreciate the benefits of practising whispering.

As we shall see, whispering is grounded in a Wilberian approach that leads to a new framework for understanding *what* successful managers do and need to do, and *why*. In other words, it is not enough merely to focus on the exterior quadrants, observing and cataloguing what successful managers currently do (see Longenecker and Simonetti, 2001). At best, this only leads to pale imitations. Furthermore, imitation does not survive for long; for something to become a permanent feature, one must also focus on the interior quadrants. This leads to a deeper understanding of why something works. It also leads to a clear and systematic framework that underlies what works.

All Whisperers are Alike

All whisperers are alike (Hogg, 2001; Roberts, 1997; Owens, 1999). They are devotees and practitioners of the same philosophy. Independently, they have discovered and developed the same principles for rearing healthy horses and dogs. This does not mean that there are no important differences between whisperers; however, for the purposes of this essay, the differences are not essential.[1]

Along the way, whisperers discovered one of the most important truths of the human condition: there was more to learn from their so-called 'students' or 'trainees' than their 'students' had to learn from them. In effect, their respective roles were been reversed: the students or trainees became the teachers and trainers, and vice versa. This is not to say that the individual perspectives, and different strengths that each contributes, are ignored. Rather, what each brings is treated with equal respect – its equal value is acknowledged.

At the same time, something even deeper was occurring – an indissoluble bond and partnership was being formed. The lines between whisperer and the horse or dog were being dissolved, so that in effect their interiors were distinguishable or differentiated as separate entities only in their outward or exterior appearance. Through long hours of working together, not only had mutual respect and understanding developed, but in effect a new being – a deep integration between trainer and trainee – had been formed. From a Wilberian perspective, this new unity or entity is what transcends and includes both of the separate entities.

Whisperers have demonstrated that horses and dogs, and by extension human beings, do not need to be physically and mentally abused – 'broken' – to be well behaved and healthy members of animal and human communities. The art of whispering demonstrates that trainer and trainee alike require a method that will allow them to jointly become healthy. Without a whisperer it is impossible for a horse, dog or human being to be healthy.

---

1   There are as many differences between horse, dog and baby whisperers and trainers as there are among the practitioners of any field. This is especially the case as the field calls for a profound life-commitment from those who devote their entire being to it. Thus, in conducting interviews for this essay, it was extremely common for the different practitioners to demean one another. In many cases, merely mentioning the name of a particular person was enough to elicit derogatory comments, such as 'So-and-so doesn't really understand a thing about training'. Thus when we say that 'all whisperers are alike', we are thereby referring to what whisperers share in common and what rises above the everyday squabbles that separate them.

Fundamental Lessons

The following sections of this essay outline the two fundamental lessons that whisperers have discovered – namely, the need to embrace polarities and to integrate mind, body and spirit. These two principles are interconnected: the integration principle builds the capacity and the maturity to transcend and include polarities.

As we will see, one of the most important lessons is that animal and human needs are organized in terms of opposites – for example, the need for stability versus the need for constant novelty and change. The tension between these opposites is as perpetual as it is necessary. Whisperers have discovered how to satisfy both needs at the opposite ends of the spectrum simultaneously. They have also discovered that if one attends to only one need at the expense of the other, then one does violence to the complexity of the animal or human. Whisperers have discovered methods for meeting the complexity of animal and human needs that are simultaneously both gentle and firm. Thus they have discovered not only that animal and human needs are organized in terms of opposites, but also that meeting these needs does not involve an either/or, but rather a both/and. Any method of instruction that emphasizes one need at the expense of the other is doomed to fail. In itself, this insight explains why the vast majority of efforts to change organizations fail.

Another of the basic lessons that whisperers have discovered is that, when a horse enters the ring for training – or when a human being walks in the door of their workplace – the whole animal or the whole person enters at the same time. The brains *and* the emotions of the animal or person arrive simultaneously, and not one at the expense of the other. In Wilber's terms, all of the quadrants, or both the interiors and the exteriors, arrive and are present simultaneously. And yet the vast majority of training and educational programmes and organizations assume not only that one's 'reasoning capabilities and needs' can be met independently of one's 'emotional needs', but also that one's emotions must not be allowed to contaminate one's 'rational' decisions. Whisperers regard this idea as complete and utter nonsense.

Whisperers consider the separation between thought and emotion to be nonsense for another fundamental reason as well (Zajonc, 1984; Lazarus, 1984). Horses are uncanny barometers of what people are feeling *and* thinking. While horses are obviously not mind-readers, they are nonetheless incredibly sensitive not only to behaviour (exteriors) but also to the emotional *and* cognitive state (interiors) of a person. For this reason alone, the separation between thought and emotion makes no sense. It certainly makes no 'horse sense'.

In some cases, horses are subjected to working conditions and training methods that cut them off from their essential, integrated nature. Take, for example, the string horse that has been conditioned to follow along and to subjugate its emotional responses and spiritual essence in the service of highly routine work (see boxed example below).

What does it take to create conditions for unlearning? Patience and persistence on the part of leaders working towards the goal of 'breaking' the patterns and structures that reinforce 'string' behaviour and an environment of support and

---

Several years ago, Terri Egan's then 12-year-old daughter, Brook, fell in love with an older mare named Flatlander. 'Flat' (as we came to call her) had been a trail horse for several years when Brook met her. As a trail horse, Flat spent part of her time on the string. String horses carry inexperienced and often insensitive riders along established trail systems. Each horse closely follows its nearest neighbour, and they all follow the lead horse and rider, thus forming a 'string' of horses. String horses are conditioned to ignore both their rider's cues and their own instincts, as they must avoid reaction to disturbances in the environment that would otherwise stimulate curiosity and perhaps anxiety in a healthy horse. Weary of the routine of trail, Flat had developed the ability to evade working on the string by running to the top of a hill in the pasture and avoiding being 'caught' by the wranglers. After a while, the wranglers got tired of chasing Flat, and she spent most days by herself or in the company of one other horse.

Brook developed a special relationship with Flat, and, through a combination of patience and persistence, Flat would allow herself to be 'caught', and she and Brook would ride out on the surrounding mountain trails. Several years passed, and we had the chance to purchase Flat and bring her home. Brook was excited about having her dream horse, and we hired a trainer to work with them both.

Initially, Flat fell into her old patterns: she avoided capture and responded with a routine set of behaviours befitting the demands of a string horse – albeit ones disconnected from her own desires and Brook's and her coach/trainer's requests. Gradually, however, Flat's underlying personality began to re-emerge, and Brook found herself challenged by an equine partner who was intelligent and full of spirit. A series of challenges ensued, in which Flat made Brook prove her trustworthiness and loyalty before she revealed additional layers of her essential personality. After about six months, Flat had remembered what it meant to be a horse and had unlearned the lessons of the string.

challenge where experimentation and risk-taking are encouraged, failures are met with patience, and desired outcomes are consistently rewarded.

What Whisperers Have to Teach

A lone trainer steps into a 'round-pen' – an enclosed ring 18 metres in circumference. Inside it an unbroken, potentially dangerous horse is kicking wildly. And yet in less than half an hour, the horse will not only let the trainer approach him, but allow her to saddle and ride him. The trainer will accomplish this by first gently flicking a rope at the horse to engage his curiosity and then by performing a highly complex and sequenced set of looks and body movements back and forth between herself and the animal. At no point in this process will the trainer either abuse or threaten him. Nonetheless, in one thousandth of the time that it once took to 'break' a horse through the earlier conventional, but abusive, methods, the trainer will have 'civilized' him and, in the process, herself as well.

A dog trainer has devised a method that is built on the fundamental principle that dogs and their carers have the same set of basic needs. As a result, he is not only able to 'civilize' both the trainer and the trainee in a much shorter period of time, but in a more humane way as well.

A horse trainer who strongly eschews the 'whisperer' label nonetheless follows their procedures to a tee. He conducts 'equine sessions' in which people who have had little or no contact with horses, and as a result may be afraid of them, are taught to approach them gently and safely in order to groom them. Later, they join the trainer in the middle of the 18-metre round-pen on an individual basis; here, they learn to get a horse to trot and to gallop around the ring without issuing any explicit vocal commands. They also get the horse to stop and change direction merely by changing the position of their bodies.

Ian Mitroff has personal experience of this; he is one of those who have stood in the centre of such a ring. To get there he had to overcome years of fear and anger. Weighing over 450 kg, a horse is a daunting, if not terrifying, animal, especially for someone who has ever fallen off one and sustained a serious back injury as Ian did years earlier. In such cases, an individual will have stored up years of anger and fear as well as other emotions that they might not be aware of until they enter the training ring. In order to bond with a horse, an individual must first confront and overcome their negative emotions. It is for this very reason that horses are often used in therapy to reconnect people to themselves and the outer world.

Two of Ian's greatest prizes are an honorary doctorate and a certificate testifying to the fact that he and his dog, Henry, have successfully completed dog obedience training. The honorary doctorate is from the Faculty of Social Sciences at the University of Stockholm, Sweden. It was awarded in recognition of a lifetime of work in the social sciences. The formal degree itself is a large, impressive-looking document written entirely in Latin. It was conferred amid great pomp and circumstance on 29 September 2000 in the Stockholm Town Hall, the venue for the annual award of the Nobel Prizes. The dog-training certificate was conferred in a small park in Southern California on 17 September 1994 when Henry was around a year old.

If the honorary doctorate represents recognition for a lifetime of professional academic accomplishments, the certificate represents recognition for a successful partnership between a human and an intelligent animal. Of course, the two are not equal in significance; there is no sensible way in which to compare an important intellectual accomplishment with an important social one. And yet, in a fundamental sense, both *are* equally significant. They attest to two distinct forms of intelligence that are critical to success in one's career and life. Whereas the honorary doctorate is evidence of intellectual attainment, or cognitive IQ, the certificate is evidence of emotional and social accomplishment, or emotional IQ.

Terri Egan has found that horses are excellent facilitators of personal and organizational learning. Horses have the ability to deliver 'feedback' in a way that transcends the typical communication between human beings. Horses, in contrast to humans, have nothing to gain from 'gaming' the relationship. They respond in a most authentic way to a variety of human emotions. Working with horses, self-aware whisperers soon understand that they must get beyond the mask of impression management in order to establish a real relationship.

The Organization of Human Needs

The work of whisperers demonstrates that human and animal 'needs' come in a small number of pairs or opposites.[2] These opposites are continually in tension with each other, such that the satisfaction of one member of the pair leads to the dissatisfaction of the other. Thus what is called for is a method that gives equal

---

2   More generally, the organization of human needs in terms of pairs or opposites follows from the work of developmental psychologists: see Wilbur (2000).

recognition to both members of the pair without doing damage or violence to either one. We have identified five core coupled needs which both whisperers and managers must hold in dynamic tension. These are:

1.   the need for *structure* and *stability*

2.   the need for constant *novelty* and *change*

3.   the need to know when to *lead* and the need to know when to *follow*

4.   the need to *cooperate* and the need to *look after self-interest*

5.   the need to integrate our *spiritual needs* with our *work life*.

In each case, a dynamic balance between these polarities must be met if development is to occur. We offer the stories of Henry and Possum as illustrations of the tension between the need for stability and the need for change.

THE HENRY PRINCIPLE – THE IMPORTANCE OF STRUCTURE AND STABILITY

The vast majority of efforts to achieve organizational change – the estimates vary between 60 and 90 percent – not only fail, but fail miserably (see Beer, 2001; Collins, 2000). Given the intense worldwide competition for survival amongst all organizations, we need not only to explain why most attempts at change fail, but also to learn what can be done to dramatically improve the percentage of successful efforts. This is precisely what we have named 'the Henry principle' helps us to understand.

Henry exhibits all of the normal characteristics of dogs. For instance, if one throws a red ball into the air, then Henry vigorously chases after it. However, if, while he is chasing after the red ball, one throws a blue one into the air, then Henry stops dead in his tracks and chases after the blue ball. If one throws both a red and a blue ball into the air at the same time, then Henry also stops dead in his tracks; in this case, he chases after neither ball because he is totally confused.

There is a remarkable parallel between Henry's behaviour and the numerous 'balls' or 'programmes' that we constantly throw at people in organizations. The result is the Henry principle: *without intensive training, neither people nor animals can chase or pursue more than one ball, or programme, at the same time.*

It is not just the consistency of the commands and the trainer that are critical in animal training. It is also the fact that the trainer needs to learn to 'connect deeply' with the animal, so that meaning, trust and mutual understanding are established. Without them, training is virtually impossible. In today's vernacular, we would say that a 'deep spiritual' element has to be present before any training can succeed. This truth holds equally for dogs and people.

If we want to succeed in dog training and socialization, we wouldn't dream of switching trainers and the meanings of commands in midstream. We expect that we will have to repeat the same commands over and over again until a dog learns to obey them consistently. Herein lies a fundamental truth about people and organizations.

The most common command for 'sit' is the extension of the right hand immediately above a dog's head, with the thumb touching the middle two fingers as if one were about to give it a piece of food. Most dogs will instinctively raise their heads to receive the 'food'. At this point, one lowers one's right hand, pushing, if need be, the dog's behind gently but firmly into a sitting position with one's left hand. The latter is especially necessary if the dog has not itself assumed the sitting position, which most dogs normally do. Presumably all one then has to do is to repeat the process some hundreds of times, saying 'sit' at the same time, until the dog performs the desired behaviour perfectly and consistently on cue. But imagine how miserably the process would fail if we changed the verbal command for 'sit' and the accompanying hand signal every time we attempted to train the animal. Our dog would be hopelessly confused. If we then blamed or punished it with shouts or, even worse, with physical punishment, we would produce a frightened and abused animal.

Working with young horses follows a similar pattern. Consistency, while difficult to achieve, is the basis for creating a foundation for future learning – the kind of learning which allows the animal to adapt to environmental inconsistencies and generate higher-order responses. While horses can and do deal with inconsistencies – witness the patience and tolerance of the 'school' horse trained to deliberately ignore miscues from novice riders – nevertheless the highest levels of performance can only come through careful and consistent communication between horse and rider. This communication begins with a process of support and challenge in which the bond between horse and rider is established before the rider even sits in the saddle.

If we want to produce a trained and healthy animal, then we have to be consistent and proceed slowly. We have to reward and constantly praise our dog when it does something right, and utter a firm 'no' or 'stay' when the animal does something we don't want (see The Monks of New Skate, 1991).

THE POSSUM PREDICAMENT – THE NEED FOR NOVELTY AND CHANGE

Possum is a three-year-old paint horse, eager to learn, and poised to begin his formal training. After two months with a reputable trainer, Possum comes home, and his human partner continues his training by working with him on a regular basis. The first several times that she steps into the round-pen with Possum, all goes as expected. As time passes, she begins to notice that Possum doesn't wait for any cues before beginning his routine. He enters the round-pen, waits for his human partner to make any last-minute adjustments to his tack and launches into his routine. None of this routine has much to do with his human partner's expectations or, more importantly, with Possum's natural strengths. Rather, his early training has conditioned Possum to perform a routine in response to what he perceives his trainer (read: manager) requires. The structural cues of the round-pen have superseded the independent desires of both horse and human.

Subsequent sessions in the round-pen focus on re-establishing a relationship based on mutual communication and introducing choice into the training environment. The predictability of the round-pen is replaced with a series of choices based on an environment that more closely represents the world that Possum will operate in as a mature horse. Six months later, Possum has a strong foundation resulting from the consistency of his early training as well as the ability to thrive in novel circumstances due to his later training.

These principles do not mean that people need to be trained to exhibit blind obedience; this would draw the worst parallel between people and animals. Rather, people need special training if they are to accomplish anything significant. And in many cases, where organizations have dehumanized people, trust, patience and persistence are required to 'unlearn' default behaviours in order to make way for advanced learning.

While this may be a truism, it does not in any way detract from its importance: animals and humans all need structure if they are to function and make sense of their world. What is far less obvious and clear is that they need 'appropriate structures'. 'Appropriate' in this case means structures that embody both firmness and gentleness. The purpose of structure is to give needed direction, not to brutalize or cause pain. By laying down clear and deliberate structures – rules, procedures, separate departments in a complex organization – a foundation is being laid for trust and for innovation. Thus when one is ready to depart from the initial structures, one has a clear base to fall back on.

Intentionally or unintentionally, most organizations violate just about every known principle of change. Even with the best of intentions, introducing one programme after another accomplishes little. Indeed, it often makes organizations worse off than before they began. On the one hand there is the need for *control over* others and on the other hand there is the need for the *relinquishing of control.*

KNOW WHEN TO LEAD AND KNOW WHEN TO FOLLOW

The tension between safety and freedom plays out in myriad ways when one is perched on a horse racing along at breakneck speed. Safety (or control) can be an overriding concern, but it doesn't take long for a rider to realize that if they want to move beyond being a mere passenger, they must let go of the need for control and let the horse be a horse. Moving beyond the illusion of control requires that we 'let go of the horn' and join the horse in a partnership. The concept of knowing when to lead and knowing when to follow is precisely the condition of understanding the polarities of having control and relinquishing control.

Recently, a client in one of Terri's Saddle Sojourns workshops came to a clearer understanding of this tension. As a respected physician, her ability to control others was well established. She came to the workshop hoping to gain insights into how her leadership style contributed to the dissatisfaction of her support staff. She picked an equine partner, Driftless, and they began a series of challenges that required the client to establish a relationship with her horse and work with several other groups of horses and riders. When one challenge became difficult, the client found that she could not rely on her traditional method of leading and found herself paralysed. Her response was to disconnect from her equine partner, and seek a solution from another human. In this case, the counsel she sought was unsound, as her 'mentor' was giving advice based on a set of assumptions that didn't hold in the current environment. Unable to re-establish her relationship with her horse, the client 'bailed' and found her lesson punctuated by the arena sand.

Clearly, the client had lost the ability to function in the face of losing control. Rather than relinquishing control to her equine partner, she sought answers from another human. This is an all too familiar scenario in organizational life, where the espoused value of empowerment fails to hold up under pressures to retain control. On the one hand, we have the constant need for communion or connectedness with our fellow creatures and to the broader human community and, on the other hand, we need to maintain and recognize the uniqueness, distinctiveness and independence of each individual, including their agency or separateness.

THE HERD AND THE PACK – CODING FOR CONNECTEDNESS (COMMUNION) AND INDEPENDENCE (AGENCY)

Horses are among nature's sternest disciplinarians. They do not tolerate for one instant the 'antisocial' behaviour of the other members of a herd. Indeed, the head – typically a mare – ruthlessly enforces the 'rules' of the herd's behaviour. Those who do not conform to these rules are often expelled, and rather violently. This does not mean that the violence necessarily escalates in an uncontrolled fashion. Instead, the offending member is encouraged through a deliberate and prolonged series of actions to 'blend in' if he or she is to remain with the herd. Only after gentler means have been tried repeatedly and unsuccessfully does the head turn to more aggressive means of enforcing behaviour. As horse trainer Carolyn Resnick puts it:

> A herd counts on every member to spot mountain lions or wolves. A horse sometimes will run off another member seemingly without provocation. Usually, Resnick says, it means one horse is disciplining another for not returning a glance, not paying attention.
>
> (Marsh, 2001: E4).

The point of the above is certainly not that humans are justified in using violence to expel antisocial beings from organizations. Quite the contrary: it merely emphasizes that we do a disservice to ourselves and to our fellow humans by thinking that gentleness is the polar opposite of firmness.

The lesson that emerges repeatedly from the study of humans, animals and babies is that they need appropriate structures that will not only enable them, but are also necessary if they are to grow and develop. As the monks of New Skate (1991: 153–55) put it:

> Packs do not hold together automatically. Since wolves are carnivores and must hunt to survive, a great deal of cooperation must exist for the

pack to achieve its food requirements. Most of the wolves' natural prey (moose, elk, caribou, and reindeer) are too large to be brought down by a single wolf and require a strategic, coordinated plan of attack by a number of them. Refined communication, as well as a tight social structure wherein each member knows its proper role is essential.

This explains why leadership is so important for wolves. Every pack has a pair of leaders, one male and one female. These alphas are dominant over the other members of their particular sex. [The male's] firm dominance preserves order by eliciting submission and respect from subordinate pack members using appropriate deferential body language.

Beneath the alpha wolves, there is a loose dominance hierarchy into which each pack member fits with a particular spot and role. [It] appears that wolf packs are stronger, more secure and smooth-running, to the extent that the alpha is secure and confident in its leadership, for such dominance inspires fewer challenges. It is when there is no clear authority within the pack, as in times of leadership change, that the pack is unstable and may break up. Wolf packs function best when there is clear leadership, and this is just as true in your relationship with your puppy.

The herd and the pack form a natural structure for the whisperer to work within – one that offers both support and challenge. In our efforts to 'manage' others, we often espouse the virtues of empowerment, while our actions reinforce the underlying philosophy of 'follow me', or 'don't worry, I'll take care of you'.

Horses have a strong sense of herd (community) and, under healthy circumstances, they are also quite willing to act independently. After Terri had competed for a season with her horse, Rudy, in a number of endurance rides – events ranging from 40 to 105 km – she began to believe she had established a special relationship with her equine partner. Rudy clearly enjoyed the partnership. After spending six to ten hours at a time riding in beautiful settings, they began to establish a relationship that was based on the needs of both horse and rider. There was an ongoing give-and-take between Rudy's need for speed and Terri's need for safety. Establishing it presented a real challenge at the beginning of each race, when Rudy would pick up on the energy of the 75 or so other horses – all primed to move out as quickly as possible. In fact, Rudy's nickname became the 'dancing Arabian' as he spun and pranced at the beginning of each ride. On a recent ride, Terri intended to start late and slowly pick up speed, passing competitors along the way until she and Rudy were well ahead of most of the pack. One problem: in her rush to implement her strategy for 'managing' Rudy, she missed several cues that he was sending, as well as changes in the environment. After about three kilometres, she found herself up an embankment, lost her balance and fell to the ground. As she lay stunned on the ground, several horses passed. This represented a natural opportunity for Rudy to join a herd of fast-running horses. Instead, he looked down at his human partner, and patiently waited for her to get up, clear her head, remount and ride on.

By resisting his natural herd instinct, Rudy had allowed his rider to recover and rejoin the race. In a sense he had demonstrated a far greater degree of emotional intelligence than his single-minded rider.

THE UNNATURAL SPLIT BETWEEN WORK AND SPIRITUAL SATISFACTION

There is nothing as disheartening as seeing a horse that has lost its fundamental sense of what it means to be a horse. A colleague and whisperer acquired Gus from a well-regarded training stable. Gus had been kept in an enclosed stall and handled with utmost care to ensure his value as a show horse. As he aged, his coat took on an unusual colour, which disqualified him for the show ring. Without a real 'job', Gus became something of a liability; benign neglect ensued, and his education stopped. Separated from his 'herd' and his natural instincts, he developed a series of neurotic behaviours. Out of compassion he was sent to live with the whisperer in the hope that he might find peace. Before even beginning to work with Gus, the whisperer turned him out with a herd of her own horses, and Gus reconnected with his essential horse nature. Eventually, if it suits him, Gus will join the whisperer's other equine companions as an endurance horse.

The endurance world is in fact full of stories of horses that have failed at their initial 'employment', only to find a sense of purpose in the world of distance riding. For example, Driftless was once considered slab-sided and stubborn when viewed from the vantage-point of the arena. However, after months of hard trail-riding, he emerged as an endurance horse that went on to win a coveted best-conditioned award at a nationally recognized race. Interestingly, after finding his 'calling', he found his focus in the arena and has become the kind of equine partner that beginner riders find irresistible. Perhaps this outcome arises from the nature of endurance riding, in which horse and rider spend hours working together. This builds a real relationship based on communication and mutual respect, and in this way delivers an experience far more satisfying for both parties.

We ask humans to leave their spirituality at home when they enter the world of work. Gus's and Driftless's stories are all too familiar to many people working in contemporary organizations. When people are asked to separate their essential humanness from their work identity, the possibility of spiritual fulfilment in the midst of the pursuit of material gain seems preposterous.

Any programme for human and organizational development which ignores any of the five pairs of needs is doomed to fail. Any programme which ignores either member of the pairs is also doomed to fail. These considerations alone account for why up to 90 per cent of efforts to change both individuals and organizations fail dramatically.

The Relevance of Whisperers

Horse and dog whisperers have not only discovered each of these five pairs of needs, but in addition they have also discovered unique ways of satisfying each pair, and each member of each pair, at the same time. First and foremost, in training animals and humans, it is of the utmost importance to acknowledge, respect and educate the *whole* animal, infant or person, and not just one of their aspects.

Most educational and training programmes fail because they divide humans and animals into separate parts, or bounded containers – for instance, their 'brains' to the exclusion of their 'emotions'. Such an approach supposes that the separate parts don't interact or influence each other. As a result, it neither recognizes nor attempts to train the whole person or animal.

This critical lesson about respecting and educating the whole animal or person emerges not only from what we have recently learned about animals, but also from the latest research on human neurobiology and neurophysiology (see Damasio, 1994). The more we study neurobiology and neurophysiology, the more we learn that the division between the so-called 'rational decision-making' aspects of humans and their 'emotions' is, at best, artificial and thin. The 'rational' and the 'emotional' aspects of the human mind are so intertwined and highly interdependent that there can be no such thing as cognition without emotion, and vice versa. In short, if humans had no emotions, then they would not be able to make decisions, period! The point is that animals *and* people respond to the whole person. For instance, when animals directly encounter humans, they don't separate each human's cognitive functions from their emotions. Rather, the animal responds to the person's 'aura' as a whole.

Animals and humans use deliberate and highly structured 'languages'. In the case of animals, these 'languages' are not to be taken in the traditional sense of the term: they are neither written nor composed of formal, abstract symbols. Nonetheless, there are very distinct languages that animals and humans 'speak'. Indeed, these languages consist of highly complex and patterned nuances in facial and bodily expressions, as well as overt physical movements. To train and educate animals, infants and adults, one must spend hours observing their 'natural languages' and 'decoding' them. Fortunately, whisperers have already done much of this decoding for us.

If one wants to share the responsibility of control with an animal, or with one's fellow human beings, then it is absolutely imperative to understand both their spoken and unspoken languages. The various languages that human beings speak go far beyond the traditional ones called English, French, German and so on. These other languages are rooted deeply in the whole organism. If we are to speak these languages, we must learn how to listen to and speak to the whole being.

As well, animals and humans exhibit a clear, step-wise progression through different levels of development. In the case of humans, this progression is from the physical level, through the mental and moral, to the spiritual level. The evidence is also strong that none of these different levels or stages can be skipped or rushed. In dog training, for instance, there is a rule of thumb known as 'the 80 per cent rule'. When a dog has learned to sit approximately 80 per cent of the time when he or she has been given the appropriate command, then the animal is ready to move on to other commands. Furthermore, when the animal has mastered a basic set of commands, such as 'sit', 'stay' and 'come', then the trainer can move on to higher levels.

The first thing one aims for is extension or duration. That is, one trains the animal to sit for longer and longer periods of time before it is released. Once this is accomplished, the animal is trained to obey commands at greater and greater distances. The same holds for humans, although at much more sophisticated and 'higher' levels of development. In fact, the highest levels of human development involve universal ethics, justice and spirituality.

FADS: WHY MOST ATTEMPTS AT CHANGE FAIL

Although it is not commonly recognized, focusing on just one of the five pairs of needs, or on only one member of a pair, is precisely what defines a fad. This narrow focus also helps explain why fads are so popular. Fads represent the flawed attempt of humankind to avoid dealing with the complexity of humans and organizations. In other words, they point to our failure to recognize and come to terms with the human condition in all its fullness and complexity.

Through our work with managers and executives, we have been able to see that the same principles that whisperers have discovered apply equally to humans and organizations. Hopefully, this understanding not only leads to our breaking the seemingly fatal grip that fads have held, but also explains why whispering itself cannot be allowed to become another fad.

Concluding Remarks

Whispering not only demands incredible patience; it is the quintessential method of patience. Unfortunately, this fundamental aspect of whispering is at odds with the latest research on fads (Carson et al., 2000), which shows unequivocally that the time between fads is shrinking precipitously. Moreover, the duration of fads is also shrinking – fads are coming and going much faster. Simultaneously, the time between major crises is also shrinking precipitously, while their length or duration is increasing (see Mitroff and Anagnos, 2000)!

All of this has had the unfortunate effect of making patience even more necessary and important. Yet, at the same time, the conditions that make patience possible are diminishing: the fact that fads come and go with greater speed is further increasing the pressure for 'instant change', making patience even less likely to manifest.

Thus one of the key requisites of change – patience – is evaporating, and at an ever-increasing rate because of the unrelenting pace of social change. Whispering not only goes against the grain, but against the very tide itself. However, although whispering faces formidable challenges, it is not impossible – and it offers the hope of changing our organizations and ourselves.

References

Beer, M. (2001), 'Why Management Research Findings are Unimplementable: An Action Science Perspective', *Reflections*, 2:3, 59.

Carson, P. et al. (2000), 'Clearing a Path through the Management Fashion Jungle: Some Preliminary Trailblazing', *Academy of Management Journal*, 43:6, 1143–58.

Collins, D. (2000), *Management Fads and Buzz Words: Critical–Practical Perspectives* (London: Routledge).

Damasio, A. (1994), *Descartes' Error: Emotion, Reason and the Human Brain* (New York: Avon Books).

Hogg, T. (2001), *Secrets of the Baby Whisperer: How to Calm, Connect, and Communicate with your Baby* (New York: Ballantine Books).

Lazarus, R.S. (1984), 'On the Primacy of Cognition', *American Psychologist*, 39, 117–23.

Longenecker, C. and Simonetti, J. (2001), *Getting Results: Five Absolutes for High Performance* (San Francisco: Jossey-Bass Publishers).

Marsh, A. (2001), 'Life Lessons on the Ranch', *Los Angeles Times*, 20 July, E4.

Mitroff, I. and Anagnos, A. (2000), *Managing Crises before they Happen* (New York: AMACOM).

Owens, P. (1999), *The Dog Whisperer: A Compassionate, Non-Violent Approach to Dog Training* (Holbrook, MA: Adams Media Corporation).

Roberts M. (1997), *The Man Who Listens to Horses: The Story of a Real Life Horse Whisperer* (New York: Random House).

The Monks of New Skate (1991), *The Art of Raising a Puppy* (Boston: Little, Brown & Company).

von Rust McCormick, A. and McCormick, M.D. (1997), *Horse Sense and the Human Heart: What Horses Can Teach Us About Trust, Bonding, Creativity, and Spirituality* (Deerfield Beach, FL: Health Communications).

Wilber, K. (2000), *Integral Psychology: Consciousness, Spirit, Psychology, Therapy* (Boston, MA: Shambhala).

Zajonc, R.B. (1984), 'On the Primacy of Affect', *American Psychologist*, 39, 117–23.

8

In Search of the Future: Notes for Spiritual Adventurers

Dexter Dunphy

This chapter confronts some of the central issues we face as humans on this planet: the nature of individual identity; how to build with integrity on a self created in the past while living in the present, and to do this in such a way as to reshape ourselves for an uncertain future; how to maintain hope for the future of humankind in the face of violence, force and greed; how to escape from the determinism of an inherited 'Newtonian world-view', and to contribute to an emerging world-view that supports a more sustainable future for ourselves and for other species; and how to act on this vision to help redesign corporations so that they sustain the social and natural worlds instead of exploiting and degrading them. I illustrate these issues with some of my poems – markers in the personal struggle of one spiritual adventurer – and with organizational examples that represent the attempts of other spiritual adventurers to grapple with these issues in the practical world of business.

Present, Future and Past

The future lies all around us. Its shape is already discernible in the swirling mystery of our dreams, emerging from the careless gestures of our play, staring at us from the blank canvas of our art, emerging in hasty decisions as we face overload at work. We are surrounded by fragments of the future. All we have to do is recognize them, pick them up like shards of coloured glass, assemble them and let the light shine through to reveal what we have made with our own hands.

The future is forming here in our minds, in our hearts – slipping through the door of our soul to shape the actions of our hands, moving our reluctant feet forward. The future is our shadow stretching before us in the morning or afternoon of our lives, drawing us on. The future is a living presence now.

Yet so is the past. And we cling to our past for security. It may or may not have been so much of a past – a happy or unhappy childhood, an episode of violence or depression, a time of strange happiness, a relationship that lit up our life or engaged us in a struggle for our identity. Whatever past we experienced, it offers us the security of the known. The past shaped us; from it we fashioned the fond illusion of a constant self, offering us a haven of security, a certainty in imagining that we know who we are.

The future, on the other hand, challenges this supreme achievement of our lives – selfhood – and threatens to throw all into chaos again. The present, the now, holds both our past and our future in precarious balance. This is a balance I have struggled to express in the following poem, written during a time of personal transformation when my very identity, my core sense of self, seemed under threat:

Future Find Me

Future find me.
Yet you may
raise echoes of forgotten days.
I reach for memories
but you make
of flowing forms
another shape:
the shape of hope
the hue of green
life springing out
to the unseen;
life stretching back
to the before
and bridging forward
to the more.
Past, I thought
that you were lost –

Future found
and grew you
vast.

Only as we respond to the future does the meaning of the past disclose itself to us. Paradoxically, only by relinquishing the security of the known – by letting go and choosing the unknown – can we be fully in the present and realize the potential of our past.

The challenge we face is to become spiritual adventurers creating, along the unexplored path, the new meaning and new identities through which we grow.

Living in the Now

There is a Zen story that illustrates the importance of the now in our lives.

A man is hunting for food in the woods when he becomes aware that a tiger is stalking him. He tries walking quickly, but the tiger also speeds up and is drawing closer. He breaks into a run, and so does the tiger. The distance between them narrows – he can hear its rapid breathing, smell its foetid breath. Just as the tiger is about to spring, the man finds himself at the edge of an abyss. To escape the tiger, he flings himself over, falls through space, and lands on a tree growing from the cliff face halfway down the precipice. He recovers, pulls himself together, looks up. The tiger is peering over the edge of the cliff above him, hungry and growling. He looks down to see the precipice dropping away below him – he can just make out the jagged rocks far below. There appears no way to climb down. He looks at the cliff face. Just near him, he sees a small strawberry plant growing from a crevice in the rock, and on it is growing one perfect ripe strawberry. He reaches over, picks the strawberry and relishes its juicy sweetness.

Now is the time to live, yet we cannot ignore the future. As Mark Twain said, 'I'm concerned about the future, for that's where I'm planning to spend the rest of my life.' In that spirit I will concentrate on what we can learn about the future now, what we can do about the future now. I want to start to pick up some of the fragments of the future that lie about us – to start to piece them together and to ask what is in store for us. And, more importantly, I want to ask how we can act now to fashion a future closer to our heart's desires – a future that will fulfil the deepest needs of our souls and resonate with the integrity of our past experience. I will be emphasizing that what we do now is all that matters. The now is the bridge that joins past to future. We build this bridge for ourselves, we build for society, we build for future generations. What we build *matters*; how we build matters even more.

Why Try?

But this raises the question whether we can realistically contribute to the design of the future. Does what I do or what you do matter? In the face of the principalities and powers of this world, of presidents and princes, terrorists, drug lords and arms merchants, multinational magnates and media barons, star war scenarios, germ warfare and genetic manipulation, what's the value, if any, of *my* puny actions?

It's easy to despair. Why not give up and sit in front of the television, beer can in hand, yelling insults at the referee? Or spin out on speed while bathing in metronome pulses of strobe light? In the face of violence, oppression and ignorance, why continue to engage with the world at all? I wrote the following poem after watching the film *Captain Corelli's Mandolin* on a flight from London to Australia. The film graphically portrayed the destructive power of violence in human life, and the poem expresses my own struggle to accept the reality of human evil while not acquiescing in it:

    Cycle

    earth
    accepts the blood of the slaughtered
    transforms to green of grass, leaves, vines
    flowers of crimson
    poppies
    roses
    desert pea
    armies of dead
    taken in battle
    fallen in unyielding rows
    in the confused tangle of fearful flight
    in sleep
    barely roused

before the downward thrust of swords
stops their beating hearts
earth
takes the severed limbs
battered skulls
ashes of martyrs
splayed bodies of innocents
shattered and strewn on killing fields
earth
receives them all
tenderly
persistently
transforms their deaths to life again
still tyrants come
drunk on power
violence
surrounded by hordes of armed angry men
with uniforms
flags
speeches
crowds
trumpets
strutting power
causes blessed by priests
rhetoric of righteousness
still they come
those men who would be gods
xerxes, cromwell, attila, mao, pisarro, hitler, ramses,
napoleon, bismark, sargon, tojo, alexander, tamerlane
caesar, darius, cortes, genghis khan
stalin, ulysses, danton, constantine, pol pot …
no end to warrior tyrants
stalking out of history
lusting for
worship
women
gold
power
taken with
torture

rape
slaughter
blood
earth
patient
covers all with green
flags the place of pain with crimson
no end to life
but what of us
who neither conquer nor are conquered
who turn aside
the sword in our hearts
and reach out to gather
the crimson flowers of defiance
what can we do
but throw the stubborn ounces of our weight
against the indifference and violence of this world
and cry for
the lost
the lonely
the betrayed

We can't ignore the endless violence of history, our collective failure to learn from experience, the extreme vulnerability of love and compassion. Despair, cynicism and conservatism are our natural responses when we are faced with these realities.

Our main problem in becoming co-creators of the future is that we live in the present with a mind map drawn in the past. Our mental models are worn hand-me-downs from bygone generations. These models and maps also carry with them inbuilt action programmes that have passed their use-by dates. The past structures the very categories of our perceptions, so we are mired in the residues of philosophical models that were once fresh and vibrant but are now irrelevant for understanding the new age bearing down on us. So often we move forward in time like zombies, programmed by the past, our sensitivity deadened by the media, substituting slogans for thought, habit for experience, sullen conformity for innovation.

The Origins of our Current World-view

We stand today at an intellectual watershed. The foundations of the Newtonian world-view that has dominated Western thought and action for four centuries have been shattered by new scientific discoveries and discourse. The Newtonian world-view itself replaced the medieval world-view that preceded it. In 50 years our grandchildren will find it impossible to understand the world-view we now take for granted, just as *we* find it impossible to understand the world that monks, knights and peasants took for granted in the Middle Ages. Think, for example, of the medieval debates about how many angels could dance on the point of a pin: 'What kind of nonsensical debate is that?' we ask. And yet for highly intelligent medieval scholastics this was the critical philosophical question. In their world-view there was a natural order and a distinct supernatural order; the question of how they intersected – spiritual angel with material pin – was the central issue to be resolved.

So I'll take a detour to examine the foundations of the world-view *we* take for granted, one which still dominates our actions and obscures our view of the evolving future that will be dramatically transformed from the present.[1] In 1641 René Descartes' *Meditations* announced a fundamental departure from the medieval world-view – already severely challenged by Copernicus. Descartes laid the basis for the new world-view that would dominate Western thinking for the next 400 years and which lives on in popular thought today. He took us outside nature into an objectivist stance and, as people began to look through his eyes, the world of angels and saints began to fade. Science became possible.

The next formative influence came from Newton, who created an intellectual model of a clockwork universe subject to universal mathematical laws. As machines proliferated and people became familiar with them, the machine became a metaphor for understanding the world. Science bought this model and thrived through its application. There was, of course, the problem of what to do with God in this model. He was conveniently assigned to the role of the clockmaker who designed the clock, wound it up and then stepped back to let it run.

Darwin was the third great thinker who contributed to our current world-view. He added the superstructure for understanding the living world – a superstructure tacked on to the Newtonian model of the physical world.

---

1 Amongst other sources, my thinking here has been influenced by Goerner (1999) and Wilbur (1998).

Darwin's principles of random mutation, natural selection and the survival of the fittest were taken up not only by biologists, but also by social thinkers. There is a direct line from Darwin to today's economic rationalists.

What is a world-view? It's a constructed model of reality that is eventually taken as reality itself: it becomes *the truth*, a set of working assumptions that are unquestioned because they are taken for granted. We know we have a world-view when we act as if this is simply the way the world is. Like fish swimming in water, we are unaware of how it dominates our lives. So what were the central features of the clockwork universe and why is it under threat today?

The Clockwork Universe

First, it enthroned analytical thinking. If the universe is a kind of clock, then it makes sense to set about understanding it by taking it apart, dividing it into its constituent elements and then reassembling it. So physicists, for example, adopted a reductionist approach; they tried to understand matter by identifying atoms, which they thought were the basic building-blocks of the physical world, and then studied their characteristics. Surely if we understood the bits, we could understand the whole. In vain Wordsworth wrote, 'We murder to dissect': in other words, if you tear the living world apart, you destroy the very essence of what makes it distinctive – its life.

Scientists went on trying to explain higher-level systems in terms of their constituent elements, instead of explaining the constituent elements in terms of the properties of the whole system. Modern Western medicine exemplifies this approach: 'You have high blood pressure? Here are some pills for that.' 'You have high cholesterol levels? Don't worry – we have pills for that too.' We are treated as collections of isolated symptoms, not as dynamic, complex and evolving whole systems.

The results are catastrophic. I spent some time working with the matrons in charge of NSW hospitals who were seeking to improve patient care. In the course of the exercise I found that there were patients on as many as eight or even 13 separate drugs, even though scientists can't assess the interactions between them. The fourth major reason for admission of patients to hospitals is the side-effects of doctor-prescribed drugs, and many patients in hospital die because of the drugs administered to them there. The medical system itself has become a virulent disease. Modern medicine could learn from Voltaire's view of how medicine works; he wrote, 'The art of medicine is to keep the patient amused while nature effects the cure.'

In the clockwork universe God eventually disappeared from the paradigm, or became an optional extra. As early as 1882 Nietzsche declared, 'God is dead. And we have killed him.' The statement was a death knell not only for God, but also for the dominance of the previous medieval world-view in which God was the director of the drama of good and evil.

We humans replaced God with ourselves; *we* were now the masters of the universe, operating as God had done, on nature from the outside. Science undergirded everything we did and drove out superstition, magic, mystery and love – sorry, 'object relations'. Science existed to help us control, dominate, exploit and redesign the world for our own ends. We were no longer part of the web of life; we stood outside and above it. Genetic engineering is just the latest example of atomistic thinking and the advocacy of human mastery over the environment.

Over time, the addition of Darwinism to the heady cocktail of ideas was used to justify imperialist expansion and elite control. Within human society, the powerful were seen as fitter than the weak, the rich fitter than the poor. Material success became the measure of a person's worth and of a nation's right to dominate the world. Why not, in a universe without purpose?

As a result of these new views, society was reorganized. Commercial activity became central to society. In the skylines of cities, the soaring glass towers of financial institutions dwarfed the cathedrals. On 11 September 2001 the terrorists chose their prime target, the World Trade Center twin towers, demonstrating exquisite sensitivity for the fulcrum of our beliefs.

But they need not have been so impatient: that world-view which seems so triumphant now is doomed anyway. Through much of this new century, intellectual heresies have been breaking out everywhere, and an intellectual revolution is in full swing. The basis for the current world-view is disintegrating, but the trouble is, most people don't realize it – for them it is just reality. But it is a reality as fragile as the towers of the World Trade Center. Those who *do* understand the fragility of the prevailing world-view are lost because they don't know what to replace it with. World-views are tightly woven webs of mutually reinforcing beliefs; they grow over time rather than being invented in one piece. You can't pick up a new one at Kmart.

Some people, of course, would like to return to a world-view dominated by God – fundamentalists, for example, alarmed at the impending future, imaginatively construct a fictional form of past spirituality which offers certainty and security. Others indulge in wistful nostalgia when they feel times are tough, as epitomized by Woody Allen's remark: 'I wish God would give me a sign. Like making a large deposit in my name in a Swiss bank.'

A revolution has been taking place in the field of physics, for example, since early last century. Those fundamental particles, the atoms, didn't turn out to be so fundamental after all, as scientists began to investigate protons, neutrons and electrons. That Newtonian model which seemed set to explain everything, collapsed. The emergent field of quantum mechanics sucked it in and imploded it. This new discipline is now rewriting the story of the universe (Wilbur, 2001). And similar revolutions have been taking place in biology, ecology, mathematics, economics, the study of the brain and the social sciences. At first glance these mini-revolutions may seem independent and unrelated, but they are marked by some emerging common themes that point us forward to the future. It is as though the shared reality of living in this moment in history is revealing the emerging mindset for the new century.

The New World-view

So can we piece together some fragments that point to key elements of the emerging world-view? Can we discern some common themes when we look across the intellectual revolutions in fields of knowledge that will shape the future?

In its simplest form, the new world-view is about seeing everything as an ecology. For example, your body is an ecology, an energy-driven web of living cells, working together to survive, thrive and reproduce. The world is a fractal series of such ecologies, nested spheres of life rising to self-awareness and collective purpose. In this new world, understanding context is critical to generating meaning and purpose. The whole gives purpose to the parts.

It's a web world too. In the new paradigm, connectedness is central; interdependence is the fundamental reality. The world is complex, interwoven and mutually determining, but also open-ended. New tools are allowing us to study and model this: computers handle immense numbers of variables; computer modelling allows us to trace emerging trajectories; new mathematics allows us to go beyond simple causality to study the effect of multiple variables on each other; and we can even follow thought processes flickering across the brain. And all is in flux. The emphasis is on evolving complexity, the intricacy of systems that are dynamic, but sometimes delicately balanced.

There is order emerging from chaos, and chaos is breaking up order. Order and randomness are characteristic of the world, but (and here's the catch) often we can't predict or control the emerging order. The problem for us is how to live in a world that has elements of both chaos and order. Dee Hock (1999) has written a book called the *Birth of the Chaordic Age* that poses the question of how managers can simultaneously manage the chaos and order that characterize organizations today. These new insights are emerging alongside a radical rethinking about the origin of the universe and all forms of organization within it. We can't control the pattern of the future – we are only a small part of the process – but we can contribute to the emergence of order by being active and spontaneous, and joining the dance of life, rather than trying to control everything. Ironically, joy gives us the greatest influence over our future. Joy is the natural expression of the freedom we feel as we join the unfolding pattern of life rather than fighting it. The attempt to stand apart from life and control it springs from fear – and fear leads to rigidity and, ultimately, to defeat.

Another feature of the emerging world view is purpose. As Charles Birch (1990) suggests, life is purposive, and life-forms band together in systems of increasing complexity. These systems are purposive in the sense that they show increasing effectiveness in coding and processing information from the environment, generating and deploying energy, and developing higher forms of consciousness. Life becomes ever more intricate and flexible in its environmental adaptation. Collaboration, not competition, lies behind evolutionary leaps. Species co-evolve – humans and cows, for example – and most similar species don't become locked into a battle for survival. They avoid competition by eating different foods and occupying different environmental niches. To take another example, wasps lay their eggs in figs that nurture their progeny, but the different species of wasp each relate to a different type of fig and, of course, the figs need the wasps for their survival too. It's a pretty good deal all around.

In this emerging paradigm, love, caring, compassion and spirituality – once dismissed as superstition and delusion – find a central place. Life-forms are collections of self-ordering, committed communities of cells. In higher species, emotional bonding – love – is fundamental to continued life, to physical and mental health, and to the creation and maintenance of complex, self-sustaining communities and organizations. Love creates the 'we' from the 'I'.

In the new world-view there is a greater place for subjective human experience – for smells, tastes, sounds, feelings, fantasy – and being intuitively attentive and sensitive to one's place in the biosphere. We can admit once more to enjoying the poetry of life, even writing it! And we can abandon scientific reductionism and legitimately start to interpret less complex life-forms in terms of what we know about more complex ones. If *we* have awareness, then slugs, spiders and birds have it too. The shaman and the horse whisperer come into their own again. Like Dr Doolittle, we can talk to the animals if we enter empathetically into their world. Humans are members of this world, not masters of it.

We are one species among many, subject as the other species are to the physical and ecological forces of the planet. Despite all the advances in science, we still live in a mysterious and wonderful universe we barely begin to comprehend. In the face of this mystery, humility and awe and respect for the beautiful blue and green globe we inhabit are more appropriate attitudes than pride, dominance, exploitation and manipulation. If we are to survive, we must act with integrity – that is, with respect for the whole. (The root of the word integrity means 'whole'.) That means we must act responsibly so as to sustain and nourish the whole. Leadership is working at the active edge of the emerging paradigm, working to help usher in the new age – becoming 'pilgrims in search of the unknown' (Coelho, 1999).

Now to another poem that arose out of my puzzlement when reading an advertisement in a newspaper a few years ago. On glancing through the advertisement section, my eyes picked up a job ad which read: 'Wanted: Wrought Iron Men'. What they wanted, of course, were men to work wrought iron. But the phrase stuck hauntingly in my mind:

'Wrought iron men … wrought iron men….' The words resonated with my experience of growing up in a world where men's lives were dominated by the premium placed on emotional repression – where the only thing a man could legitimately feel like was a Tooheys, in the words of the Australian brewery's well-known advertising slogan. In struggling to find more emotional freedom for myself, I discovered that repression manifests itself in what Wilhelm Reich called 'body armour' – rigid musculature that imprisons the human spirit.

The rigid structures of the Newtonian world – the bureaucracies, the hierarchies, the emphasis on control, the fear (particularly in men) of emotion – had in fact created generations of wrought iron men, and more recently, as women move into higher organizational positions, some wrought iron women as well. Nature, however, is different. It invites us to grow, to expand, to change shape, to evolve, to live, to die. It treats our attempts to control it and ourselves with quiet contempt. So to my poem …

Wrought Iron Men

Those who fear the force of flowers
also flee summering and sunshine –
the golden glow of light burning ocean
into voluptuous vortexes of riotous cloud.
They seek dark and fear flowers
for the lively burst of stems to blooms
breaks walls, fissures paths and patios,
upends boulders and in the end
wreaths the wrecks and ruins of civilizations.
Us too it wrecks within.
This growing life bends habits of years,
breaks old bonds
and melts with unexpected tears
walls built to protect us,
safe paths laid through the wild world.
Wrought iron men, fear rather
for the fragility of machines
and for concrete, metal and glass artifices
poised precariously against life.
And fear for yourselves
whose bodies copy their iron shapes
walled stiffly into hard lines;
whose minds are boxes
taut with wire, bar and chain.
Is that why you stand tense in the shadows,
hating the plushy push of petals,
the delicate levers of groping grass,
the grasping tenderness of spiralled tendrils
leaning lovingly, learningly
to warmth and light?

Do you sense where the ultimate power lies?
And you others,
who stroke petals gently,
afraid to believe:
listen …
listen through the stillness
to crickets celebrating
the irresistible thrust of life.

So if we are willing to step out of our inherited world-view (which is now in a state of collapse) to abandon its fake security, to go unarmed, undefended and vulnerable into the dark, allowing ourselves to respond to life, we will find that the darkness is light enough. Just as, when camping in the bush, we step out of the circle of firelight: at first we experience blindness, but as we wait our eyes adjust to the faint starlight, and we can walk or run with confidence, even where there is no path. The dark is light enough.

Lessons for Corporate Life in the Future

So how will these themes I have identified coalesce into a unified world-view for this century? And how will these themes affect corporate life? Each century has a central focus – a core defining issue around which much of the debate, human effort and conflict revolve. The central focus of the last century was economic growth; all social ideologies favoured it. Capitalism, communism, socialism and fascism all supported economic growth from industrialization. Two quite different but famous women have expressed this clearly. Karl Marx's wife, Jenny, commented after his death, 'I wish that dear Karl had spent some time acquiring capital rather than writing about it.' More recently, Sophie Tucker remarked, 'I've been poor and I've been rich. Rich is better.' The aspiration of the majority in the last century (and still of many now) was simple: to gain a larger share of the wealth created by the Industrial Revolution for themselves, or at least for their children. What capitalism, fascism, socialism and communism disagreed about was how to distribute that wealth. By the end of the twentieth century the issue was resolved in favour of the capitalist solution.

The central focus of this century will be *sustainability* – that is, how to redesign society and our organizations within it to sustain, rather than damage, the biosphere and to create a just and equitable social order. This is not only the idea of a couple of prophets in the wilderness. At the end of the last century the authors of a worldwide survey commissioned by the Millennium Project concluded, 'Never before has world opinion been so united on a single goal as it is on achieving sustainable development' (Glenn and Gordon, 1998).

I don't have space here to review the evidence for the current crisis of the modern capitalist economy and its industrial base. However, it's enough to say that we can't continue to plunder and pollute the planet without jeopardizing the future of generations to come. We live in an interdependent world. There is no secure fortress for the wealthy to hide from the envy and anger of the starving millions of the world. To survive and thrive on this planet we must create both a viable social fabric for a global society, and technologies of wealth creation that give us quality of life while enhancing the fragile ecology on which life depends. And that brings us to the role of corporations in society. Corporations have played a large part in creating the current problems and so they must be part of the solution. The concept around which the new solution is emerging is precisely sustainability – the major philosophical challenge to the old clockwork model of the universe and to the economic rationalism that has emerged from it.

What is Sustainability?

Sustainability is a contestable concept – it's more a symbol, a rallying point, for a challenge to the dominance of neo-liberal economics than a clearly worked out philosophy. The debates and conflicts of this century will give shape to this emerging philosophy and define what it means for social organization. There is no agreed definition yet, but here's a start: sustainability results from actions we take, individually and collectively, that:

- enhance the planet's ability to maintain and renew the viability of the biosphere and protect all living species;

- maintain a decent level of welfare for present and future human generations; and

- extend the socially useful life of organizations so they can contribute the resources needed to achieve these goals.

Organizations are the enablers, the tools we need to ensure that we have a healthy society on a healthy planet. Genuinely sustainable organizations engage in activities that contribute to that ideal. We can no longer act as if the economy is a separable entity from society and the ecology. Organizations are the fundamental cells of the society and the ecology, as well as of the economy. The growing realization that this is so is changing the way business does business.

Why this redefinition of organizations as such, including corporations? There are increasing pressures on businesses to take responsibility for their impact on the world. In addition, new technologies are already dematerializing production processes and reducing energy consumption. Whatever the causes, business leaders themselves are providing much of the momentum for change.

Economic rationalism (economic neo-liberalism) has been the prevailing economic philosophy in the West for the last 30 years. Now it is increasingly under challenge for its emphasis on short-term returns and lack of concern for long-term consequences; for its philosophy of 'greed is good' which emphasizes material wealth rather than fulfilment and spirituality; for its pursuit of shareholder wealth and neglect of the firm's other stakeholders; for its willingness to 'externalize' to the general community the social and ecological costs of business decisions; and for its bypassing the collective good for private gain.

But is it possible to create sustainable enterprises? Isn't this just some esoteric flight of fancy – a luxury that business can't really afford? To begin to answer these questions, I will briefly describe some of the achievements of a relatively small, but important, operation that is part of the worldwide Fuji-Xerox Corporation. The particular plant I will describe is the Fuji-Xerox Eco Manufacturing Centre, located in Zetland, not far from the University of Technology, Sydney, where I work. As I have said, the future is just down the road if we care to look.

The parent company, Fuji-Xerox Corporation, is one of a growing number of multinational companies that have instituted a philosophy of sustainability. As part of its commitment to a sustainable future, the senior executives in the parent company decided to move from selling to leasing office equipment, and to recycling component parts of their products. In 1998 some Australian managers saw this development as an opportunity, and designed and established a new plant, the Eco Manufacturing Centre. The Centre takes used products, reprocesses their components and rebuilds used office machines.

This is not as simple as it sounds, since different manufacturing processes are needed to rebuild used equipment that has been subjected to factors such as heat and vibration.

The plant pioneered these remanufacturing processes and also developed new technology for diagnosing faults in returned parts. As a result, component design is continually improved so that 'second-hand' reconditioned machines perform better than the originals.

In the past, faulty equipment was simply trashed and went into landfill. But it was not only potentially valuable equipment that was being trashed; throwing away whole machines or components meant also throwing away valuable information about the reasons for equipment failure – that is, data that could help the manufacturer redesign the equipment for better long-term performance. This data now provides a major input into research and development on product redesign – it helps the manufacturer redesign the equipment for enhanced quality and durability. And newly designed products are sent from other Fuji-Xerox plants around the world to be tested on the equipment developed in this plant – a major R&D pay-off. The parent company regards the plant as embodying best practice in eco-manufacturing worldwide, and teams from Japan and the United States have visited the plant to learn from it and to help diffuse its innovative practices.

The community also benefits. As all parts are reused or recycled, there is no waste sent to landfill. And what is 'waste' from the company's perspective becomes a resource for other companies. For example, the plant developed a CO_2 dry-cleaning process to draw off carbon deposits on used equipment. The waste carbon is taken by the steelmaker BHP and used in the process of steel manufacture. Communities will increasingly deny business the right to dump waste as landfill. In Japan, for example, it is now illegal to dump white goods and computer equipment into landfill. Those companies that develop sustainable technologies before legislation is introduced will have a significant strategic advantage worldwide as this trend spreads.

Developing this plant has also brought a transformation in the workforce culture. The workforce had a history of adversarial trade unionism, but it now has an entirely different culture of voluntarism and commitment. The sustainable plants of the future require a new culture to operate effectively, new levels of professional skill and new approaches to participatory problem-solving. To achieve ecological sustainability, the social system of the plant must be sustainable too.

So what has all this cost Fuji-Xerox? Far from *costing* a fortune, the plant is *making* a fortune. The savings in 2000, the first year of operation, were AU$25 million, and AU$30 million in 2001. (And that's not counting what is saved by extending the lifespan of office machines – estimated to be worth at least as much again.) The operation has achieved 20 per cent year-on-year growth since then. It now exports 'as new' remanufactured parts to nine countries in Asia, thus making some contribution to reversing Australia's balance of trade deficit (Benn and Dunphy, 2004).

How can these savings be explained? In the past, for example, a circuit board that was inoperative was simply thrown away, although it might be worth $10,000 and only two of the board's components might have been malfunctioning. The new equipment designed at the plant can now identify the specific malfunctioning components, which may be worth a mere AU$250. Replacing the components rather than the entire board achieves a saving of AU$9,750 – on one board. Multiply this a thousand times and you can see where the profit comes from. Then add the fact that Fuji-Xerox Australia doesn't have to buy a new replacement machine from the United States at the current exchange rate, and you can see how the company managers in Australia are laughing all the way to the bank.

There are many managers who believe that, in highly competitive markets, it is too costly to pay attention to issues of sustainability. But, in reality, the traditional industrial process and the traditional office are extremely wasteful of resources. Reclaiming and recycling these resources create wealth, lay the foundation for a learning organization, provide satisfying work with meaning, and contribute to a healthy community and natural environment. Note that the case study exhibits many of the characteristics of the new world-view I outlined earlier. The managers at the plant were conscious of interconnectedness; they took a systems view and used modern technology to study the interconnectedness within their business and between their business, other businesses and stakeholders. They worked collaboratively with others in the organization and with key stakeholders; they were purposive but not controlling; they tried different approaches and learned as they went, imposing no preconceived ideas. The plant is, therefore, the future made manifest in the now.

The Fuji-Xerox case is only one of thousands around the world today (Dunphy, Griffiths and Benn, 2007; Hargroves and Smith, 2005; Staib, 2005;

Starik and Sharma, 2005). Operations like this are glimpses of an emerging world in which we will think in system terms and live in harmony with each other and with nature.

We have achieved the wealth we enjoy today by using global resources at a rate unsustainable into the future, particularly with rising expectations and global population growth. Continuing economic success and a sustained quality of life depend on developing a different relationship with the natural world (Sheldrake, 1990). We have been living as if there is no tomorrow and, unless we change the way we use resources, there may be no tomorrow we would wish to contemplate. Tim Flannery (1994) refers to the human race as 'the future eaters', and our future-eating behaviour threatens the livelihood and quality of life of the generations to whom we bequeath the world. We have discovered the secret of creating wealth on a large scale but, like Midas, we are finding that we cannot live on gold alone.

Currently, our success in developing efficient technologies for gathering and processing the world's natural resources is threatening the planetary life-support system we have previously taken for granted. We are depleting the seas of fish, logging the forests out of existence, changing the world's climate, polluting and degrading the soil and water. Our profligate waste of non-renewable resources like oil and natural gas is creating a looming environmental crisis. Nature cannot forever absorb the massive and expanding impact of traditional production and consumption processes. Nor can communities withstand the vicious cycle of hunger, war and desperation. A planet under threat means the end of business as usual (Diamond, 2005; Meadows and Randers, 2004; Wright, 2004). So, managers in particular must rethink the current approach to wealth creation by moving from an exploitative to a regenerative mode, reducing resource use, recycling products and eliminating waste.

This shift requires a rather more sophisticated approach to managerial leadership than that which has prevailed in the past. That doughty old oil magnate Paul Getty was once asked for his formula for business success. 'Simple,' he said. 'Rise early, work late, and strike oil.' Well, corporate leaders today need a lot more than hard work and luck to succeed.

But financial success and environmentally-friendly practices can be combined. Von Weizacker and his colleagues (1997) have provided many examples of businesses that have more than quadrupled their productivity while halving their use of resources. Far from reducing productivity and profits, these companies found that introducing ecologically sustainable practices provided sustainable success. Their experience is being verified by the superior returns of the expanding ethical investment funds. There are solutions at the national and international level too – solutions that can support the evolution of a truly sustainable economy and society; but this means rethinking the prevailing economic paradigm which is based on spiralling material production (Lowe, 2005). However, the deepening global crisis of climate change (compounded by population growth, resource depletion, inequality and war) presents us with a narrow window of opportunity to undertake the paradigm shift in thought and behaviour. We are running out of time (Dunphy, 2006).

We must learn to live harmoniously and in peace with each other, as well as with nature, not play games of 'my god is better than your god, so I'll kill you', or 'my culture is superior to yours, so I'll reject you', or 'my lifestyle and language are so great that I'll expect you to live in poverty and serve my needs', or 'you're poorer than I am, so go away and die somewhere else'. Social justice is an essential element of any meaningful approach to sustainability. Individuals can combine to make transformational change in their collective endeavours – for example, to build new organizational cultures based on constructive behaviour and self-understanding. Recent research in organizational settings shows that this improves performance and leads to improved business outcomes (Jones et al., 2007). Caring for each other and the natural world does, however, require more self-knowledge and reflexivity, as well as higher levels of interpersonal sensitivity and skill.

Finally I return to my original theme: can we dare to be co-creators of a future reality based on care for each other and for the natural world of which we are an integral part? To do this we must face and let go of our fear of uncertainty and chaos. As the Buddha emphasized, chaos, violence, sickness and death are inescapable facets of the human condition. When we were born, we weren't issued with a certificate of exemption from life's great challenges. We can run from these things, but we can't escape them. Wisdom lies in acceptance and from acceptance flow joy, spontaneity and freedom. On the spiritual journey we are not alone. There are more spiritual adventurers around than we realize – most of them look like you and me and travel incognito. A critical mass is forming; the tide of the spirit is returning to flood our world with new meaning. All that is required is that we expand our awareness and travel in hope, despite our fear.

My last poem was written after walking at dawn along a beach on the South Coast of New South Wales. As I walked barefoot on to the cold sand, the dawn light penetrated the mist and I experienced an intense sense of being simultaneously separate from, yet at one with, the mystery of continuous creation:

Travelling Companions

Over the grey edge of sand
sea mist is moving
stirred by the rising sun.
Shellfish glued to rock
glisten in the retreating tide.
Gull flaps along the beach –
first wings to challenge
night's lingering silence.
Crab edging from its bolthole
offers a perfect sphere of sand
to the new day.
Bird, shellfish, crab and I
Share this moment of time –
fellow travellers sculpted
by sea, sand and sun.
Shell, carapace and bone
record our histories;
co-evolved,
bound by ancient choices
unknown to us.
Let us hold a convention here,
gull, crab, shellfish and I
to ponder the meaning
of our brightening world.
We pluck so little from it
when we go alone.
How shall we speak to each other?
How shall we share
what it means for us to be
on this earth together?
What can we learn

you and I?
Shall we consult
the sea's oracle too?
Now
light and tide combine
to unveil the mystery.
Carpe diem,
my small companions!
From this home
experienced in diverse ways,
a larger truth emerges
to shape the coming day.

References

Benn, S.H. and Dunphy, D. (2004), 'A Case of Strategic Sustainability: The Fuji Xerox Eco Manufacturing Centre', *Innovation: Management, Policy and Practice*, 6:2, 258–68; Fuji Xerox Australia Sustainability Report 2006, at: www.fujixerox.com.au.

Birch, C. (1990), *On Purpose* (Sydney: University of New South Wales Press).

Coelho, P. (1999), *Confessions of a Pilgrim: A Biography by Juan Arias* (Sydney: Harper Collins).

Diamond, J. (2005), *Collapse: How Societies Choose to Fail or Survive* (London: Allen Lane/Penguin).

Dunphy, D. (2006), 'Running Out of Time' in C. Barker and A. Payne (eds), *Speed @ Work* (Sydney: AIM/Wiley).

Dunphy, D., Grffiths, A. and Benn, S. (2007), *Organizational Change for Corporate Sustainability* (2nd edn), (London: Routledge).

Flannery, T. (1994), *The Future Eaters* (Sydney: Reed Books).

Glenn, J.R. and Gordon, T.J. (1998), *State of the Future: Issues and Opportunities* (Washington, DC: American Council for The United Nations University, The Millennium Project).

Goerner, S.J. (1999), *After the Clockwork Universe: The Emerging Science and Culture of Integral Society* (Edinburgh: Floris Books).

Hargroves, K.C. and Smith, M.H. (eds) (2005), *The Natural Advantage of Nations* (London: Earthscan).

Hock, D. (1999), *Birth of the Chaordic Age* (San Francisco: Berrett-Koehler).

Jones, K., Dunphy, D., Fishman, R. and Larne, M. (2007), *In Great Company: Unlocking the Secrets of Cultural Transformation* (Sydney: Human Synergistics).

Lowe, I. (2005), *A Big Fix: Radical Solutions for Australia's Environmental Crisis* (Melbourne: Black Inc.).

Meadows, D. and Randers, J. (2004), *Limits to Growth: The 30-Year Update* (White River Junction, VT: Chelsea Green Publishing).

Sheldrake, R. (1990), *The Rebirth of Nature: The Greening of Science and God* (London: Rider).

Staib, R. (ed.) (2005), *Environmental Management and Decision Making for Business* (New York: Palgrave Macmillan).

Starik, M. and Sharma, S. (eds) (2005), *New Horizons in Research on Sustainable Organizations* (Sheffield: Greenleaf).

von Weizacker, E., Lovins, A.B. and Lovins, L.H. (1997), *Factor 4: Doubling Wealth – Halving Resource Use* (Sydney: Allen & Unwin).

Wilbur, K. (1998), *The Marriage of Sense and Soul: Integrating Science and Religion* (Melbourne: Hill of Content Publishing).

Wilbur, K. (ed.) (2001), *Quantum Questions: The Mystical Writings of the World's Greatest Physicists* (Boston: Shambhala Publications).

Wright, R. (2004), *A Short History of Progress* (Melbourne: Text Publishing).

9

Humanistic Management Education: Richness, Challenges and Possibilities

Ana Maria Davila Gomez and David Crowther

In the West, just as much as in Eastern civilizations, a concern for respectful behaviour, and thus for the mutual and complementary development of all the participants involved in an activity, has been a moral tenet for more than two millennia. For the individual, this premise has had the practical implication that others' desires and accomplishments are as important as one's own. As an example of this valuing of mutual co-development, European humanistic thinkers have written about the need for a humanistic orientation in any social cooperation; in this context, the work of Rousseau (1712–78) and Montaigne (1533–92) is especially notable. The American philosopher John Dewey (1963) has explored this orientation in more recent times. Moreover, within this humanistic tradition, other philosophers such as Socrates (as related in Plato's works) and Kierkegaard (1941[1851]) reflected on the responsibility for taking any action in the light of the whole; actors need to consider the meaning of existence as the soul expresses it, since purposeful human action impacts on a total, interrelated development. These writers bear witness to the need to explore the meaning of actions, the results they seek and their actual consequences.

We know from experience that actions have repercussions which result in either distress or satisfaction for other beings that interact with the actors concerned. Hence actors must accept accountability for their actions and the consequences of their decisions. In this sense, repercussions may be treated as the 'meanings' of actions, both as results and as transcendent explanations of the spirit. From this holistic standpoint – and in a world that needs more justice and more responsible organizational behaviour (Crowther and Rayman-Bacchus, 2004; Aktouf, 2001) – managers as potential agents for proactive change are called upon to develop behaviours informed by consideration of others. The 'others' in question are not only human beings, but also other life-forms and the biosphere as a whole. In this perspective, we can conceive of the manager as an integrated being whose human development includes the spiritual enhancement of the whole person. We thus need to look for approaches that help to develop not only managers' intellectuality (so prized in the occidental tradition of technical and functional expertise), but also their morality and ethics. Some previous research (for example, Davila-Gomez, 2003; Chanlat, 1998) shows us that these kinds of needs relate more to the development of attitudes (such as comprehension, compassion and sensitivity) than to the reinforcement of technical and mechanical abilities. Hence more open human and social perspectives need to complement today's dominant, pragmatic organizational paradigm of functionalism.

One way of furthering this aim is through the role, contents and practice of management education, given that a part of the development time of future managers is spent inside the classroom where educators may influence future managers' awareness of the issues and needs we have discussed. In order to advance a human orientation within management education, we need to reflect on some pertinent pedagogical and educational approaches. Our literature review suggests that humanistic educational thinkers such as Rabelais (1494–1553) and Rousseau took up aspects of our concern for human integration in students by promoting justice and consideration towards others and nature. Similarly, Montessori (1870–1952) and Pestalozzi (1746–1827) treated in depth the inescapable connection between humans and nature, as well as the need for equality, compassion and mutual understanding. These two thinkers applied their precepts in elementary schools, and their methods are still practised today. Valett (1974, 1977) proposed a set of guidelines for integrating the emotional stages of a student's growth. While there is a strong corpus of philosophical works on humanist education, the problem we find is that their precepts (and, in some cases, practical guides for teachers) have yet to be included in, or developed for, university courses in management education.[1] Most of their applications remain confined to elementary schools. Hence there is a continuing need to explore the possibilities and challenges of introducing a humanistic orientation into management education.

---

1   Probably the only exception to this generalization is the work of Freire and his school (Freire, 1970; Escobar et al., 1994), especially in his denunciation of authoritarian teaching in favour of shared learning experiences.

Piaget's work has exercised the greatest influence on contemporary Western education. He and his followers – for instance, Doise, Mugnet and Perret-Clemont (Dillenbourg, 1999) – developed the concept of constructivism, based on the relation between student and educator (or child and parent), which is established in the subject–object interaction. Piaget's (1977a, 1977b) precepts have been very valuable, not least in his deepest focus on the cognitive field – the development of intelligence. However, his approach does not adequately develop the issue of awareness of other subjects' needs and meanings, including ecological factors.

In order to adapt and develop the insights of these humanistic educators, then, we need to include relationships based on a *subject-subject* interaction. In educational psychology, the work of the Russian thinker Lev Vygotsky (1978, 1997), a contemporary to Piaget, is significant though internationally little known. He explores the concept of social aid in learning as a continuous development of the human being, although his followers, Grangeat (1998) and Jonnaert and Vander Borght (1999), and especially Mercer (cited by Dillenbourg, 1999), introduced his ideas under the rubric of socio-constructivism, which emphasizes social interaction. While they developed Vygotsky's thought, the latter typically remained for the most part within the confines of elementary schooling. For them, students and educators develop together and establish the bases of future continuous improvement. For us, the humanistic orientation – in which the concept of wholeness inheres – melds with the notion of continuous social co-construction, given that both encapsulate the inevitable repercussions of each being's actions for all others. The two concepts complement each other, as they both explore the ideals, initiatives and human qualities that humanistic education must develop and how that might be achieved.

We will apply these themes to management education and present our argument in the following order. First, we will discuss the appropriateness and need for a humanistic orientation in management education, noting in particular the importance – already explored by others (for instance, Reynolds, 1999; Boje, 1996) – of inculcating a reflective mindset. Second, we complement this by exploring ways of introducing humanistic values in management education, above all sensitivity towards others, a sense of responsibility for and togetherness with nature, and identification with the entire planet and its future. Managers must be willing to behave humanely if today's drastic and growing global inequities are to be addressed at source – that is, in organizational behaviour. For that purpose, third, we identify some human qualities (for example, compassion, comprehension, thoughtfulness, sharing and caring, among others) whose development in managers may help them (and us as facilitators in the formal process of education) to behave more responsibly. Fourth, our search will encompass the need for an affective and enthusiastic relationship between educators and students, if the latter are to internalize the new humanistic values. We will conclude by insisting on educators' acting with coherence and integrity and themselves setting a good example, in order to generate credibility and inspire students to pursue those orientations which their courses would introduce.

The Meaning of Actions

What does a humanistic orientation mean? Following Gusdorf (1988) and Ortiguez (1984), we suggest that a humanistic orientation expresses the concern for equality of opportunity in seeking an equitable development of every human being, as well as a life in harmony with nature. That equality implies, among other things, respect for different viewpoints and ways of life. It has ramifications in managerial practice, education and in scientific fields; a humanistic approach seeks the enhancement of human capacities in what is sometimes called 'human realization'. In alluding to the latter, some recent authors refer to what earlier thinkers, such as Socrates and Rousseau, called 'realization of the spirit', in the sense of aspiring to act in ways conducive to a coherent and meaningful life.

These humanistic ideas arose between the fifteenth and eighteenth centuries, an epoch of intellectual movements in revolt against the denial of freedom and insistence on ideological and behavioural conformity, and against a social order in which only the powerful few could achieve self-actualization at the expense of the less fortunate majority. Modern history teaches us that these movements succeeded in promoting a more equitable world. In reality, they built on ideas that Greek thinkers (primarily Socrates) developed many centuries earlier. Socrates himself fought many battles for justice and the virtues, although even he lived in a developed civilization – one much admired nowadays. We still need to fight the same battles today in a world marked by gross inequities.

Montaigne exemplifies the intellectual revolt in question; he advocated the individual's right to personal judgement, including the right to identify what is meaningful in life and worth working and fighting for. The individual must exercise the right to interpret and reflect, he argued. Throughout his *Essays* (1952[1580]), Montaigne wrote of the need for liberation from the mental chains forged in a culture of fear based on coercive religion and political doctrines that allowed monarchies to commit injustices – ideologies that normalized brutality and injustice throughout Europe. Montaigne asserts the right of the subject to achieve actualization and, by the same token, their obligation to respect and encourage the actualization of others. From the standpoint of education theory, we can read Montaigne as preferring the development of an intelligence that encompasses both rational and emotive aspects; in such a process the quality of the student–educator interaction is far more important than its outcomes in terms of cognitive memory.

From a humanistic perspective – and without straying into religious areas – we interpret the recurring concern for the 'spirit' in terms of advancing the right of every human being to an authentic way of life. Thus we refer to aspirations in the true sense – in other words, the meaning individuals attach to their deeds and life work. In short, any individual's spiritual aspirations are as valid as anyone else's. Furthermore, following the argument of such classical humanists as Pestalozzi (1951), realization is as crucial for a human being as survival is for an animal or ecosystem. In adopting the notion of realization that Montaigne and the others developed, we suggest that it can be treated as coterminous with the idea of enlightenment that some Eastern religions and Western idealist philosophers extol (for instance, Plato – see Durbin, 1988; Schelling, 1800; Hegel, 1977). These approaches have in common a philosophical orientation towards compassion, trust and openness to others' perspectives. Thus when discussing managerial challenges, we point to the need for individuals who will manage in the light of these values.

As we look for the intellectual antecedents of a humanistic approach for education, we find the works of Rabelais, Rousseau and Pestalozzi between the fifteenth and eighteenth centuries especially significant, as well as the recent contributions of Dewey (1963) and Valett (1974, 1977). For instance, in his second book, Rabelais (1930) describes the contribution Gargantua makes to the development of his son Pantagruel. Here, the mentor sets out to mould an individual who brings forth his entire potential in order to maximize his contribution to society, and this agenda includes cultivating reflectivity, self-knowledge in identifying personal goals, a capacity for independent judgement and a sense of the objective context within which he must make decisions and carry them out. In effect, Rabelais prioritizes the actor's right to (and need for) subjective reflection in whatever activity they pursue in the wider world. Certainly Gargantua imparts to Pantagruel the importance of reflecting on the meaning of any intended action before he takes it, at each stage in his life. Each time Pantagruel follows this advice he embellishes the skill of *learning to learn* – an accomplishment now known as metacognition. This skill makes use of abstract thought, past experiences and moral considerations; when applied, it will lead not only to prompt problem-solving decisions, but ones that express the decision-maker's generative values. These sorts of decisions and the practical actions they lead to will thus contribute to the agent's sense of ultimate meaning, including on political and social issues. Although Rabelais uses a father–son relationship to model this approach to education, he also thereby provides a template for an educator–student dialectic comparable to that which Plato, among other ancient Greek philosophers, established in the institution of the Lyceum. The latter constituted an ongoing forum in which teachers and students could freely interact and discuss philosophical, moral, social and political matters (see Ozmon and Craver 1999).

Much later, Rousseau wrote one of the most cited works about education, *Emile: or, On Education* (Rousseau [1778]1979), which is mostly cited in the context of primary schooling. In this book, he wrote about the individual's continuous personal development. This journey starts in the womb and takes in birth, childhood and adolescence, finishing when the individual has a strongly established character enabling them to act as a reflective adult who is conscious of their social responsibility. In all those developmental stages, Rousseau highlights the emergence of sensitivity, the personal nature of education and the value of contact with nature. Especially when he points to the need for the individual to experience nature and maintain contact with others, he identifies what are now important desiderata in the education of management students, if the executives of the future are to act out of awareness of their social responsibility.

We rank Pestalozzi's contribution in *Le chant du cigne* (The Song of the Swan) (1947[1827]) alongside Rousseau's. As Pestalozzi explained his educational method, it follows much the same lines as Rousseau's. He also implemented Rousseau's precepts in the kindergarten in which he formalized teaching from a humanistic perspective. His practices included reflection in groups and excursions to the world outside of the classroom, where he was fascinated by the sensitivity that children expressed in contact with nature and by the profound questions they could thus put to their teachers.

Contributions to Individuals' Development and Educational Challenges

These reflections indicate the need to work not only on the specific skills to be imparted to management students, but also on the formation of integrated human beings who interact constantly in society and, in doing so, transform the world we all share. Hence we also suggest the need to incorporate the concept of 'the zone of proximal development' that Vygotsky elaborated in *Mind in Society* (1978: 79–91):

> [T]he zone of proximal development ... is the distance between the actual developmental level as determined by independent problem solving and the level of potential development as determined through problem solving under adult guidance or in collaboration with more capable peers ... [H]uman learning presupposes a specific social nature and a process by which children grow into the intellectual life of those around them ... [L]earning is not development; however, properly organized learning results in mental development and sets in motion a variety of developmental process that would be impossible apart from learning. Thus, learning is a necessary and universal aspect of the process of developing culturally organized, specifically human, psychological functions ... [T]he developmental process lags behind the learning process; this sequence then results in zones of proximal development.

From this perspective, the educator as a social facilitator should encourage students to transcend what has been taught, to explore and generate more than that already presented as the formal content of a theory. The way in which educators approach students and the activities experienced (such as the direct contact with nature proposed by Rousseau and Pestalozzi) help to generate more reflective thinking in the student. Hence adequate management education requires institutions to contribute to the continuous development of students not only through association with teachers with the right intellectual attainments, but also through the ability to challenge their students so as to bring forth in them an inquisitive and sensitive spirit of discovery – the spirit that society needs its future managers to embody. In another text, *Thought and Language*, Vygotsky (1966) held that the continuous development of each individual depends on their evolving world-view and increasing awareness of their own motivations, and that this development depends on social confrontation. We can compare the latter to the process of dialogue proposed by Socrates and introduced formally by Plato in his text, *The Lyceum*.

These observations indicate that a humanistic approach in management education enriches reflection and inputs into organizational life. Thus we agree with Borrero (1995: 111–12):

> The education of a student should not be based on projects conceived merely for the execution of specific duties to perform, with no consideration of the spiritual, intellectual and moral development of the individual. The university may be the answer to general societal needs as well as to organizational needs in a specific way, but only if it forms men and women with well-developed personalities ... Some professors manifest the ontological intention of opening the individual to the possibility of learning, of being and becoming, while others are concerned to develop the more intellectual and creative capabilities of the student: learning to learn, comprehension, creation and production. That also covers the social meanings of education, such as learning to coexist with others, and with nature which is the underpinning of every life, as well as the acquisition of a spirit of adaptation and the art of leadership.

Borrero (1995) argues that a good curriculum includes not merely theoretical or practical knowledge, but also the art of shaping those things that we learn to do. Hence administration and management comprise more than duties to perform; they also encompass interactions with others and with nature, and therefore require creativity and sensitivity. With Bédard (1995), we suggest that the art of management must rest on a philosophical orientation (such as the humanistic one we propose) that allows for the individual's self-expression and sense of meaning (ontology), as well as the social values and implications of any action they take (axiology). Management education should contribute to the individual's capacity to interact, to question, to reflect and to anticipate the individual and social outcomes of organizational behaviour. A spiritual and moral learning should thus be taking place every time a managerial concept is discussed between educators and students. Moreover, they should never lose sight of axiological considerations whenever they analyze the consequences of managerial decisions.

The Need to Overcome Dominant Theories and Practices in Management

So far we have argued that a humanistic approach is an imperative for any quality management school. This applies even to financial subjects, the content of which many scholars might consider antithetical to reflection (see Dewey,

1960); but in reality the more practical areas need a humanistic input the most. For example, in financial courses at both undergraduate and graduate levels, the evaluation of the students' learning should not stop with demanding that the students reproduce the mathematical formulas to increase financial growth, but should be accompanied by reflection on the social consequences that a profit-oriented decision may carry for the community and employees (see Crowther, 2004).

The major problem in management education, then, is that the majority of management courses inculcate practical competencies and pragmatism in the absence of any broader reflection. This narrowness appeals to the proprietorial interest in financial growth without regard for social and human issues. Reynolds (1998) criticizes Kolb's (1991) influential organizational psychology that supposedly introduces 'human aspects' on the ground that it still promotes pragmatism at the expense of critical reflection on the consequences of managerial decisions. As Crowther and Davila Gomez (2005) also suggest, in most instances in which academies claim to treat 'the human aspect', such as in 'organizational behaviour' subjects, they simply encourage the individual's motivation and collaboration in the organization's profit orientation while ignoring the substantive ontological and axiological content of the humanistic dimension. The dominant paradigm implies that motivation can be artificially constructed without reference to the students' human subjectivity and capacities.

Notwithstanding institutional pretensions to the contrary, the humanistic element – including ethics based on reflectivity – remains conspicuous by its absence from management education. A reflective ethic of the kind we propose would extol the need for respect, mutual understanding, development of awareness of others' needs and aspirations and ecological sustainability – in a world currently rife with inequities and outrages against other species and the ecosystem. Current management education is also rife with rational discourses to justify the utilitarian exploitation of some people for the benefit of others, and these discourses rule our organized socio-economic behaviour (Crowther and Davila Gomez, 2006). Corporations are social constructions built around the self-interest of their individual owners, rather than the neutral, impersonal entities depicted in the dominant theory of the firm. Corporate actions are perpetrated by individuals – either the powerful or those who must obey them – and they carry consequences for people and the environment outside the corporation itself. Contrary to the neo-liberalism evangelism, profit maximization necessarily involves emotions, meanings and actions.

Without the broadening and deepening influence of a humanistic education, managers – like everyone else – have available to them very limited inputs and perspectives. In such cases their interpretations are moulded by past experiences, and the influence of people they happen to have interacted with. The latter include family members, schoolteachers and, later in life, work colleagues and superiors who are not necessarily those whom they would normally admire and seek out. This does not mean that every unchosen association will be unfruitful; sometimes they are surprisingly enriching. But without a humanistic education, we may be so stuck in the utilitarian mindset that we will not be receptive to these positive chance influences.

From a psychoanalytical viewpoint, Klein and Riviere (1964) explain that our attitudes of trust, mistrust or openness are forged in the earliest stages of our lives. Early formative experiences generate patterns of behaviour in future situations, resembling those we have known before. For instance, most of the violence and hatred we experience nowadays is the work of adults stuck in earlier authoritarian family relationships that ruled out rebellion and self-expression. In childhood our guides and role models – those we relied on to protect us from the unknown – were physically and morally more powerful than we were.[2] Klein and Riviere (1964) refer, then, to the paradox of someone feeling love for another who nonetheless evokes stress and sometimes even hatred in the former – a situation Laing (1969) calls the 'double bind'. The individual needs an internal reconciliation, and, in the process of achieving it, their character is forged. Each individual may react differently to the same situation, depending on previous experiences and the earlier love objects.

For instance, we do not necessarily love our superiors or colleagues in organizational life. However, if we have already developed a friendly

---

2   Freud (1976, 1977) held that most aspects of identity are laid down in early childhood and that the attempt to integrate the various conflicting facets of childhood experience leads a person to act in particular ways. Part of this conflict is based on parental influence, which leads to the development within the child of the concept of the ideal self as the perfect being to strive to become in order to win parental approval. This ideal self is, of course, unattainable; but much of adult life, and the actions undertaken by adults, spring from an unconscious motivation to achieve this ideal self and thereby secure respect. This motivation has been expressed by psychoanalysts as the drive towards individuation, and explains the continual need for reassurance, self-respect and the respect of others. For some people this drive can be reflected in a tendency towards conformity as a means of escaping from the isolation of the self (Fromm, 1957). In extreme circumstances this can result in a person resorting to madness by attempting to hold what Laing (1969) describes as an untenable position. When these individuals are managers of organizations their personality disorders inevitably have implications for those organizations as well. Sievers (1994) has described this situation as leading to organizational psychotic behaviour.

relationship with them, we may experience a subsequent act of unfriendliness from one of them as treachery, but not necessarily as a formative experience, given that the individual concerned is no longer our mother, father or primary-school teacher whom we loved in the past. We now see colleagues and superiors as our equals in terms of physical strength and rights. So we may fight our own battles – although we might equally refrain from doing so in the face of other sources of domination, such as hierarchical power or internalized intellectual paradigms.

As Mintzberg (2003), Alvesson (1996) and Aktouf (2001) have highlighted, power and domination in organizations are survivals of historical elite domination, as well as evidence of a social permissiveness towards the self-interested conduct of those who have power, especially managers and owners. In childhood we have learned to accept the mores imposed on us by those more powerful than us (parents and teachers), as well as those who personify our career goals – for instance, directors whose lifestyles we aspire to.

Even though this ingrained elitism and self-interest may be the most common way of life, not least in child-rearing and organizational life, some thinkers throughout history have produced alternative models. Although managers make up part of the elite, the dissidents suggest, they are not exempt from their social responsibility towards others. What might trigger our awakening to alternative values when most of our education and emotional life have been coloured by uncomfortable experiences of violence and abuse? One way is through higher education, including management education, through some alternative to the mainstream paradigm of pragmatism.

The Imperative of Attitudinal Change

This change would require us to concentrate our efforts on cultivating a specific philosophy and strategy for attitudinal change, one resilient enough to challenge prefigured patterns of response based on childhood experiences. The strategy would rest largely on those responsible for contributing to a continuous development of character in individuals who will come to play a key role in organizational life. In other words, the responsibility falls not only on educators in the business administration discipline, but also on the directors of the educational institutions in which they work. As Reynolds (1998) suggests, reflection is not enough: we need to change curricula to neutralize the existing pedagogical orthodoxy that excludes all considerations other than productivity and experiential pragmatism. In line with Reynolds' position, our previous research (Crowther and Davila Gomez, 2005, 2006; Davila Gomez, 2003) uncovers the roots of current organizational psychology in Kolb's theory, which in fact follows a behaviourist approach to the individual and sees motivation as something induced by external stimuli – such as higher salaries, promotion and other economic rewards, as well as attainment of organizational goals – rather than as something that expresses our own individuality, our own inner meanings and bearings. To empower the latter, management education would need to stimulate what Reynolds (1999, 1998) refers to as a broader 'critical reflection' – one that demands emancipation and social change.

As teachers we need to convince our students that sensitivity towards humanity and the whole planet is acceptable. As Winnicott (1965) and Klein and Riviere (1964) show, it is only when our emotions are engaged that we can carry through genuinely transformative actions. Mature people will change their attitudes towards animals, for example, not only by learning about their natural habitats or their importance for the world, but also by being with them when they manifest distress. This example accords with the core of the humanistic education premise: contact with nature teaches us to feel and experience what other beings and species must face as challenges and difficulties. The experience awakens sensitivity, openness and thoughtfulness.

Even though Rousseau and Pestalozzi focused on childhood education, their precepts apply equally to any adult education which seeks to bring about changes in attitude. Although he concentrated on children, Pestalozzi expressed a concern for humankind as a whole and for its relationship with nature. Indeed, in *The Education of Men* (Pestalozzi, 1951: 4–5), he not only talks about education for children, but also about lifelong education for adults:

The good instincts of mankind, in their pure state, are more than gifts of art or chance. Their fundamental qualities lie deeply buried in man's nature. All men feel the need to develop these powers, and the paths along which nature reveals them must be kept clear and easy of access. To achieve wisdom and tranquillity, the processes of human education must be kept simple and be of universal application.

Pestalozzi makes a compelling case for the possibility of an education based on sensitivity, respect, openness and thoughtfulness. At the same time, of course, education should be accessible for all. Management education today falls well short of this potential, which can only be realized through changes in institutions and governments. One aspect of the reform process would be the democratization of education, opening it up to people with few economic resources, including the use of distance education that exploits new technological possibilities for its delivery (see Crowther, Barnett and Davies, 1998). As a contrast to Pestalozzi's advocacy of educational simplicity, we note how business schools are becoming increasingly dependent on arcane technology, abstruse theories and research, and myriad academic publications – all of it marshalled to impart an essentially unchanging agenda of maintaining unfairness and inequities in the workplace.

The question is, then, whether we the educators are forever bound by the prerogatives of the dominant elite and its interest in preserving the world as it is, or whether we possess the academic freedom to break with the hegemonic paradigm and teach alternative contents using alternative methods, including critical reflection and a humanistic orientation. University directors, as well as academics, are also human beings; their behaviour follows the same patterned reactions, such as the fear of being fired for not following the institutional order and, in the case of public universities, of losing public funding. In a sense, these ultimately self-imposed barriers are what allow many of us to think, talk and write, but not necessarily to act. As Pestalozzi (1951: 6) puts it:

> *To accomplish good in this our world takes more, much more, than merely to suggest it, dreamlike, to the human soul, that it marvel thereon, and glory in the image; men must be brought to pick out the thread by which the good thus shown them will ultimately lay rein upon their inner life, their inclinations, and their aspirations; and, as it were, take over their eyes, their hands, their tongues, and all their outward powers.*

If we are to succeed in the reform of management education, we will need determination and authenticity. We will need to reconcile the inner self (soul, meaning, the whole person) with our past conditioning and future aspirations, and so gain the determination to act consistently and coherently out of a concern for others and for the consequences of our actions.

In organizations this human orientation implies that managers must respect others' opinions, ideas and actions as being as valuable as if they were their very own. It implies the need to overcome the residues of past experiences of violence, repression and ridicule perpetrated by the powerful against the powerless. A great deal of organizational violence, perpetrated by powerful agents, fulfils their felt need to oppress others to compensate for their own childhood humiliation, so making others pay the price of that original abuse. As managers of organizations, we become others' role models at the same time as we model ourselves on our own superiors and we should assume responsibility for the message we impart by the way we manifest in our organizational roles. Respect, concern and sensitivity towards what others might feel are no longer simply a question of awareness, but an imperative of the inner self. Thus when managers make promises they later renege on, others feel disappointment, and the initial empathy perhaps developed in the first weeks of work is broken. If this pattern recurs, morale falls, and what functionalist organizational theory calls 'identification with the corporate culture' will not develop. Corporations may unfurl their explicit written axiology on their websites, whilst their power-holders commit routine abuses that contradict their official credos. In such cases, employees just as routinely experience the inconsistency, which triggers feelings of abandonment with resonances to their childhood experiences and the powerful others who acted hypocritically and incoherently back then.

Institutional Accountability

Not far from this corporate reality, we experience a similar situation in business schools, as they are also organizations. Our citizen-clients are the students, and we as teachers may either reproduce coercive power relations or considerate human ones. As we have pointed out above, as educators (and sometimes as directors of institutions) we also carry our past psychological conditioning that is in continuous reconstruction and readjustment. We might harbour frustrations deriving from the way in which we have been treated by others, and we may have chosen to mete out the same treatment to our students. Or we might have experienced autocratic and hierarchical power from others in different instances, and we may have then chosen to inflict bureaucratic insensitivity on a subordinate out of a desire to see another suffer as we have done. Where, then, is the compassion? Where is the sensitivity? For these are the feelings we must foster in order to obtain attitudinal change in aid of a better company, community and – even more – a better world and future for the generations to come.

When we teachers act in unreconstructed ways, we must realize that students are paying us to be mistreated because they have no alternative in the near future, as organizations will employ them only if they have passed the approved university courses. Routinely abusive educator–student interaction is then socially acceptable, even though we feel it is wrong. As Montessori (1965) pointed out, our methods are so authoritarian that the will of the student is almost forgotten. Students are forced to follow the teacher's (and institutional) precepts and, in the process of doing so, they receive a pedagogy of repression and instructionalism, totally opposed to dialogue, debate and the students' self-discovery. On this path, most students choose to follow the precepts out of fear of disappointing their parents, of being confrontational, or simply the fear of becoming social misfits. They then silently endure this pedagogy of oppression (Freire, 1970), even though they feel mistreated. It is not surprising that the work of a revolutionary woman like Maria Montessori in the early twentieth century was so difficult! Nowadays, however, we can find some primary schools that follow her method based on love, compassion and comprehension (see Montessori Foundation, 2005). Nevertheless, the need to extend this kind of pedagogy to adult education remains, not least in business schools with their predilection for elitist organizations.

As alternatives we have discussed the introduction of critical reflection and a humanistic and respectful interaction between teachers and students. As learning by example powerfully assists the development of new behaviours, this kind of learning can help students gain faith in a new humanistic paradigm. In order to generate compassion and generosity in our students, we need to model these qualities in our teaching relationships.

As Reynolds (1999) argues, we need less hierarchical approaches and more emphasis on the overall development of the individual. As teachers follow new orientations, new challenges arise for educational institutions to bring about the continuous development of their personnel. Here we agree with Dewey (1975[1909]: 8–9) on the need to integrate morality and ethics in any educational process:

> *The social work of the school is often limited to training for citizenship, and citizenship is then interpreted in a narrow sense as meaning capacity to vote intelligently, disposition to obey laws, etc. But it is futile to contract and cramp the ethical responsibility of the school in this way. The child is one, and he must either live his social life as an integral unified being, or suffer loss and create friction … The child is an organic whole, intellectually, socially and morally, as well as physically. We must take the child as a member of society in the broadest sense, and demand for and from the schools whatever is necessary to enable the child intelligently to recognize all his social relations and take his part in sustaining them.*

Dewey's precepts are widely applicable to management education; they reinforce our emphasis on the continuous development of the whole individual as against the mere inculcation of specific technical skills.

As a practical example of the proposed pedagogy, we could ask students to gain a lived experience of 'organizational realities' side by side with people who already work in organizations. This exercise would go beyond the traditional experiential learning aimed at developing skills: it would also require the students in their class assignments to reflect on the impact of existing arrangements they have experienced on the workers they have encountered while they were working beside them. A complementary exercise might be to ask students to visit working organizations and interview subjects from the different levels of the personnel, from directors to employees, so as to gain access to the different vantage points and experiences in the same organization. In this way we would require more of the students than is traditionally asked of them; we would be asking them to empathize with people occupying contrasting positions in a hierarchical organization. Their later engagement in strategic planning could then draw on ethical considerations on which they would now enjoy a range of vivid perspectives. Educators working in this way would need the support of the institution to gain the necessary cooperation with industry and other organizations, which in turn would admit students to undertake visits and probationary periods. Those who control the study programmes would also have to support the change, because nowadays curricula are so tightly controlled and rationalized as to deny teachers the freedom and room to manoeuvre they would need. Much of the time we teachers are also victims of the excess of rationalism, including the abuses of what we ourselves taught about 're-engineering', because the old norms are already implicit in all the written procedures and policies, including those prescribing evaluation processes, contents and tasks to require of the students.

When we look for entry points for sensitivity and the opening of the mind in management education, we need to insist that the students develop the habit, desire and taste for humanistic social attitudes and values. As Winnicott (1965: 73) put it:

> The word 'concern' is used to cover in a positive way a phenomenon
> that is covered in a negative way by the word 'guilt'. A sense of guilt
> is anxiety linked with the concept of ambivalence, and implies a degree
> of integration in the individual ego that allows for the retention of good
> object-imago along with the idea of destruction of it. Concern implies

*further integration, and further growth, and relates in a positive way
to the individual's sense of responsibility, especially in respect of
relationships into which the instinctual drives have entered. Concern
refers to the fact that the individual cares, or minds, and both feels and
accepts responsibility.*

As Winnicott also explained, this sense of concern (that is, the sense
of responsibility we seek in managers) may not initially be well developed,
depending on childhood experiences, but it can grow during the continuous
development of the individual in adult life. When we teachers receive students,
it might well be that this concern is deficient in some, and we will not make
up this deficiency merely through imparting the theoretical corpus of our
discipline. Once again, then, we come up against the need for the humanistic
desiderata – contact with nature, and direct experience of organizational reality
side by side with other human beings. In this way, we ourselves may come
to enjoy a more human relationship with our students so as to offer them
alternative experiences that can lead them to a critique of coercive power as
the supposed be-all and end-all of effective leadership. As Klein and Riviere
(1964) make clear, the psychoanalytic perspective on human development
demonstrates how much more is involved in teaching than the dominant
paradigm suggests.

The wider pedagogical perspective mandates forethought and a new ethical
grip, not only in the case of teachers, but also that of the directors of educational
institutions. More examples of humanistic practices in organizations and in
teaching are needed. More experience and contact with the world are essential
in order to contribute to the development of the critical thinking of students as
well as human and social attitudes of concern and responsibility. We recognize,
of course, that this places a considerable responsibility on people (such as
ourselves), who are engaged in the education of managers and future managers.[3]
We suggest, however, that such education is more open, as it sets out to provide
opportunities for all and to introduce a concern for society as a whole, rather
than with merely reinforcing and reproducing existing hierarchies of power.
It is a broader education than one simply concerned with task proficiency
and knowledge transfer, because it extends the approach started in primary
education into higher education. Moreover, it does not place the educator and

---

3   This, of course, opens up a considerable discourse regarding the role of education and the role
of educators in the process. We do not intend in this chapter to engage with this discourse to
any great extent, instead restricting ourselves to the arguments we have made concerning the
need for humanistic education.

the student in a hierarchical power relationship; rather, both work together and learn from each other. The result is more challenging, but also more satisfying for educator and student. This is laudable in its own right, but what we are particularly concerned with is behaviour in the workplace. Our argument here is that the provision of an enhanced education for managers has a key role to play in reforming institutions. A more holistic, humanistic education for managers and potential managers will help move the workplace towards a socially responsible environment in which those working there are valued as people and not just as factors of production.

References

Aktouf, O. (2001), 'Mondialisation et Post-mondialisation: implacables logiques de marginalisation?', *Cahier de recherche du Centre d'études en administration internationale (CETAI)*, September (Montréal: Ecole des Hautes Etudes Commerciales (HEC)).

Alvesson, M. (1996), *Communication, Power and Organization* (Berlin: Walther de Gruyter).

Bédard, R. (1995), 'Les Fondements philosophiques de la direction', doctoral thesis (Montréal: Ecole des Hautes Etudes Commerciales (HEC)).

Boje, D. (1996), 'Management Education as a Panoptic Cage', in D. Boje, J. Gephart, T. Thatchenkery (eds), *Postmodern Management and Organization Theory* (London: Sage).

Borrero, A. (1995), *L'Université aujourd'hui* (Paris: Centre de recherche pour le développement international).

Chanlat, A. (1998), *Les deux Bourque: côté cour, côté jardin – Grandeurs et misères de la matière du dirigeant.* (Québec: Presses de l'Université Laval).

Crowther, D. (2004), *Managing Finance: A Socially Responsible Approach* (London: Elsevier).

Crowther, D. Barnett, N and Davies, M. (1998), 'Using Multimedia Technology for Teaching: A Case Study Approach', in M. Henry. (ed.), *Using IT Effectively* (London: UCL Press)

Crowther, D. and Davila Gomez, A.M. (2005), 'Is Lying the Best Way of Telling the Truth?', *Social Responsibility Journal*, 1:3/4, 128–41.

Crowther, D. and Davila Gomez, A.M. (2006), 'I Will if You Will: Risk, Feelings and Emotion in the Workplace' in D. Crowther and K.T. Caliyurt (eds), *Globalisation and Social Responsibility* (Cambridge: Cambridge Scholars Press).

Crowther, D. and Rayman-Bacchus, L. (2004), 'The Future of Corporate Social Responsibility', in D. Crowther. and L. Rayman-Bacchus (eds), *Perspectives on Corporate Social Responsibility* (Aldershot: Ashgate), 229–49.

Davila Gomez, A.M. (2003), 'Hacia un Management Humanista desde la educación a distancia: intersubjetividad y desarrollo de cualidades humanas', doctoral thesis (Montréal: Ecole des Hautes Etudes Commerciales de Montréal (HEC)).

Dewey, J. (1960[1933]), *How We Think – A Restatement of the Relation of Reflective Thinking to the Educative Process* (Lexington, MA: D.C. Heath and Co.).

Dewey, J. (1963), *Experience and Education* (Indianapolis: Kappa Delta Pi Ed)

Dewey, J. (1975[1909]), *Moral Principles in Education* (Illinois, IN: Southern Illinois University Press).

Dillenbourg, P. (1999), 'What Do You Mean by "Collaborative Learning"?', in P. Dillenbourg (ed.), *Collaborative Learning – Cognitive and Computational Approaches* (Oxford and Amsterdam: Pergamon/Elsevier).

Durbin, P. (1988), *Dictionary of Concepts in the Philosophy of Science* (New York: Greenwood).

Escobar, M., Fernandez, A.L., Guevara-Niebla, G. and Freire, P. (1994), *Paulo Freire on Higher Education: A Dialogue at the National University of Mexico* (Albany, NY: State University of New York Press).

Freire, P. (1970), *Pedagogy of the Oppressed* (London: Penguin).

Freud, S. (1976); *Jokes and their Relation to the Unconscious*, trans. A. Richards (Harmondsworth: Pelican).

Freud, S. (1977), *On Sexuality*; trans. A. Richards (Harmondsworth: Pelican).

Fromm, E. (1957), *The Art of Loving* (London: Unwin).

Grangeat, M. (1998), 'Lev S. Vygotsky (1896–1934) – L'apprentissage par le groupe' in J.C. Ruano Barbalan (ed.), *Éduquer et former* (Paris: Editions Sciences Humaines).

Gusdorf, G. (1988), *Les origines de l'herméneutique* (Paris: Payot).

Hegel, G.W.F. (1977), *Phenomenology of Spirit*, trans. A.V. Miller (Oxford and New York: Oxford University Press).

'Johann Heinrich Pestalozzi', *Encyclopaedia Britannica Online, 2005*, at: http://britannica.com.

Jonnaert, P. and Vander Borght, C. (1999), *Créer des conditions d'apprentissage – un cadre de référence socioconstructiviste pour une formation didactique des enseignants*, (Bruxelles: Editions De Boeck).

Kierkegaard, S. (1941[1851]), *For Self-examination and Judge for Yourselves!*, trans. W. Lowrie (Princeton, NJ: Princeton University Press).

Klein, M. and Riviere, J. (1964), *Love, Hate and Reparation* (New York: The Norton Library).

Kolb, D. (1991), *Organizational Behaviour: An Experiential Approach* (5th edn) (Englewood Cliffs, NJ: Prentice Hall).

Laing, R.D. (1969), *Self and Others* (London: Penguin).

Mintzberg, H. (2003[1893]), *Le pouvoir dans les organisations* (Paris: Editions d'organisations).

Montaigne, M. (1992[1580]), *Les Essais*, ed. C. Pinganaud (Paris: Editions Arléa).

Montessori, M. (1965), *The Advanced Montessori Method – Spontaneous Activity in Education* (Cambridge MA: Robert Bentley Inc.).

Ozmon, H. and Craver, S. (1999), *Philosophical Foundations of Education* (New York: Prentice Hall).

Ortiguez, J. (1984), 'Sciences humaines', *Encyclopaedia Unversalis* (Paris: Encyclopaedia Unversalis).

Pestalozzi, J. (1947[1827]), *Le chant du cigne – suivi de mes destinées*, trans. V. de Léon (Paris: Baconnière).

Pestalozzi, J. (1951) *The Education of Man: Aphorisms*, trans. H. Norden and R. Norden (New York: Philosophical Library).

Piaget, J. (1977a), *Mes idées* (Paris: Denöel Gonthier).

Piaget, J. (1977b), *El nacimiento de la inteligencia en el niño* (Barcelona: Critica)..

Plato (1997), *Complete Works*, ed. J.M. Cooper. and D. Hutchison (Indianapolis, IN: S. Tacket Publishing Company).

Rabelais, F. (1930) *The Works of Rabelais*, Book II, trans. W. Ives (New York: Tudor Publishing).

Reynolds, M. (1998), 'Reflection and Critical Reflection in Management Learning', *Management Learning*, 29:2, 183–200.

Reynolds, M. (1999), 'Critical Reflection and Management Education: Rehabilitating Less Hierarchical Approaches', *Journal of Management Education*, 23:5, 537–53.

Rousseau, J-J. (1964[1778]), 'Discourse on the Origin and Foundations of Inequality among Men' in *The First and Second Discourses*, ed. R. Masters, trans. R. Masters and J. Masters (New York: St Martin's Press).

Rousseau, J-J. (1979 [1778]), *Emile: or, On Education*, trans. A. Bloom (New York: Basic Books).

Schelling, F.W.J. (1800), *System of Transcendental Idealism*, trans. P. Heath (Charlottesville: University Press of Virginia).

Sievers, B. (1994), *Work Death and Life Itself. Essays on Management and Organization* (Berlin: de Gruyter).

The Montessori Foundation (2005), *The Montessori Foundation and the International Montessori Council*, at: http://www.montessori.org.

Valett, R.E. (1974), *Affective-Humanistic Education – Goals, Programs and Learning Activities.* (Belmont, CA: Lear Siegler/Fearon).

Valett, R.E. (1977), *Humanistic Education – Developing the Total Person* (St Louis: C.V. Mosby Co.).

Vygotsky, L.S. (1966), *Thought and Language,* trans. E. Hanfmann and G. Vakar (Cambridge, MA: MIT Press).

Vygotsky, L.S. (1978), *Mind in Society – Development of Higher Psychological Processes* (Cambridge, MA: Harvard University Press).

Vygotsky, L.S. (1997), 'Ethical Behavior' in *Educational Psychology* (Boca Ration, FL: St Lucie Press).

Winnicott, D. (1965), *The Maturational Processes and the Facilitating Environment: Studies in the Theory of Emotional Developments* (New York: International University Press).

10

Standardizing Corporate Social Responsibility

Winton Higgins

Twenty years ago, the development and publication of rules and codes in the form of written standards was mainly the work of specialized national and international standards bodies. Almost all their standards addressed technical matters such as railway gauges, seat belts, methods of tests, design, building and installation codes, network standards needed for interoperability and so on. Standardizers have played an essential role in the development of mechanized production, technology transfers, the facilitation of trade, and, from the 1970s, in giving effect to organized consumers' demands for safety, reliability and accurate information about consumer durables. In short, standardizers made an essential but modest contribution to our standard of living, quality of life and safety.[1]

From the late 1980s, however, standardization took a turn that qualitatively boosted standards bodies' importance in national and global governance. In 1987 the International Organization of Standardization (ISO) published its suite of quality management standards (coded ISO 9000), and many of its affiliated national standards bodies (NSBs) adopted it as national standards. It quickly became a runaway success, boosting the fortunes and prestige of both ISO and the NSBs. ISO 9000 prescribed how an organization – but, in the first instance, a corporation – should be managed, ostensibly so as to attain a nebulously conceived 'quality', but more importantly in the event, to achieve auditability and thus certified probity in the 'globalized' economy. This suite of management standards (and the audit and certification industries it spawned) plugged the gaps left by the shift away from nation-states' 'hard regulation'

---

1   See Higgins and Tamm Hallström (2008a) for a brief history of formal standardization since 1875.

and the declining relevance of reputation in local business cultures for firms that were 'going global'. It provided a new way for them to announce their virtues globally.

In this way ISO 9000 proved the icebreaker for a new *kind* of standard – 'administrative' or 'system' standards – that has since risen to prominence in global governance and, some might even suggest, come to inform corporate behaviour. ISO and the Western NSBs have sought to repeat the success of ISO 9000 by producing administrative standards covering such aspects of corporate governance as records keeping, knowledge management, risk management, regulatory compliance and complaints handling. But ISO's most ambitious projects of this kind since ISO 9000 are its suite of environmental management standards (ISO 14000), published in 1996, and the ongoing project, at the time of writing, of developing a standard for social responsibility (ISO 26000). The latter emerged from a proposal for a standard covering corporate social responsibility (CSR), but ISO decided that social responsibility (SR) concerned all large organizations, not just corporations.

By the time ISO entered these two fields, they were already occupied by other organizations and consortia; after all, standardizers can only get their teeth into a project after the initial innovation is in place and their constituents have actually called for it to be standardized. And, naturally, those pioneering organizations and consortia already in the fields in question had mixed feelings about the newcomer. Nonetheless, ISO could claim that its institutional *gravitas* and *modus operandi* could make a unique contribution to these fields. After all, standardization was a long-established and universally accepted 'technology' for making things happen and getting things done. The standards development process within ISO and the Western NSBs could lay unique claim to the virtues of transparency, representativeness and consensus; the product itself was voluntary and, above all, came in commodity form – you could buy it off the shelf in the marketplace. Finally, in most cases, management standards were auditable and certifiable, which meant that their purchasers could, after implementing the standards, unfurl their good corporate citizen status on their websites – the kind of 'street cred' that matters in the global market.

In this chapter I will evaluate the claim that standardization could prove an effective means for making private enterprise socially responsible. First, I want to present an historical overview of private enterprise's real and imagined relationship with moral responsibility, to show how successive attempts to make this troubled relationship work eventually ended up in various proposals for instilling SR in corporations from outside them. Then I want to look at the emergence of standardization as a technology of government in order to test its likely effectiveness in tackling a very old problem that now threatens every living being on the planet – the impact of private, self-interested calculations on the needs of others, and on the resources and environments that human beings and all other species have to share.

As we shall see, those who have sought to make private enterprise compatible with basic decency and sociability – and ultimately with planetary survival – could choose between trying to make corporations into inner-directed moral agents, on the one hand, and imposing external legal, financial and cultural constraints on them to make responsibility a factor in their own survival, on the other.

Historical Background

The project of bringing the profit motive endemic to corporate life into some working relationship with morality – to say nothing of spirituality – has a long and usually dismal history. The latter includes the exercise of legislative *force majeure* on to the commercial world when even financial disincentives to immorality have not worked. An early case in point is the UK Slave Trade Act of 1807, which set out to stymie the slave trade by fining sea captains £100 for each slave found on their ships. Their subsequent practice of throwing their slaves into the sea to avoid the fine whenever Royal Navy vessels appeared on the horizon led to the outright abolition of slavery in the tougher Slavery Abolition Act of 1833. Similarly, child labour and the other horrors of the nineteenth-century factory system forced the British legislature to pass no fewer than nine Factory Acts between 1802 and 1891.

A handful of early entrepreneurs and companies who were temporarily shielded from the winds of competition pursued their own projects of social amelioration for their workforces. They included mill-owner Robert Owen (1771–1853), and companies such as Cadbury's, Rowntrees and Guinness (UK), and Hershey's (USA). But these experiments were temporary and signally failed to inspire other captains of industry. Rather, mainstream entrepreneurial behaviour bore out Marx's argument that capitalists were mere bearers of social relations – appendages of their capital, just as they made their wage-workers into mere appendages of factory plant. Put simply, entrepreneurs either followed the logic of profit maximization or faced personal ruin. Indeed,

Adam Smith, the father of political economy, had already implied as much in his 1776 classic, *The Wealth of Nations*: it is economic activity based on self-interest alone that animates 'the invisible hand' of the market so that it in turn coordinated production and distribution, thus maximizing aggregate wealth. But it has been Marx's appendages-of-capital thesis about corporate behaviour that has constituted the case to answer whenever corporate decision-makers have laid claim to effective high-mindedness.

Even before Marx was cold in his grave, along came the savagery of the 'robber barons' (Astor, Rockefeller, Carnegie, Ford and J.P. Morgan among others) in the development of US industry in the later nineteenth century, including their deployment of spectacular violence against workers by private armies of thugs – above all, the Pinkertons.

In the 1930s those who were trying to append a fig leaf of decency on to real-world corporate behaviour thought that they had found the perfect adhesive in the 'managerial revolution' thesis, not least when it later received magisterial support in Joseph Schumpeter's otherwise unsettling classic, *Capitalism, Socialism and Democracy* in 1942. All that money-grubbing, antisocial corporate behaviour was now sheeted home to the pioneering entrepreneurs that the robber barons exemplified. But these people represented a passing phase in the development of the essentially benign private-enterprise system, the story went. Now their firms had grown too large and complex for them, and they were being replaced at the helm by civilized managers, engineers and other experts who did not own the corporations they controlled. This supposed managerial revolution split the function of control off from that of ownership. The new masters were thus no longer constrained by the profit motive and could be expected to behave in socially and morally responsible ways. They were, after all, university-educated and could thus be presumed to be scholars and gentlemen, or at very least to have acquired a veneer of civic culture. In the jargon of the time, the bad old entrepreneur-dominated company had now metamorphosed into 'the soulful corporation'.

This idea gained renewed cachet during the Cold War and still underpins much of today's rhetoric around business ethics and CSR. Back in the Cold War, the uses of the soulful-corporation thesis went beyond business posturing to become an important trope in the ideological defence of capitalism itself: it contributed to what C. Wright Mills (1956) famously called 'the Great American Celebration' of the uncritical American social-science academies. It is worth quoting the influential statement of the thesis written by Carl Kaysen of Harvard University in 1957, at the height of the Cold War:

> *Ownership is disappearing ...With the sublimation of ownership, management has become professionalized. Managers are not owners ... [A] characteristic of the behavior of the modern corporation is the wide-ranging scope of responsibility assumed by management. No longer the agent of proprietorship seeking to maximize return on investment, management sees itself as responsible to stockholders, employees, customers, the general public, and, perhaps most important, the firm itself as an institution ... its responsibilities to the general public are widespread: leadership in local charitable enterprises, concern for factory architecture and landscaping, provision of support for higher education, and even research in pure science, to name a few ... The modern corporation is a soulful corporation.*
>
> (Kaysen, 1957: 312)

Note here that the new corporate masters are not presented as mere philanthropic individuals, but rather as bearers of 'responsibilities' to their employees, the general public and so on. The idea of CSR was already emerging.

Unhappily, the soulful corporation has distinguished itself by its absence from the real world. During the Third Reich (1933–45), for instance, management-led firms like Volkswagen used slave labour as enthusiastically as did family-owned ones like Krupp and Siemens, while management-run IG Farben realized large profits through supplying the death camps with Zyklon B gas pellets. General Motors' management was as pleased to provide trucks and artificial-fuel technology to Hitler as family-owned Ford was. But such examples of corporate lapses of soulfulness were trumped by management-governed IBM's development and monthly leasing of its Hollerith punch-card machines (forerunners of computers) to German authorities, so making the highly bureaucratized Holocaust achievable.[2] We should not be too surprised, then, to find the US giant ITT planning and bankrolling the military coup against Chile's elected government of 1973, which ushered in one of the bloodiest dictatorships of the postwar period.

Today we live with recurring revelations of how Western corporations with leading brand names in the clothing and footwear industry exploit the Third-

---

2   This case has been exhaustively researched in Edwin Black's (2001) prize-winning *IBM and the Holocaust*.

World producers of their wares – to say nothing of those involved in the arms trade and a wide range of activities contributing to global warming, species loss and pollution. In short, the changing composition of senior management has had no impact whatever on corporate malfeasance.

Thus far, then, the appendages-of-capital thesis is well ahead on points, and turning corporations into reformed characters looks like a forlorn prospect. No matter who runs the firm, the financial forms of calculation it deploys are those that the capital markets (not least today's hyperactive stock exchanges) force on it. Ever since the incorporation of joint-stock companies, Western jurisprudence has treated them as 'artificial persons'. However, while mature real persons establish their integrity through assuming responsibility for their morally significant actions, thus becoming inner-directed moral agents, profit-seeking artificial persons clearly fail to achieve any immanent moral agency. These days a specialized managerial argot suppresses reference to the moral significance of corporate decision-making as such, as a number of critics have pointed out by publishing 'dictionaries' that decode it (see Saul, 1994; Watson, 1994). Moreover, the bureaucratic structures of large corporations positively invite their functionaries to displace moral responsibility on to others, or simply on to 'the firm', as if its actions were independent of their own acted-out choices. Given this institutional disengagement of the individual conscience, the professed commitment of functionaries to religious or moral codes, be they ever so grand, make no difference to real-world outcomes.

The Rise of Soft Regulation

Regulators and interest groups who have sought to curb corporate destructiveness have accordingly come to understand that only external sticks and carrots that impinge on corporate forms of profit-seeking calculation will work. Those who have undertaken the difficult task of setting up these constraints have commonly conflated two moral issues, although they have perhaps gained a tactical advantage by doing so. The first issue focuses on *probity*: how to keep corporate managements honest enough to uphold the minimal trust required to sustain the flow of investment, commerce and trade between firms. Corporate corruption that leads to such global ructions as the 2003 Enron collapse hurt other corporations, which themselves then have a material interest in forms of regulation – 'hard' or 'soft', depending on whether they have the backing of a nation-state – that make such events less likely.

The other issue goes much more to the heart of the moral problem: how to prevent corporations from acting in socially and environmentally destructive ways and, if possible, harness at least some of their activities to ameliorative ends. So long as the distinction between mere probity, on the one hand, and altruism and societal responsibility, on the other, is not sharply drawn, external regulators and interest groups have a chance of influencing corporate behaviour by appealing to corporate self-interest.

These regulators and interest groups have enjoyed another advantage, too. Whereas an individual corporation's potential moral restraint or altruism can blunt its competitive edge, it is not at all disadvantaged by following rules that also bind its competitors. On this basis, transnational bodies have, especially over the last three decades, launched a number of attempts to devise voluntary (or at least non-coercive) codes governing corporations' treatment of employees, trading relations with vulnerable groups and countries, and impact on the environment. The problem with such mechanisms has always precisely been how to win compliance for rules in the absence of criminal sanctions. That problem raises the issue of the moral authority of transnational organizations such as ISO, whose standards lack the backing of either nation-states' coercive powers or financial muscle (Tamm Hallström, 2004).[3] As we shall see in the next section, however, recent trends in global governance have greatly bolstered the authority of bodies like ISO.

Early versions of this kind of 'soft regulation' relied indirectly on the imprimatur of nation-states, starting with the labour commission set up by the Paris Peace Conference in 1919. Its recommendations laid the basis for the charter under which the International Labour Organization (ILO) – initially the creation of the Treaty of Versailles, but now a specialized UN agency – was established. The ILO still issues conventions and recommendations on social justice, human and labour rights, and standards for minimum labour conditions. Its recommendations and standards have enjoyed clear moral authority, especially in progressive states willing to incorporate them into their national legal frameworks, and they equally clearly refer to important aspects of corporate behaviour.

In the postwar period similar initiatives followed, now under the auspices of the United Nations and the ambition it embodied to create a new world order based on democracy, human rights and economic progress. The new

---

3   The issue of authority was acute as ISO undertook a particularly long drawn-out decision-making process over whether to develop an SR standard (Tamm Hallström, 2006).

economic framework included such powerful institutions as the IMF, World Bank and the General Agreement on Tariffs and Trade (GATT), which much later evolved into the World Trade Organization. Though it is a non-government transnational organisation, ISO itself has its origins in 1946, as a creature of this postwar new world order, and its more recent activities have squarely targeted corporate operations. A sign of the times, which melded human-rights issues with economic management, was the UN Economic and Social Council's (UNESCO's) establishment of the Human Rights Commission in 1946. Two years later the Commission's Universal Declaration of Human Rights made compliance not only the duty of states, but also 'every individual and organ of society'.

The world thus became accustomed to norm-setting transnational organizations, consortia and fora that issue rules, recommendations and standards with no direct coercive means to enforce compliance: the problem of authority remains endemic for the bodies concerned (Tamm Hallström, 2004). Flouting these rules nonetheless has increasingly become 'not a good look' for corporations, with palpable effects in consumer preferences and the attitudes of governments and potential business partners. Developments in communications – not least the Internet – have meant that bad corporate behaviour, as measured against the new norms, can quickly become notorious and invite boycotts.

In this way, a new theme, 'the business case' for CSR, grew in importance (ISO, 2004: 20–21; 34–35). Put simply, it claimed there was a dollar to be made by being responsible and a bottom-line penalty to be paid for irresponsibility. 'The business case' for shouldering social responsibility would become a vital part of ISO's motivation for undertaking its own SR project and a key argument with which it eventually won over its corporate stakeholders. Of course, 'the business case' also tacitly affirms the appendages-of-capital thesis: corporations will only take responsibility if it maximizes profits. Social responsibility for its own sake still has no place in corporate forms of calculation.

The new rules, or 'soft regulation', came to cover more and more areas of corporate behaviour, not least with the establishment of the UN Environment Programme (UNEP) in 1972. It has in turn issued a number of important norms (starting with its 1973 Convention on International Trade in Endangered Species), but in more recent years it has launched such high-profile initiatives as the 1992 Earth Summit and the 2002 World Summit, both focused on the goal of sustainable development. ISO's 1996 environmental management standards (ISO 14000) could thus draw on many preceding initiatives.

ITT's complicity in the 1973 Chilean coup triggered ambitions to curb the worst behaviour of multinational corporations as they manipulated the governments of weaker states and manoeuvred to evade the stronger nation-states' regulatory regimes. In 1976 the OECD published its *Guidelines for Multinational Enterprises* on responsible business behaviour; the updated 2000 version carries the admonition that the guidelines are to be applied by corporations wherever they do business in the world, not just in the OECD area.

Fragile corporate soulfulness attracted more and more self-appointed guardian angels, such as the ethical investment movement, Social Accountability International (SAI), founded in 1997, and the Ethical Trading Initiative and the Fair Labor Association, both established in the following year. In 2000 representatives of business, organized labour, civic organizations and governments committed themselves to the UN Global Compact, a voluntary code of 'corporate citizenship' (ISO, 2004: 14–15).

Today's most forceful guardian angel, the Global Reporting Initiative (GRI), a collaborating centre of the UNEP, emerged soon after. Though not an 'official' standards body, it too has links to UNEP, is a multi-stakeholder organization, and – significantly for our story – publishes standards for corporate behaviour called 'sustainability reporting guidelines'.

In this development, the concept of CSR crystallized. Yet another participant in its evolution, the UN Conference on Trade and Development (UNCTAD) declared that CSR:

> ... *concerns how business enterprises relate to, and impact upon, society's needs and goals... Discussions relating to TNC [transnational corporation] social responsibility standards and performance therefore comprise an important component of efforts to develop a stable, prosperous and just global society.*
>
> (UNCTAD, 1999: 1)

For its advocates today, corporate social responsibility expresses the goal of sustainable development and privileges three dimensions of corporate activity and its impact – the economic, the environmental and the social ('profits, planet and people') (ISO, 2004: 31).

Neo-liberalism and Globalization

A profound shift in how government is exercised has been proceeding since the 1970s; it has bolstered what some researchers have called 'the new regulation', especially the proliferation of management standards in it.[4] The change is best understood in terms of the analysis of 'the rationalities of government' proposed by the school of social analysts who have followed Michel Foucault into this area.[5]

This school looks at the actual *practices* of government – 'the conduct of conduct' – no matter who or what undertakes them, rather than continuing to focus exclusively on the workings of state *institutions*. Historically, it argues, both 'public' and 'private' bodies have worked together to make government effective. The practice of government during the modern period (that is, from the sixteenth century in the West) has rested on changing conceptions ('rationalities') of government, and each rationality in turn conjures forth specific practices (or 'technologies') of government. The ascendant rationality over the last 30 years has been neo-liberalism.

Foucauldians use 'neo-liberalism' neutrally to denote a particular approach to the art of government, rather than a political ideology that invites a positive or negative partisan response. Neo-liberalism, unlike its predecessors, eschews social processes as such and any attempt to ameliorate or regulate them. On this basis, under the rubric of 'deregulation', it dismantles a great deal of public institutional regulation. It then seeks to 'govern at a distance' through a series of 'relays', such as 'partnerships' between state organs and 'autonomized groups', which neo-liberal governors tend to call 'communities' – for instance, the medical, academic, accounting, legal, business and even standards 'communities'. The features of this new rationality of government are the ones often taken to characterize globalization – a reminder that globalization is itself a (neo-liberal) political project and not something spontaneous that 'just grew like Topsy' or otherwise arose independent of the concerted action of dominant nation-states.

Rule-setting and compliance mechanisms have thus come to depend on these new networks of government – or 'govern*ance*', to use one of the neo-liberal buzzwords from the 1990s. To the greatest possible extent, neo-liberalism insists,

---

4   'The new regulation' is, *inter alia*, the name of a large research project that the Stockholm Centre for Organizational Research is undertaking.
5   For a succinct presentation of this approach, see Rose and Miller (1992). For its application to standardization, see Higgins and Tamm Hallström (2007).

relationships within these networks should be monetized and 'marketized' so as to conform to the commercial business model of human interaction. 'The new regulation' thus calls forth a market in rules: rule-setters compete on an apparently free market by offering a variety of 'soft' regulatory regimes for sale. A veritable 'rule explosion' and a new 'golden era of regulation' have resulted (Ahrne and Brunsson, 2004; Levi-Faur and Jordana, 2005). Naturally, when rule-takers get to exercise their new consumer sovereignty over which set of rules to buy and comply with, a temptation arises to select the least onerous and most lightly policed option.

Two important and related technologies of government employed by neo-liberalism are standardization and audit. As noted earlier, standards are commodified rules ('deliverables', in standardizers' jargon) that can be bought off the shelf and compete with the rules of other 'communities', such as the ILO, the OECD, the UN Global Compact and GRI, mentioned above. In most cases, management standards are auditable, which also offers the purchaser the accolade of certified compliance (Higgins and Tamm Hallström, 2007). Like their competitors, standards bodies have to constantly shore up their authority as rule-setters, but they enjoy a competitive edge in the rule market through their 'partnerships' with public authorities – including nation-states and the EU superstate – and their long-standing associations with their (usually corporate) 'stakeholders'.

The practice of audit – that other neo-liberal technology of government – has also 'exploded', according to one of its most prominent practitioners and critics, Michael Power (1994, 1999: 42–60), who identifies ISO 9000 as its main detonator. In the tart subtitle of his second book on the subject, *The Audit Society* (1999), he calls audit 'rituals of verification'. Audit looks at matters of form, rather than substance, he argues, and it forecloses public questioning and debate rather than informing them as is usually claimed (Power, 1999: 138, 143). Audit and the ensuing third-party certification deliver the usual pay-off for purchasers of management standards. But as we shall see, ISO has initially taken a surprising turn away from this mechanism in developing its SR standard.

ISO 26000 – What Difference Will it Make?

From the time ISO's Consumer Policy Committee suggested the development of a CSR standard in May 2002, the organization has suspended its usual routines for considering a recommended project and developing it once it gains the approval of the effective decision-making instance, the Technical Management Board (TMB). The latter set up a special advisory group to explore the proposal, and it held large international meetings over the ensuing two years in Geneva, São Paolo, Munich and Chicago.

Predictably, the idea of an ISO standard on CSR turned out to be highly controversial. Out of the discussions emerged an impressive 90-page report that exhaustively rehearses the conflicting opinions and arguments over whether ISO should proceed and, if so, on what basis. Among its other recommendations, it opted for the broader SR concept instead of the narrower CSR one, and it advocated a break with the pattern of earlier management standards by suggesting that the new standard take the form of a 'guidance document' *not* subject to third-party certification (and thus audit). The enormous growth of the third-party audit and certification industry on the back of management standards was inducing a certain cynicism about the motive underlying the development of these standards; thus, cutting that industry out of the SR field in this way could help ISO to retake the moral high ground.

Interestingly, the report commended a range of probity issues, beside the 'profits, planet and people' ones, to be addressed by the proposed standard. They include normal transparency and reporting requirements, as well as protection of whistleblowers (ISO, 2004: 70, 75–76). Once again, we see the pragmatic conflation of probity issues with requirements on corporations to respect the needs and rights of others.

The report underpinned energetic discussion at a large conference in Stockholm in June 2004, opened by no less a personage than Crown Princess Victoria of Sweden. In its aftermath the TMB gave the project its imprimatur, but the standard's development was not entrusted to a conventional technical committee; rather, it was handed to a special international working group answerable directly to the TMB.[6] At the time of writing, the development process is continuing, during and between major international meetings of the working group, the most recent one in January 2007 in Sydney. ISO 26000 is likely to appear in 2009.

---

6   For a detailed discussion of the decision-making process and issues, see Tamm Hallström (2006). Higgins and Tamm Hallström (2008b) provide an overview of ISO's normal standards-development routines.

It would be invidious to try to second-guess the final contents of ISO 26000 in advance. But we need to face the fact that ISO is seeking to develop a 'deliverable' – a marketable set of rules that can attract buyers despite the allure of other options that the 'market in rules' already makes available. In line with a point made above, ISO's working group will face pressure to produce a bland, lowest-common-denominator standard. Whether the exclusion of audit as a 'ritual of verification' will hold in practice is also a moot point. Auditors and certifiers with links to standards bodies commonly offer firms a 'one-stop shop' – a single audit to cover compliance with a range of management standards – and many firms might seek added credibility by bundling ISO 26000 with other management standards against which they seek certification.

In today's global 'communication society', it may well be that the new SR standard's real usefulness to human, social and environmental well-being will be the contribution it – and the long, intense discussion leading up to its publication – makes to an emerging culture of holding corporations morally accountable for their activities in the eyes of the world. Nowadays corporate social irresponsibility, as measured against published norms of the kind that the new SR standard will hopefully articulate, can quickly lead to notoriety and a painfully diminished 'bottom line'. The latter, at least, is a central term in senior management's native language.

References

Ahrne, G. and Brunsson, N. (eds) (2004), *Regelexplosionen* [*The Rule Explosion*] (Stockholm: Stockholm School of Economics).

Black, E. (2001), *IBM and the Holocaust: The Strategic Alliance between Nazi Germany and America's Most Powerful Corporation* (New York: Crown).

Higgins, W. and Tamm Hallström, K. (2007), 'Standardization, Globalization and Rationalities of Government', *Organization*, 14:5, 685–704.

Higgins, W. and Tamm Hallström, K. (2008a), 'Technical Standardization', in A. Iriye and P. Saunier (eds), *The Palgrave Dictionary of Transnational History* (London: Palgrave Macmillan).

Higgins, W. and Hallström, K.T. (2008b), 'The International Organization for Standardization' in C. Tietje and A. Brouder (eds), *Handbook of Transnational Economic Organizations* (Leiden: Martinus Nijhoff).

ISO (International Organization of Standardization) (2004), 'Working Report on Social Responsibility', prepared by the ISO Advisory Group on Social Responsibility, 30 April.

Kaysen, C. (1957), 'The Social Significance of the Modern Corporation', *American Economic Review*, 47:2, 311–19.

Levi-Faur, D. and Jordana, J. (2005), 'The Rise of Regulatory Capitalism: The Global Diffusion of a New Global Order', *Annals of the American Academy of Political and Social Science*, 598, 200–17.

Marx, Karl (1976[1867]), *Capital: A Critique of Political Economy*, vol. 1, trans. Ben Fowkes London: Penguin/NLR)

Mills, C.W. (1956), *The Power Elite* (Oxford and New York: Oxford University Press).

OECD (2000), *The OECD Guidelines for Multinational Enterprises*, at: http://www.oecd.org/dataoecd/56/36/1922428.pdf.

Power, M. (1994), *The Audit Explosion* (London: Demos).

Power, M. (1999), *The Audit Society: Rituals of Verification* (Oxford: Oxford University Press).

Rose, N. and Miller, P. (1991), 'Political Power beyond the State: Problematics of Government', *British Journal of Sociology*, 43:2, 173–205.

Saul, J.R. (1994), *The Doubter's Companion: A Dictionary of Aggressive Common Sense* (New York: Free Press).

Schumpeter, J. (1976[1942]), *Capitalism, Socialism and Democracy* (London: Allen & Unwin).

Smith, A. (1982[1776]), *An Inquiry into the Nature and Causes of the Wealth of Nations* (Oxford: Oxford University Press).

Tamm Hallström, K. (2004), *Organizing International Standardization – ISO and the IASC in Quest of Authority* (Cheltenham: Edward Elgar).

Tamm Hallström, K. (2006), 'ISO Enters the Field of Social Responsibility (SR) – Construction and Tension of Global Governance' in G. Folke Schuppert (ed.), *Global Governance and the Role of Non-state Actors* (Berlin: Nomos).

UNCTAD (UN Conference on Trade and Development) (1999), *The Social Responsibility of Transnational Corporations* (New York and Geneva: United Nations).

Watson, D. (2004), *Watson's Dictionary of Weasel Words and Other Meaningless Managerial Phrases* (Sydney: Knopf).

Index